Consuming Texts

Also by Stephen Colclough

READING EXPERIENCE 1700–1840: An Annotated Register of
Sources for the History of Reading in the British Isles

Consuming Texts

Readers and Reading Communities, 1695–1870

Stephen Colclough

First published in 2007 by
PALGRAVE MACMILLAN
Houndmills, Basingstoke, Hampshire RG21 6XS and
175 Fifth Avenue, New York, N.Y. 10010
Companies and representatives throughout the world.

PALGRAVE MACMILLAN is the global academic imprint of the Palgrave Macmillan division of St. Martin's Press, LLC and of Palgrave Macmillan Ltd. Macmillan® is a registered trademark in the United States, United Kingdom and other countries. Palgrave is a registered trademark in the European Union and other countries.

ISBN-13: 978–0–230–52538–2 hardback
ISBN-10: 0–230–52538–5 hardback

This book is printed on paper suitable for recycling and made from fully managed and sustained forest sources. Logging, pulping and manufacturing processes are expected to conform to the environmental regulations of the country of origin.

A catalogue record for this book is available from the British Library.

A catalog record for this book is available from the Library of Congress.

10 9 8 7 6 5 4 3 2 1
16 15 14 13 12 11 10 09 08 07

Printed and bound in Great Britain by
Antony Rowe Ltd, Chippenham and Eastbourne

Contents

List of Figures

Acknowledgements

This book began as a research project on reading in the long eighteenth century that was designed to add material to the Open University's Reading Experience Database project. I owe great thanks to the project's director, Simon Eliot, for his guidance and support, and to William St Clair, who encouraged me to investigate his collection of early-nineteenth-century manuscript books.

I would also like to thank Tony Brown, Michela Calore, Justin Edwards, Maurice Hindle, Mark Hutchings, W. R. Owens, Sharon Ruston, Ceri Sullivan, Caroline Sumpter, Stephen Thomson, Ian Willison, Alexis Weedon and all of the students who took the 'Historical Reader' option on the MA in the History of the Book at the University of London between 2001 and 2005. Their input has been invaluable. Thanks, in particular, must go to Bill Bell, Ian Henderson, Dirk Van Hulle, Giles Mandelbrote, Wim Van Mierlo and Adam Smyth, who encouraged me to give conference papers on many of the readers referred to in this study. And to Karen Waring, without whom it never would have been started in the first place. This book is for Cyril Burtonwood (1933–2006), the family reader.

Earlier versions of sections of this book were published as 'Consuming Texts: the Reading Experience of a Sheffield Apprentice, 1798' in *Book History*, 3 (2000) and 'A Grey Goose Quill and an Album: the Manuscript Book and Text Transmission 1800–1850' in *Owners, Annotators and the Signs of Reading*, ed. by Robin Myers, Michael Harris and Giles Mandelbrote (British Library, 2005). I am grateful to both sets of editors for allowing me to rework that material in this volume. Permission to quote from unpublished manuscripts was generously granted by the British Library, Hackney Archives, London and Nottinghamshire Archives, Nottingham.

Introduction: Consuming Texts

In the 25th chapter of *Candide* (1759), Voltaire's hero is shown into the library of the Venetian nobleman Pococurante, where he compliments his host on the 'magnificently bound edition' of Homer that he finds on its shelves. Pococurante's reply is significant because it draws attention to the material and ideological contexts in which this book is read: 'I've sometimes asked men of learning if they found it as boring as I did. The honest ones admitted that the book used to drop from their hands, but said that you had to have it in your library, like an ancient monument, or like those rusty medals that have no commercial value'.[1] The book is described as bound in a style designed to reflect the opulence of the nobleman's home and is contained within a library that is part of a system of display. The 'men of learning' guard its canonical status, but even they, Pococurante suggests, share his boredom with its contents. This anecdote is important because it hints at just how difficult it is for the historian of reading to recover the complexities of reading experience from traditional sources such as library catalogues and probate inventories. These sources may well reveal that books and medals were displayed side by side, but they cannot account for the reader's emotional engagement with the text, the excitement and boredom of reading, or discern the underlying set of practices that helped determine this reading.

Many books must have undergone the partial reading described by Voltaire, and many more, perhaps, were never removed from the library shelf. Of course, Pococurante is being used by Voltaire to represent a figure too easily bored by the cultural artefacts that he owns. He is an 'intradiegetic reader', a reader within the narrative, who is used to correct Candide and direct the reading of the 'actual reader' of the novel.[2] As this episode suggests, representations of reading can tell us a great deal about past reading practices, but like Jacqueline Pearson, I think that we need to maintain a distinction between the 'historical reader' (because 'historical moment' colours 'all questions of reading') and the reader *within* the text, who is ubiquitous throughout the period covered by this study.[3]

Leah Price has noted that much recent work on the history of reading has tended to concentrate on the consumption of literary texts and that this inevitably 'skews the generalizations that we draw about reading'.[4] *Consuming Texts* looks at more 'historical' readers than 'intradiegetic' readers because it is concerned with the investigation of a range of different sources, from commonplace books through to auto-biographies, which reveal evidence of individual readers, only some of whom consumed literary texts. The following, entered into the journal of the East Anglian farmer William Coe (1662–1729) sometime in 1721, is a fairly typical example of the kind of evidence being dealt with throughout this book: 'My black mare fell down and threw me over her head, but God be praysed I got not the least harm. I rode a slow trott reading the Northampton news paper'.[5] Like someone reading at the wheel in a modern day traffic jam, Coe appears to be a reader keen to distract himself during an all too familiar journey, but this sort of evidence needs careful analysis before we make any generalisations about either his reading or the experience of reading in the 1720s. Coe only noted that he was reading the newspaper because he managed to survive being thrown from his horse while doing so without injury. His recollection of this event is part of a list of 'mercy's received' during 1721, which includes notes on his daughter's survival of several domestic disasters. Neither newspapers nor reading on horseback are mentioned anywhere else in a journal that regularly refers to his reading of a limited number of religious texts. Coe compiled annual lists of 'mercy's received' because he was encouraged to do so by these texts. Evidence of his horseback reading is thus a chance survival, but it is one that shows just how partial the evidence used to reconstruct past reading practices can be. It makes us ask what other kinds of reading never made it to the page.

As this example suggests, no source simply offers an unmediated insight into reading. The genre or convention of the source (in this instance the journal of religious salvation) helps to define and construct the historical reader who is uncovered. Each chapter of *Consuming Texts* looks at one or more of these sources in detail. Chapter 2 discusses the commonplace books and personal miscellanies compiled by wealthy readers in the early years of the eighteenth century; Chapter 3 looks at reading further down the social scale by examining journals of religious salvation, reading diaries and annotated books; Chapter 4 examines the private journals of two young readers from the 1790s in the context of contemporary representations of the circulating library and other institutions of reading; Chapter 5 explores the range of manuscript books created by readers in the late Romantic period as well as Anne Lister's private letters. The final chapter describes the emerging genre of working-class autobiography before moving on to look at the 'Answers to Correspondents' columns that were a feature of the new penny press.

Where possible, I have used a combination of these sources to produce a complex picture of the individual reader.

Most of the individuals dealt with in this book are 'common' readers, in Jonathan Rose's sense of not having reading books for a living, and it has been my intention throughout to pay equal attention to the materiality of the source being investigated and the 'historical specificity of the reader as a complex subject'.[6] Given the nature of the evidence, which is often partial or vague, I have positioned these readers in a variety of contexts drawn from recent work on the construction of reading in works of art (including literary texts, paintings and engravings) and the history of text production and distribution. I am also, of course, in the enviable position of being able to draw on a number of major studies of readers and reading practices completed during the past twenty years. Chapter 1 provides an overview of much of this recent work.

1
Reading Has a History

'Reading has a history. But how can we recover it?' Since Robert Darnton posed this question 20 years ago, historians, book historians and literary scholars have done a great deal to recover the history of reading.[1] Most studies of reading in Britain completed during the mid-twentieth century focused on improvements in the production and distribution of texts. For example, R. D. Altick's *The English Common Reader* (1957) traces that emergence of the 'mass reading public' during the period 1774–1900 by looking at changes in copyright law, the provision of education, printing techniques and distribution methods. Using a wide range of printed sources, Altick worked to rediscover the best-selling books and periodicals of the period, from the cheap editions of British Classics published by Cooke and Bell after the abolition of perpetual copyright in 1774, through the great increase in the circulation of weekly newspapers in the 1840s, and on to the 'cheap journalism' and 'sixpenny reprint novels' of the 1880s and 1890s.[2] Altick's work is heavily reliant upon publishers' estimates of circulation figures, government reports and contemporary articles on the cheap press, but as William St Clair has noted, it does at least provide some 'quantified' information on the formation of readerships.[3] Altick also often gives rather contentious summaries of what a text was like. For example, *Household Words* 'which began its career in 1850 with a (short-lived) circulation of 100,000' is described as 'sometimes banal and over sentimental ... with little appeal to the average working-class reader'.[4] Although in this instance he provides no evidence for their rejection of Dickens's weekly paper, Altick was particularly interested in the way in which working-class readers made sense of texts. As Jonathan Rose notes 'only one chapter of his book actually deals directly with the common reader', but Altick's use of working-class autobiography to explore the reading practices of 'intellectually ambitious workmen' has been widely influential. His conclusion that working-class readers had little access to contemporary authors before the 1850s is one that is endorsed by several recent studies.[5]

The English Common Reader was one of a number of studies published during the mid-twentieth century that tried to produce a much more sympathetic account of the working-class reader than anything which had gone before. Indeed, Altick's work needs to be placed in the context of R. K. Webb's *The British Working-Class Reader* (1955), Richard Hoggart's *The Uses of Literacy* (1957) and Raymond Williams's *Culture and Society* (1958).[6] These studies, Williams argued, were part of a rejection of earlier descriptions of modern print culture, such as Q. D. Leavis's *Fiction and the Reading Public* (1932), which tended to 'concentrate on what is bad and to neglect what is good' about 'popular culture'.[7] Hoggart's demand 'to know very much more about how people *used* much of the stuff which to us might seem merely dismissible trash' has proved an inspiration to many historians of reading including Jonathan Rose.[8] Roger Chartier has argued that *The Uses of Literacy* was important because it showed that 'the culture of the popular classes, far from being reduced to that embodied in the productions of mass culture, was characterised by a relationship of defiance and defensiveness vis-à-vis the messages it received and consumed'.[9]

During the past 20 years the work of Altick on print production and Hoggart on consumption has been revised and refined. As James Raven, Helen Small and Naomi Tadmor have argued, 'major cataloguing projects and the specialist work of a new generation of historical bibliographers have meant that is now possible to chart with far more accuracy the timing and character of the upturn in English domestic publication from the early modern period onward'. The development of national bibliographies, such as the *English Short Title Catalogue* (ESTC), has allowed a comprehensive reconstruction of print production to 1800. These catalogues reveal a rapid escalation in the number of titles published during the eighteenth century – from 21,000 during the 1710s, to more than 56,000 in the 1790s – but they only provide a partial picture of the reading culture of the period.[10] The short title catalogues 'do not fairly represent what was collected, read, or acted upon' because they exclude books printed outside Britain and cannot (of necessity) take account of material circulated in manuscript, or via the second-hand trade.[11] Detailed studies of auction records, private library catalogues and probate inventories have gone some way to filling in these gaps in our knowledge.[12] A book owned is not necessarily a book read, of course, but work on the private collections of Sir Thomas Cornwallis (1509–1604), Elizabeth Puckering (1607–1677) and

Samuel Jeake (1623–1690) has revealed a wealth of information about the ways in which libraries were assembled and put to use during the sixteenth and seventeenth centuries.[13]

Without knowledge of average print runs, prices and sales, it has always been difficult to derive useful information about the size and construction of past readerships from sources such as the short-title catalogues, but recent work on archival sources, such as the surviving ledgers of printers, publishers and booksellers is beginning to fill this gap, too. For example, by drawing on a vast range of these sources William St Clair has accumulated enough information about print runs, prices and purchasers to be able to talk with some confidence about those books which were most widely available during the period 1780–1840.

St Clair's investigation of book prices reveals that even the most popular *new* books produced during the Romantic period had short print runs and sold in relatively small numbers because they were staggeringly expensive to buy. For example, the first quarto edition of *Childe Harold* (1812), the book that supposedly made Byron famous overnight, cost 36s bound. This was about 'half the weekly income of a gentleman', but it is the revelation that the cheaper octavo edition would have cost a serving maid the equivalent of 'six weeks' income, seven weeks if she had the book rebound' that underlines just how limited access to new books was during this period.[14] As St Clair notes, most literary histories pay little or no attention to questions of access and tend to examine only those books that were published for the first time so that the Romantic period is presented as either a 'parade' of famous authors, or a 'parliament' of texts debating with each other. Both parade and parliament models tend to assume that any text published for the first time was available to *all* readers whilst at the same time ignoring reprints of earlier works. By contrast, St Clair's own account of the expanding reading nation of the period pays particular attention to the 'brief copyright window' opened up by the change in copyright law in 1774. He argues that much of the 'sharp rise in the annual growth rate of book titles published nationally' after 1774 recorded in the ESTC can be 'accounted for by reprints of older titles'.[15] These new versions of old texts were produced in relatively cheap editions. Often issued in series, individual volumes of 'old canon' writers, such as James Thomson and Oliver Goldsmith could be bought for as little as 1s or 6d per volume by the 1810s, cheaper if they were second-hand, or split into parts. Even the chapbook trade was forced to modernise in order to compete. These books were eagerly consumed by readers who had never before been able to afford substantial texts, but St Clair notes that 'self-censorship' by the publishers patrolling 'the textual limits' of what was available in the lower price ranges meant that most of these texts were ideologically conservative. His description of the 'old canon' as the 'first truly national literature' radically alters the way in which we think about the Romantic period. Scott and Byron were amongst the best-selling modern authors of the period, but it was earlier writers such as James Thomson who were the most widely reproduced, and in St Clair's formulation, most widely read authors of the age.[16] St Clair concentrates on books and pamphlets, but other book historians have extended this concern with what was most widely reproduced to include all of those other productions of the jobbing printer. Simon Eliot has argued that by the 'the mid-nineteenth century at latest' the most commonly read objects would have been the advertising posters, handbills, tickets and newspapers that were mass produced for an industrial society.[17]

This book is deeply indebted to the work of St Clair, Eliot and other book historians who have begun to reconstruct the print culture of the eighteenth and nineteenth centuries, but like other recent studies of reading practices it is also informed by the developments in literary theory that have taken place over the past 30 years or more. Indeed, most recent contributions to the history of reading note the importance of 'reader-response' and other theories developed primarily as tools for literary analysis in changing the way in which we think about reading. For example, in *John Dee and the Politics of Reading and Writing in the English Renaissance* (1995), William Sherman notes that reader-response criticism is 'peopled with every kind of reader except the real and historical'. He lists several types of reader and the theorists who invented them, including 'the mock reader (Gibson), the implied reader (Booth and Iser), the model reader (Eco), the super-reader (Riffaterre), the inscribed or encoded reader (Brooke-Rose), and the ideal reader (Culler)'.[18] As he acknowledges, this list is derived from Elizabeth Freund's introduction to reader-response criticism, *The Return of the Reader* (1987), which also includes references to 'the actual reader (Jauss)' and 'the informed reader and the interpretive community (Fish)' that have influenced recent studies of 'real and historical' readers.[19]

I am largely in agreement with Sherman when he argues that reading theories 'must give way to, and be grounded in, histories of the reading practices of actual readers', but I want to consider these theories in some detail because they have had a particular influence over the way in which recent studies have conceived of and described these 'actual readers'.[20] Robert Darnton's 'First Steps Toward a History of Reading', for example, attempted to promote 'collaboration between literary critics and historians of the book'. After demonstrating how critics such as Wolfgang Iser reveal the 'implied' or 'ideal reader' embedded in the text, he notes that it is only by 'paying heed to history' that such critics will 'avoid the danger of anachronism'.[21] Similarly, Roger Chartier and Kevin Sharpe frequently allude to the notion of the 'interpretive community' devised by Stanley Fish, and many historians of reading, including Sherman, have found inspiration in Michel de Certeau's metaphor of the reader as poacher. St Clair's emphasis upon 'readerly autonomy' is in part derived from a modification of the reader-response theories associated with Wolfgang Iser and H. R. Jauss.[22]

Reader-response

The late twentieth century saw a revolution in literary theory that wrested control of the text away from the writer and gave it to the reader. It is significant that the final line of Roland Barthes's most famous essay argues that 'the birth of the reader must be at the cost of the death of the author'.[23] Barthes own work often suggests that the reader is involved in a hedonistic search for pleasure, but many of the post-structuralist theories developed in his wake focus on the instability of a text now freed from the authority of the author, rather than the role of the reader in the creation of meaning.[24] However, during the same period other writers such as Wolfgang Iser, Stanley Fish, Jonathan Culler, Mary Jacobus and Paul de Man made readers and reading central to their work. As Andrew Bennett has argued, Stanley Fish's question 'Is the reader or the text the source of meaning?' was the central concern of the various schools of reader-response criticism that dominated critical discourse during the 1970s and 1980s. The different answers to Fish's question, Bennett suggests, 'may be reduced to three major variants which map the limits of reader-response criticism'. One, theorists, such as Norman Holland, who approach the problem by looking at the 'particular response pattern of the individual' from the perspective of American ego psychology. Two, 'Structuralist' theorists, such as Riffaterre, who 'emphasise the ways in which the text itself 'controls the production of meaning', and three, theorists, such as Wolgang Iser, who concentrate upon 'the interactive space of reading', the negotiation between reader and text.[25]

Of the three variants, that associated with Iser has been the most influential. His work tends to suggest that although the 'actual reader' is, within reason, free to make meaning, all texts create an 'implied reader' through a network of 'response inviting structures'. It is these structures, at least in part, that determine the way in which the 'actual reader' interprets the text.[26] As Terry Eagleton argues, 'the most effective literary work for Iser is one which forces the reader into a new critical awareness of his or her customary codes and expectations'.[27] In this school of thought 'actual' readers, like the literary critics who construct them, desire reading to be a process of defamiliarisation. David Finkelstein and Alistair McCleery have argued that Iser's theories are important to those interested in the history of 'how' texts are consumed because they describe the reader as an 'active and creative participant in the creation of meaning', 'dislodging' a previous model that had concentrated upon the author and his or her intentions, but as Vincent B. Leitch has noted Iser's ideas have been easily absorbed into traditional practices of author-centred close reading because he emphasises the 'aesthetic and didactic dimensions of reading rather than the psychological, sociological, or historical aspects'.[28]

By contrast, H. R. Jausss's 'aesthetics of reception and influence' first outlined in the essay 'Literary History as a Challenge to Literary Theory' (1967) has a strong focus upon history. It argues that in the 'triangle of author, work and public, the last is no passive part, but rather itself an energy formative of history'. Jauss's most significant contribution to reader-response criticism is his reformulation of the idea of a shared 'horizon of expectations'. For Jauss each 'new text evokes for the reader (listener) the horizon of expectations and rules familiar from earlier texts, which are then varied, corrected, altered, or even just reproduced'. Once the 'expectations' of a given historical moment are established, he suggests that it is possible to measure the 'aesthetic distance' of any new work from the expectations of the reader. However, much of the evidence for the 'expectations' being reproduced or altered by the 'new text' is in fact derived from the text itself. Readers are active in this model, as references to both the 'receptive reader' and the 'reflective critic' suggest, but it is mainly concerned with establishing the 'aesthetic value' of the text. Indeed, Jauss tends to concentrate on those texts, such as *Madame Bovary*, which are deemed to have shocked their original audience, or gained only 'scattered approval, gradual or belated understanding'.[29] Jauss's work is important because it shifts the focus of reader-response theory away from the single-text-implied-reader model, favoured by Iser, towards an engagement with both texts and readers that are embedded in history, but there is a continuing lack of distinction between the 'actual' or 'receptive reader' (in itself a loaded term) and the professional critic. His main focus is still the rhetorical strategies of the classic canonical text.

Reader-response studies concentrate upon the 'reader' and the 'text' (rather than the 'author' and the 'work'), but the way in which both these terms are theorised is often problematic. The critique of reader-response staged by book historians, such as Sherman, during the mid-1990s was part of a wider dissatisfaction with the way in which the 'actual' or 'historical' reader was written about in reader-response theory. Kate Flint's assessment of 'theory and women's reading' in *The Woman Reader* (1993) argued that the models devised by Iser, Jauss and others excluded any consideration of the gender of the reader. She notes that feminist critics, such as Sally Mitchell and Elaine Showalter, have engaged in a 'necessary revisionism' centred on the idea of 'reading as a woman', but these new 'text-based definitions and discussions of women readers' are also limited because they tend to elide the difference between, say, 'the fifteen-year-old or the grandmother, the woman on a Yorkshire farm or the society hostess'.[30] Judith Fetterley's notion of the 'resisting reader' has become part of common critical discourse, but as Heidi Brayman Hackel has argued, when applied to the woman reader it sometimes 'threatens to slide into transhistorical notions of an essentialized female'.[31] Andrew Bennett's revision of Freund's list includes both 'the female reader' and 'the gay or lesbian reader', and he notes that by the mid-1990s readers were being conceived of as 'historically or socially constructed, rather than abstract and eternal essences'.[32]

Other literary scholars have chosen to move beyond reader-response by making the very concept of reading itself problematic. The work of deconstructionists such as J. Hillis Miller, Jacques Derrida and Paul de Man is particularly suspicious about the idea of reading as a communication of ideas from text to reader. De Man, for example, chooses to look at those moments in texts where the reader is given 'a choice between two interpretations, neither of which can be given priority'.[33] The work of Hillis Miller, Maurice Blanchot and others, suggests that reading can be 'an affirmative or actively creative act', but as Sherman argues 'it is virtually unconstrained by history and society, and it has no impact upon the autonomous power of the author's text'.[34] In other words, deconstruction often becomes just another form of textual analysis, but historians of reading may well benefit from its insistence that the reader as much as the text is produced in reading. Derek Alsop and Chris Walsh have noted that 'many theorists of reading who readily see the text as unstable nevertheless posit real readers as models of stability'.[35] My own work starts from the position that the reader is an 'active and creative participant in the creation of meaning' established by reader-response critics, but it also pays attention to the ways in which readers refuse to participate by misreading or actively resisting the accepted set of meanings given to a text by a particular community. Chapter 5 of this study focuses on issues of gender and sexuality.

Reading as poaching and interpretive communities

Like the majority of reader-response theorists, Michel de Certeau questions the traditional notion of reading as a passive activity by insisting that 'the text has a meaning only through its readers'. But he argues that for many contemporary theorists, including Barthes, it is assumed that this freedom to make meaning is the preserve of 'literate' readers ('only someone like Barthes can take this liberty') and is denied to subordinate groups ('the public'), 'who are carefully told "what is to be thought" '.[36] This critique can be applied to much reader-response criticism which favours or writes from the position of 'the informed' or 'ideal' reader who is imagined to make complex, intertextual links that mirrors those of the critic. For example, Alsop and Walsh have argued that the 'experienced' and 'perceptive' Victorian reader would have forged 'connections across the gaps' in Dickens's *Great Expectations* (1861) similar to, or the same as, their own.[37] By contrast, de Certeau argues that *all* readers appropriate texts for their own purposes: 'Readers are travellers; they move across lands belonging to someone else, like nomads poaching their way across fields they did not write, despoiling the wealth of Egypt to enjoy it themselves'.[38]

On the basis of contemporary debates about television and the mass media, de Certeau's work is mainly concerned with the common reader whose consumption of texts can appear passive when compared with the active reading practices of professional or studious readers. Although he is arguing for a transhistorical model of reading as appropriation, de Certeau also suggests that throughout history the liberty of the reader has frequently been constrained by social institutions (such as the Church) which have tended to control access to texts. Modern readers (or television viewers), he argues, often engage in 'transgressive, ironic, or poetical' activities. And, although such practices are rarely acknowledged because they are not in accordance with official stories about acceptable 'literate' practices, all readers engage in them.[39] As David Vincent has noted, de Certeau's idea of the reader as poacher is particularly useful to anyone investigating 'those sections of society where material deprivation imposed a constant need to appropriate and improvise'; working-class readers 'have often been lifelong poachers'. However, the idea that working-class readers frequently engaged in subversive or playful readings of the texts (and other cultural artefacts) produced *for* them needs to be historicised because it risks celebrating a subversive practice as an actual freedom. In the nineteenth century, working-class readers often 'subverted the intentions of the official curriculum' imposed by the Church and state, but this experience was not necessarily liberating. Even many of those working-class readers who left detailed records of their determined acquisition of the skills of reading and writing found that they rarely opened up 'alternative structures of power and opportunity'. As Vincent's work suggests, we sometimes need to acknowledge that working-class reading was little more than a respite from everyday struggles.[40]

Protocols of reading and the history of the book

De Certeau's ideas have been particularly important to Roger Chartier, whose work is associated with the emerging discipline of the history of the book. In *The Order of Books* (1994) he argues that historians of reading need to pay attention to two of de Certeau's propositions. First, that 'reading cannot be deduced from the texts that it makes use of', and second, that readers are not entirely free to make meaning, as their tactics 'obey rules, follow logical systems, and imitate models'. Chartier's own work argues that the reader is constrained 'by the discursive and material forms of the texts read', but he also draws upon Stanley Fish's idea of the 'interpretive community' in order to suggest that readerly freedom is limited by the 'codes and conventions that regulate the practices of a membership community'.[41] Fish's work is important because he does not deal with literary texts as though they are timeless objects unconnected with history. Indeed, his concept of the 'interpretive community', first set out in the essay 'Interpreting the *Variorum*' (1976), is controversial because it appears to make the traditional idea of the 'text itself' disappear: 'Interpretive strategies are not put into execution after reading ... they are the shape of reading, and because they are the shape of reading, they give texts their shape, making them rather than, as it is usually assumed, arising from them'.[42]

In order to elucidate this idea Fish shows how the reading of Milton performed earlier in the same essay is dependent upon a number of 'interpretive strategies' shared by contemporary literary scholars. These are not just ideas about genre and authorship (such as treating *Lycidas* as a pastoral poem by Milton), but about poetic form. He argues that his own reading of *Lycidas* pays attention to line endings because 'the strategy that we know as "reading (or hearing) poetry" has included paying attention to the line as a unit'. This way of reading poetry is so widely shared that it can appear natural ('a brute fact'), but as Fish makes clear, it is only a convention shared by an interpretive community. This means that the common conception of reading as 'disinterested perception' is impossible. All readers deploy 'interpretive strategies' which are not 'natural, or universal, but learned'.[43] The idea of the interpretive community is useful to historians of reading in two ways. It helps to explain 'the stability of interpretation amongst different readers' (they share interpretive strategies because they belong to the same community) and gives reasons for the way in which the *same* text can be interpreted in many different ways, either at the same moment in history (not all communities deploy the same strategies), or later (communities change over time, hence the frequently heard phrase, 'no one reads that way anymore').[44] Fish also suggests that groups that share a set of interpretive strategies will produce texts containing formal devices that members of the community recognise. However, in Fish's view, these 'marks' on the page do not dictate meaning and may be difficult for members of other interpretive communities to even recognise because they 'will only *be* directions to those who already have the interpretive strategies in the first place'. He does, however, refer to an edition of Milton published in the 1790s which attempted to impose a particular reading onto the text by re-punctuating the poems in order to edit out difficult ambiguities.[45]

Chartier and other historians of reading have argued that it is possible to detect the material traces of these interpretive communities because 'readers and hearers, in point of fact, are never confronted with abstract or ideal texts detached from all materiality; they manipulate or perceive objects and forms whose structures and modalities govern their reading (or their hearing), thus the possible comprehension of the text read (or heard)'.[46] Jerome McGann's widely influential work on the publishing history of nineteenth-century poetry reaches a very similar conclusion. For example, in 'The Text, the Poem, and the Problem of Historical Method' (1981) he argues that no reader ever really encounters the 'Ideal Text', 'the *Ur*-poem or meta-work whose existence is the Idea that can be abstracted out of all concrete and written texts which have ever existed or which will ever exist' that was traditionally the subject of critical discourse. Byron's *Don Juan*, for example, was widely pirated in many different forms soon after its first publication by John Murray in 1819. Readers in this period would have engaged with one or other of these texts, rather than an ideal text, and each of these versions would have allowed different readings to emerge. As one contemporary review noted, reading *Don Juan* 'in quarto and on hot pressed paper' (i.e. the expensive Murray edition) was not the same as reading it in a 'whity-brown duodecimo' (the pirated edition).[47] McGann's work has encouraged both literary critics and historians to pay greater attention to the various material forms in which a text has been reproduced (from first edition to hypertext) and to ask questions about how these forms effect interpretation.[48] Janine Barchas has argued that the basic assumption that the presentation of a text affects its interpretation, which underlies McGann's work, has 'forced literary scholars to expand their definition of "text" to include a work's visual makeup and graphic design'. Her own study of the eighteenth-century novel, for example, 'aims to contextualise the manner in which the novel genre's original audience read and experienced this new species of writing' by recovering the 'look' of these books as they were first published. Although Barchas acknowledges that eighteenth-century readers had some control over how their books looked, she concludes that 'author portraits, cacophonous title pages' and a host of other 'graphic embellishments' were used to 'entice readers and guide their interpretation'.[49] Some other recent studies have looked at the way in which the guidance given to the reader of a particular genre changes across time in order to construct a history of changing reading practices.[50]

The history of reading as a history of 'misreadings'

The work of both McGann and Chartier is deeply indebted to that of D. F. McKenzie. In 'Typography and Meaning: the Case of William Congreve' (1981) McKenzie argued for an understanding of the book as 'an expressive intellectual structure' in which typography and layout are integral to meaning. He suggests that in the case of Congreve's *Works* (1710), author, publisher and printer collaborated to construct a text that was 'intended' to direct the responses of the reader through new forms of 'typographic display', such as the division of the plays into neoclassical scenes.[51] McKenzie's work suggests that by paying close attention to the way in which texts were published (and republished) it is possible to reconstruct the dominant attitudes towards the reader during a given historical period. For example, in *Bibliography and the Sociology of Texts* (1986), he argues that 'every society rewrites its past, every reader rewrites its texts, and if they have any continuing life at all, at some point every printer redesigns them'. He calls the investigation of the bibliographic changes made each time a text is redesigned in this way 'a history of misreadings'.[52]

In a particularly witty example of how this history might work, he notes that an editorial misreading of a line from Congreve's *Way of the World* (1700) helped to legitimate a new way of thinking about texts that ignored authorial intention and bibliographical history when it was reproduced in Wimsatt and Beardsley's influential essay, 'The Intentional

Fallacy' (1946).[53] Wimsatt and Beardsley created a 'new' version of Congreve's text in order to support a new reading practice that concentrated on the text itself, ignoring authorial intention, historical context and the psychology of the reader. Their new version of the text was created by selective quotation from an edition that had already been redesigned to conform to the dominant 'critical opinion' of the early twentieth century, which 'left the text to speak for itself'.[54] He concludes that the study of each new version of a text will provide evidence of this kind of 'historical use'. Of course, Congreve's initial attempt to direct reader-response by controlling every detail of the way in which his work was reproduced suggests that he feared that most readers were free to ignore authorial intention in the construction of their own meaning. As McKenzie acknowledges, even Congreve was forced to concede 'that an author's intentions have no power to save him if an audience or reader thinks him dull'. Despite this attention to the way in which 'for better or worse, readers inevitably make their own meanings', McKenzie concludes that past readings 'can be at least partially recovered from the physical forms of the text'.[55] However, as the choice of Wimsatt and Beardsley suggests, McKenzie's methodology is perhaps more suited to uncovering the 'misreading' practices of new schools of interpretation initiated by professional readers than it is to tracing the practices of non-professional or 'common' readers.

Much of Chartier's work on the cheap texts repackaged and reprinted for a broad audience in ancient regime France shares McKenzie's assumption that changes in the purely formal, typographical elements of a text 'modify both its register of reference and its mode of interpretation'. Indeed, he argues that 'the basic specificity of the Bibliothèque bleue resided in editorial changes made in the texts in order to make them readable by the wide clientele that the publishers were aiming at'. Books which had originally come from a vast range of learned genres were shortened, simplified, cut up, and given illustrations because of the way in which 'the bookseller-publishers who specialized in that market envisioned their customers' abilities and expectations'.[56] Old works were introduced to a new, broader audience, by being given the form of texts that the publishers assumed they were familiar with. However, Chartier is always very careful not to confuse the protocols of reading laid down in these texts with the actual thoughts and actions of the readers that they were intended to direct. Texts dictated 'the norm to be respected (and sometimes even followed)', but it was always possible for the reader to adapt and appropriate these texts for his or her own needs. As Chartier describes them, texts aimed at a wide audience during this period were intended to teach, acculturate and discipline, but they also 'created uses and representations not necessarily in accordance with the desires of those who produced the discourses and fashioned the norms'.[57] He uses the protocols of reading embedded in these texts to provide a set of norms (similar to Jauss's horizon of expectations) against which actual practices can be measured. Like McKenzie, Chartier argues that the material forms of texts (their non-verbal elements, their typographical configurations) have meanings to which readers respond, but he also maintains that readers are free to miss or ignore these symbols, to misread.

However, Chartier's work is particularly valuable because he always makes it clear that historians cannot simply assume that their interpretation of the protocols of reading inscribed in a text will be the same as those of its first audience. Historians bring their own assumptions about past and present reading strategies to the interpretation of these signs. For example, he notes that although texts included in the Bibliothèque bleue catalogue often contain guidance for reading aloud, it should not be assumed that working-class readers always read them 'in common'. Indeed, he argues that the bleue are important because all levels of society read them. As Jonathan Rose has noted, Chartier provides very little evidence of actual readers engaging with these texts, but he does use the example of one bourgeois reader's unsophisticated reading of a tale of roguery as literal truth in order to warn historians against imposing contemporary assumptions about reading practices onto the past via the interpretation of signs directing the reader. Reading aloud, for which there is much direction in the bleue, was an important practice amongst bourgeois as well as working-class readers and he refers to evidence of the latter reading these texts in solitude.[58] In the chapters that follow I often draw attention to the material forms of the texts being read by the various actual or historical readers being examined, but I share Chartier's view that these readers were free to ignore or misread the protocols that authors and publishers hoped would direct them.

From interpretive communities to communities of readers

Janice Radway's work on communities of women readers in the late twentieth century exposes one of the major problems with work on the history of reading that is formulated within the text-centred practices of literary critical debate. As she notes in the revised edition of *Reading the Romance* (1987), she originally set out to interview a group of female readers of romance novels with the idea that 'textual interpretations are constructed by interpretive communities using specific interpretive strategies' very much in mind. However, the evidence that she gathered from this group made her realise that to conceive of reading '*as interpretation*' would not allow her to describe what reading actually meant to the women of this community. She notes that when interviewed they 'always responded to my query about their reasons for reading with comments about the pleasure of the act itself rather than their liking for the particulars of the romantic plot'. Reading was 'a social event in a familial context' to the women interviewed by Radway, and her work argues that historians of reading need to be able to distinguish between the '*event* of reading and the meaning of the *text* constructed as its consequence'.[59] Of course, as Radway goes on to discuss in detail, certain features of these stories were particularly important to this group of readers, but to concentrate solely on the text would be to ignore a vital part of what reading meant to this community. As she makes clear, Fish's notion of an interpretive community was useful to this study because it suggested that 'textual features are not an essential structure upon which an interpretation is hung'. Fish's work has little room for social determinants, however, whereas the 'similar set of reading strategies and interpretive codes' shared by Radway's readers were, she argues, determined by 'social location', gender and class.[60] I have also found it difficult to adapt Fish's theory to describe the way in which specific groups of readers interact. Throughout this study I have used the term 'reading community' to describe the activities of a small group of readers who might be conceived of as constituting part of a much larger 'interpretive community'.

The idea of the reading community has proved particularly important to historians of Renaissance Europe. Harold Love has investigated the scribal communities or 'court coteries' that gathered around men such as Essex, Sidney and Ralegh, where the exchange of texts informed personal and political alliances. Kevin Sharpe has noted that during the early seventeenth century, historians and antiquarians 'copied and circulated "scribally published documents" ' as part of a similar process.[61] He argues that a 'history of early modern interpretive communities' will reveal 'the many groups and texts, ideas and beliefs that made up the commonwealth' that are often represented as 'unified whole'. As we achieve a better understanding of these various communities, terms that oversimplify the relationship between reader and context, such as the 'Renaissance reader' or the 'Jacobean reader', will no longer be tenable.[62] These communities can be traced either by the books that they produced (or which were produced for them) or, as in the case of smaller groups such as court coteries, via the manuscript material that they exchanged. However, as Sharpe's work makes clear, much of the evidence that we have of broad interpretive communities tends to come from an examination of the restrictions placed upon the liberty of the reader by the text. Prefaces, dedications and title pages help to reveal 'the rules of the game and the techniques of play' rather than actual practices of readers who engaged with these texts, and the surviving evidence of smaller reading communities tends to focus on elite groups. Such studies are invaluable, of course, but they raise almost as many questions as they answer. We need to know whether readers rebelled against, complied with, or simply ignored the textual mechanisms restraining their liberty, and to find out to what extent 'shared interpretive strategies' conditioned reading practices.[63]

Case studies

An alternative to looking at the protocols of reading embedded in texts or the material traces of interpretive communities is to concentrate on the evidence of a single reader, usually recorded in reading notes or marginalia. As Sharpe states, it is 'important to acknowledge that not all seventeenth-century London burghers thought (or read) alike. Carlo Ginzburg's celebrated study of Menocchio the Friulese miller gives powerful evidence of how radically individual even a humble reader could be'.[64] Much of the best recent work on the history of reading uses the case study (or micro-history) to reveal the 'otherness' of past reading practices. For example, Robert Darnton's work on the history of reading in enlightenment France often begins by de-familiarising reading. He asks his own reader to think about Ovid's account of a love letter inscribed upon the body of a Roman slave, or the way in which the recitation of texts at a Balinese funeral is thought to ward away evil demons, in order to suggest that the reading practices of the late eighteenth century can appear similarly alien to a modern consciousness which thinks of reading as just another everyday event.[65] Case studies have also been used to question models of thinking that rely either upon overly simplistic paradigm shifts ('from manuscript to print') or restrictive definitions (the 'woman reader').

Perhaps the most influential series of case studies conducted so far have been those using the marginalia of sixteenth- and seventeenth- century scholarly readers such as Gabriel Harvey and John Dee. Lisa Jardine and Anthony Grafton have used Harvey's marginalia to argue for the existence of 'the reader as facilitator', who was employed to read in the service of others.[66] Harvey's edition of Livy's *Romanae Historiae* contains notes from the period 1568–1590 which often record the date on which the text was read, who he was reading with, what other books they consulted and the aims that they set out to achieve. For example, in 1570 or early 1571 Harvey noted in his Livy that he and the son of his patron Sir Thomas Smith spent a week reading the 'decade on Hannibal' together. Jardine and Grafton argue that this was, in Harvey's own terms, a ' "pragmatic" – or "militarie, stratagematical" ' reading, which had been agreed in advance, and that subsequent readings of the same text with different reading partners were embarked upon with very different goals in mind. Their recognition that 'a single text could give rise to a variety of goal-directed readings, depending on the initial brief' has important connotations for the history of reading. Many of Harvey's readings relied upon a close inspection of marginal commentaries, but at other times he ignored this paratextual material and drew instead upon a range of other texts on similar themes. This means that the historian cannot 'prejudge' what the 'focus or central theme' of a past reading was simply by looking at a text's generic or typographic constitution. Their conclusion that 'if we use our own understanding of the salient features of the text of Livy (say) to identify the points of crucial importance to an Elizabethan reader we are very likely to miss or to confuse the methods and objects at which reading was directed' casts doubt upon the ability of analytical bibliography to recover reading practices from a close study of typographical features, or the protocols of reading embedded in texts.[67]

Despite this suggestion that it is almost impossible to 'prejudge' the specific nature of a reading, a number of case studies have begun to establish the importance of a particular *type* of reader during this period – the pragmatic scholar for hire.[68] Other men who 'read as a form of service' include John Dee, Henry Wotton, Francis Bacon and Sir Robert Cotton. The manuscript books of John Milton and Sir William Drake provide evidence of scholarly readers who were paid to assist in the compilation of reading notes for these men. Although early-modern readers (paid and unpaid) may have read with specific goals in mind that are difficult to recover without the aid of extensive marginalia, a similar set of practices appears to have been shared by scholarly readers throughout Europe. As Grafton has noted, 'learned reading' was often collaborative. Scholars engaged in conversation as they read, and their discussions frequently resulted in the production of marginalia or books of copied extracts. The annotated books of Guillaume Bude (1468–1540) are similar to those of Gabriel Harvey in that they memorialise and archive the shared event of reading. These books were part of the 'cultural capital'

assembled by professional readers in order to help them sell their ser-
vices. Despite the changing goals at which his reading was addressed,
Harvey's methods of recording marginalia remained constant for a
period of nearly forty years. This consistency suggests that even if it is
not always possible to discern the goals at which reading was directed
we may be able to discover the underlying intellectual building blocks
out of which such readings were constructed. Harvey regularly reread
his own annotations, which when they consisted of extracts from other
texts made his books into a form of anthology. Bude created books of
extracts, 'color-coded, specialised reference works in which every phase
that struck him was copied out, translated, and analysed for its rhetorical
potential'.[69]

This practice of note-making was not restricted to readers for hire. The
majority of readers educated at grammar school or university compiled
similar commonplace books during this period. Indeed, the humanist
educational programme recommended by Erasmus and others encouraged students and scholars to produce collections of moral wisdom and
rhetorical felicity from the ancient Greek and Latin authors. Most of
these extracts were positioned under headings, sometimes dictated by a
schoolteacher or university tutor, or copied from a printed volume of
'the heads necessary for a perfect commonplace'.[70] This process of
extracting continued to be an important part of reading culture throughout the seventeenth century, by which time almost any kind of text
could be reproduced. As Kevin Sharpe's case study of William Drake
makes clear, however, they were no longer kept solely for humanist education and scholarship. As Drake's surviving manuscript compilations
and annotated books reveal, he relied upon the traditional method of
highlighting a particular sentence or maxim in a text before transferring
it to his commonplace book, but the final product was a 'startlingly
amoral catalogue of adages and proverbs about public life' quite at odds
with the humanist tradition. Sharpe does not perhaps give enough
detail about the changing nature of commonplace compilation during
the early seventeenth century in this account, but his argument that we
need to treat books of reading notes as evidence of self-fashioning is persuasive. 'Drake's bricolage of annotations from his reading was', he concludes, 'a very personal script, penned for his use as a manual for living
in a self-interested and competitive world'.[71]

As Steven Zwicker suggests, such 'dissident reading' was a product of
the changed historical circumstances of the mid-seventeenth century, but
he also argues for a 'continuum of social practices and intellectual protocols' throughout the period before the civil war via reference to the case

studies of Harvey and other Renaissance scholars: 'The detailed portraits we possess of Renaissance humanists argue not simply the active and applied agency of the intellect, but an overarching model of exemplarity that guided the reading of courtiers, aristocrats and connoisseurs, and of their professional servants and protégés'. Commonplacing, which urged this active search for examples, he suggests, 'was practised across the social spectrum of early modern literacy' and remained an important skill until well into the eighteenth century.[72] Zwicker acknowledges in a footnote that this harmonious image of reading in the early modern world excludes those who could read but not write, which included many gentry women, as well as those further down the social scale, and Heidi Brayman Hackel has argued that a history of reading which focuses on the elite (usually all male) groups described in the majority of case studies completed so far ignores both male and female readers who consumed books for pleasure. Like many other contemporary scholars she draws together a range of source materials to produce a series of alternative case studies of readers that are 'more various and less extraordinary' than those described in the studies referred to by Zwicker.[73] Brayman Hackel is right to want to show that these earlier case studies are not the last word on early modern reading practices, but the almost canonical status that they have achieved during the past decade or so shows how effective the case study can be in recovering otherwise neglected groups of readers and establishing recurrent patterns of use.

There have also been an important series of case studies of late-eighteenth-century readers. Robert Darnton's investigation of the reading of 'an ordinary bourgeois', living an ordinary life in 'provincial France during the two decades before the French Revolution' has been particularly influential. In 1774 Jean Ranson began a correspondence with a Swiss publisher of French books, the Societe Typographique de Neuchatel (STN).[74] Darnton uses the 59 titles that he ordered during the 11 years of his correspondence to provide 'a general idea about his taste and reading habits'. Ranson bought books from the five main categories found in contemporary library catalogues (religion, history-travel-geography, belles-lettres, medicine, children's books), but he was particularly interested in the work of Rousseau, even replacing the 11 volume 1775 edition of his works with the STN's own much larger edition in 1782. Darnton's essay is particularly important because it argues that 'to pass from the *what* to the *how* of reading is an extremely difficult step'. The letters that Ranson sent with his orders reveal something of the way in which he made sense of the books that he bought. By comparing them with others sent to the STN, Darnton is able to make some guarded generalisations about reading in this period. Ranson's frequent reference to the material quality of books, for example, leads him to suggest that many readers shared 'this typographical consciousness'.[75]

Ranson's letters show how Rousseau's ideas about education and childcare became integrated into his family life and that he was interested in the author's life, gathering together as much information about him as possible. By comparing this 'response' to Rousseau with those described in letters sent to the author in 1761, Darnton argues that 'Rousseauistic reading was an important phenomenon in prerevolutionary France'.[76] In this account, the Rousseauistic reader is an important *type* of reader, at the cutting edge of a new way of thinking about texts, but not typical of the age in which he read, in much the same way as Jardine and Grafton's Renaissance facilitators are only typical of one particular sector of society. Darnton's suggestion that 'Rousseau taught his readers to "digest" books so thoroughly that literature became absorbed in life' shows the kind of reading practice that he believes began to emerge at the beginning of the Romantic period, but it is also very revealing about his own methodology. Although keen to give a voice back to the reader via letters, Darnton's is still a text-centred account of the reading process. Rousseau is imagined as teaching Ranson, who is said to embody 'both the ideal reader envisioned in the text and the real reader who bought the books'.[77] Of course, some readers may indeed have responded to texts in this way, but it often feels as though by concentrating on Ranson's reading of Rousseau Darnton elides many of the complexities of his reading life.

Darnton's case study was produced in order to explore the possibility of applying reader-response theory to a historical reader, but he also uses it to stage a major challenge to one way of thinking about reading after 1750. As he notes elsewhere, historians of reading often look at the 'interplay of binary opposites' that mark a supposed paradigm shift, such as 'reading by turning the leaves of a codex as opposed to reading by unrolling a volumen' or 'reading printed texts in contrast to reading manuscripts'. In studies of the eighteenth century 'reading extensively by racing through different kinds of material' is often opposed to 'reading intensively by perusing a few books many times'.[78] This movement from 'intensive' to 'extensive' is sometimes referred to as 'the reading revolution'. This phrase was first used by Rolf Engelsing to describe changes in book ownership and consumption in urban Germany after 1750, but the term has been adopted to describe both eighteenth-century Europe and early-nineteenth-century America.[79] These studies suggest that as books became more widely available, readers moved from the 'intensive' to an 'extensive' style of reading. In the 'intensive' mode, readers had access to a limited number of books often religious in character, or designed to be read regularly. This kind of reading was often practised publicly and aloud, and recitation and learning by heart gave the printed word a strong sense of authority. By contrast, 'extensive' readers passed rapidly from text to text. Most of their reading took place privately and silently, and the written word was no longer imbued with the same power. Darnton's case study tests and challenges the 'reading revolution' hypothesis. Ranson read a wide range of texts, but he did not simply pass from one book to the next. He was 'an impassioned Rousseauist' who incorporated the philosopher's ideas 'in the fabric of his life as he set up business, fell in love, married and raised his children'.[80]

A similar challenge to the reading revolution model comes from John Brewer's case study of an English middle-class reader of the same period, Anna Larpent. Larpent's diaries record that between 1773 and 1783 she read 440 titles from many different genres. Novels and plays were often read aloud to her family, but she also engaged in regular, repeated readings of sermons and the Bible while alone in her room. Like Darnton, Brewer describes a reader engaged in a diversity of reading practices. He concludes that if a general theory of reading was to be constructed from this record it would be that 'reading practices did not become more extensive but rather more diverse'. During the late eighteenth century intensive and extensive modes 'were complementary rather than incompatible'.[81] Other case studies have questioned the progressive optimism of the reading revolution theory. Otto Van Eck, a young boy from a Dutch gentry family who kept a diary in the early 1790s, was a reluctant reader, forced to study by parents who controlled his access to texts.[82] A recent study of Samuel Johnson as reader suggests just how complex and contradictory an individual's account of his or her reading practices can be.[83] I have been careful not to impose the reading revolution model onto the sources dealt with in this study.

Beyond case studies

Anthony Grafton ends his witty overview of the different phases of the recovery of the history of reading after the Second World War with the suggestion that all future case studies should be concerned with 'local difficulties and particularities' rather than broad generalisations.[84] Other historians have worried that this recovery of the 'individuality of reading practice favours synchronic comparison and analysis rather than diachronic explanation and identification of behavioural difference over time'. James Raven has argued that one solution to this problem is 'the gathering of multiple case-studies of readers', based on personal accounts of readers and reader observers, 'in conjunction with other evidence and approaches'. Margaret Spufford, David Vincent and Jonathan Rose have all produced 'diachronic' studies of humble readers that use autobiographies to identify 'shared perspectives' and changing practices.[85] Similarly, Jacqueline Pearson has produced studies of four women readers that give some sense of the way in which women's reading changed between the late Restoration and the early nineteenth century as part of a larger study that brings together many different sources, including representations of women reading in literary texts. As she acknowledges, 'some accounts of reading and writing in the eighteenth and nineteenth centuries have too easily accepted contemporary stereotypes which developed in the service of vested interests, without checking them against the historical record', but her argument that evidence of 'the construction of the reader' can be as important as that 'provided by historical readers' is convincing.[86]

Many recent studies share Pearson's concern with 'implied readers (as Iser calls the hypothetical reader to whom the text is directed)' and the 'reader within the narrative'. Garrett Stewart's work, for example, is particularly concerned with the way in which the nineteenth-century novel inscribes the agency of its activation by 'Dearing' the reader. Pearson suggests that we add his idea of the 'conscripted reader' to the list begun by Freund.[87] However, Patrick Brantlinger's study of novel reading in the same period is suspicious of the author's ability to control an audience in the way that Stewart suggests, and he argues that 'from Henry Fielding to Henry James, the practice of authorial commentary perhaps does little more than register the nervousness of authors about how their stories may be *mis*interpreted by readers whom they have no way of knowing, much less controlling'.[88] Brantlinger is particularly concerned with writing that was anxious about the rise of mass literacy. Kate Flint has argued that 'reading provoked a good deal of anxiety during the Victorian period' especially when it was the reading of women or the working class. Her own study looks at 'the wide range of contexts in which "the woman reader" was constructed as a discrete topic' between 1837 and 1914, including 'newspapers and periodicals; medical and psychological texts; advice manuals for young girls, wives, servants, governesses; educational and religious works; autobiographies; letters; journals; fiction; verse; paintings, photographs and graphic art'. She makes the important point that the discourse of the woman reader 'affected the composition, distribution and marketing of literature'; texts were 'received, classified and interpreted by both publishers and critics within a context of what women should and should not be reading, and what they expected from their books'. The discourse of the 'woman reader' was conducted by both men and women, and the notion of the 'impressionable' female who needed to be protected against the worst excesses of contemporary print culture (often figured as the novel) helped to 'uphold and reinforce dominant patriarchal structures'.[89] Other studies have paid similar attention to the iconography of reading. Both William Beatty Warner and Elizabeth Long have noted the importance of the visual representation of the female novel reader in eighteenth-century art. Long contrasts the figure of the male reader, absorbed in scholarly study, with that of the self-absorbed female, in order to suggest that visual representations have tended to trivialise (and eroticise) women's reading.[90]

Long argues that the representation of reading as a solitary activity has led to the 'historical invisibility of reading groups'. Hers is one of several recent studies that have explored the collective reading practices of book clubs and literary societies in the light of Janice Radway's work on communities of novel readers. Both Long and Jenny Hartley place contemporary women's book clubs within the context of those groups that emerged during the nineteenth century.[91] Elizabeth McHenry has used the records of African American literary associations to show the importance of these institutions to black readers throughout the nineteenth and twentieth centuries.[92] Such studies have helped to bring otherwise forgotten groups of readers to notice. Bill Bell's work, for example, has looked at the experience of shipboard reading amongst those leaving the British Isles to settle in the New World. Once settled, they maintained links with the communities they had left behind by sending letters requesting newspapers and other texts that reminded them of home.[93] All of these studies insist that we take account of reading as a sociable rather than a solitary act. As I argue in Chapters 4 and 5, the rules and regulations governing subscription libraries, book clubs and societies help us to understand the concrete social practices of these reading communities.

Other historians have moved beyond the synchronic treatment of the individual reader by looking at how a specific genre has been read across time. Examples include D. R. Woolf on the consumption of history in the early modern period and Adam Smyth on the circulation and transmission of printed miscellanies during the mid-seventeenth century. Such studies work by producing a series of micro-histories based upon diaries, commonplace books and marginalia.[94] Heather Jackson's work on marginalia has demonstrated that it is possible to use this source to produce a broader history of changing reading practices. She argues that the annotating readers of the late eighteenth century shared a number of practices. They made extracts, constructed 'networks of information' via cross-reference and enjoyed the 'license to "illustrate" more or less ad lib'. By the mid-nineteenth century, however, the annotating reader was in retreat as 'public libraries and compulsory education joined forces to discourage note-making', which came to be 'stigmatised as antisocial'.[95]

However, not everyone is convinced that gathering this sort of evidence will produce a history of reading. William St Clair is sceptical about using 'reports of individual responses' because 'they can never be, at best, anything beyond a tiny randomly surviving, and perhaps highly unrepresentative, sample of the far larger total of acts of reception which were never turned into words in the mind of the reader let alone recorded in writing'. He goes on to argue that this kind of evidence is useful in helping to 'break out of the closed circle implicit in exclusively text-based approaches', but he believes that only a thorough understanding of which texts were most widely available will allow us to understand how ideas were communicated during a given historical period. For example, he is particularly critical of work on American literature that makes 'broad claims about the mentalities of the colonists' based only upon those books 'composed and manufactured' in the 'mainland settlements which later became the United States'. What he describes as 'a history of reading' offers instead a picture of a colonial world that imported books from Britain and other parts of Europe. 'American' texts were thus 'only a tiny proportion of the texts that were read' and cannot be used to describe colonial 'mentalities'.[96]

St Clair's major achievement is, of course, to have put this methodology into practice to produce a 'quantified' history of reading that looks at the impact of texts upon British mentalities between 1780 and 1840 (p. 439). As already noted, his investigation of the texts that were most frequently reproduced during the Romantic period, which included many reprints, radically revises traditional literary histories that tend to look only at those books published for the first time. Indeed, he uses the old canon, along with the other most frequently reproduced texts of the age, to model, or reconstruct the 'official mainstream ideology' of the period, which he also describes, in a term adapted from Jauss, as providing an 'horizon of expectations' against which 'texts and mentalities can be judged' (p. 269) Central to this mainstream ideology were 'official' texts such as the Bible, and Burn's *Justice*, which sold in great numbers, and religious tracts, many of which were distributed for free. Conduct books and volumes of literary theory, such as Blair's *Lectures*, helped to police reading practices. Religious-philosophical works, such as Blair's *Sermons*, were particularly common. Abridged, anthologised, and included in school textbooks, they were also performed in church. To be a member of the reading nation was thus to experience these texts in some fashion.

St Clair is careful not to suggest that 'weight of print' is the same as 'influence', but he argues that Mary Wollstonecraft's *Vindication of the Rights of Woman* (1792) had little influence upon the mentalities of the period because, although there were three editions published during the 1790s, it did not go on to be reprinted or pirated, and was thus 'simply overwhelmed' by the sheer weight of conduct books 'which advised against' it (p. 278). After the third edition of 1796, the *Vindication* was not published again in Britain for nearly fifty years. This is a brilliant reassessment of the cultural impact of one of the most important radical texts of the period, but St Clair also uses the notion of a mainstream horizon of expectations to theorise and account for the ways in which politically and aesthetically radical texts were read. All radical texts, if they were read at all, he suggests, would have been measured against the conservative norms constructed by the texts of the 'official mainstream ideology'. The 'virulence of the reaction to Byron and Shelley' is evidence that their work did not fit into the horizon of expectations associated with 'mainstream literature'. Readers of Byron's *Childe Harold* were confused by the poem because it appeared to them to be 'written in a deadly spirit of scorn and hate' and he gives one example of a reader so 'incensed' by Shelley's rewriting of the dominant aesthetic that he was forced to denounce it in print (pp. 288, 289).

Like Jauss's original theory of an horizon of expectations, which attempted to measure a text's 'aesthetic distance' from a normative horizon, St Clair's notion of a conservative mainstream ideology obviously favours controversial texts which break with the norm, and I think it is better suited in this instance to creating a reading of Byron (in the literary critical sense) than it is to describing the possible ways in which his work was consumed during the period. And, while the notion that a text like *The Vindication* had little influence upon the general mentality of the period is valuable – proving what was not available to be read is essential to the history of reading – this insistence on the ability of the dominant ideology to 'overwhelm' new ideas seems unnecessarily negative. It conceives of a dominant mentality, rather than mentalities. Of course, as St Clair notes, by the 1820s some politically and aesthetically radical texts, including Byron's *Don Juan*, actually enjoyed a very large audience. Such texts obviously had an influence that was much greater than earlier radical texts, such as the *Vindication*, and although he deals with what he calls 'the radical canon', the way in which these texts impacted upon or changed the mentalities of readers who had previously only experienced the old canon and official texts is not fully addressed. *Don Juan* is said to have had an important effect upon Chartists and other politicised working-class readers, but the conservative horizon appears unchanging. Indeed both the 'incensed' conservative and the Chartist appear to recognise Shelley or Byron's essential radicalism whatever the form in which they received the text, and whatever their intellectual background.[97]

The argument that the majority of cheap books were deliberately conservative in nature is a particularly important one, but I do not think that we have to assume that they were of necessity read conservatively, as St Clair's model seems to suggest. Indeed, as perhaps the most commonly reproduced printed objects of the age, the texts of the official ideology would have percolated down to a vast array of different reading communities with different competencies. Despite making references elsewhere to the 'autonomy' of the reader and the 'resisting' reader, St Clair's 'horizon of expectations' appears to leave little room for those who created radical meanings out of the very texts associated with a conservative governing ideology (p. 5). As Jonathan Rose argues, 'even when working people read books approved and provided by the governing classes, there was no guarantee that they would read those texts as their patrons wished'. Working-class autobiographies provide numerous examples of official texts being read in this fashion. The Chartist John James Bezer read Bunyan's *Pilgrim's Progress* as a tale of rebellion and found that even the contents of a Sunday school or prison library could be read against the grain.[98] Different groups of readers can read the *same* texts in very different ways. My final chapter, for example, looks at how some working-class readers used the Bible to question dominant ideas about the rights of property.

St Clair's argument that the evidence that we have of actual readers' responses can never be more than 'a tiny randomly surviving, and perhaps highly unrepresentative, sample' has to be taken seriously, however. It was only unusually articulate members of the working class who created the autobiographies examined by Rose and Vincent, and the contents of these and other autobiographical writings are often over-determined by the context in which they were published. Pearson's series of case studies of women readers includes Elizabeth 'Moral' Carter (1717–1806), whose work was carefully edited by her nephew in order to present her moral correctness. The codes restricting what it was appropriate to read even led some women to censor their own ostensibly private reading notes.[99] By the early nineteenth century even working-class autobiography had its own codes and conventions.

To accept the evidence of readers, such as Gabriel Harvey, Jean Ranson and Anna Larpent as 'typical' or 'common' would clearly be a mistake as they had much greater access to recently published texts than most of their contemporaries. However, this does not mean that we should discount the evidence of reading that they reveal. Indeed, the concept of the 'common' or typical reader has begun to appear increasingly anachronistic to scholars who are concerned with issues of difference and diversity. For Kate Flint, evidence of what 'individual women were actually reading' complicates our view of 'the woman reader' of the nineteenth century by 'challenging many of the generalizations advanced by contemporary commentators'. She goes on to suggest that such evidence 'reminds us of the specificities of circumstance, the variables of parental occupation and family affluence, of urban and rural lives, of religious affiliations, enthusiastic relatives, and modes of education which militate against establishing neat patterns of generalization whether contemporaneous or retrospective'.[100] Flint's argument is supported by Jason Scott-Warren's work on one early-modern reader whose 'eccentric' reading patterns 'could not have been predicted from the content of his books'. Indeed, such case studies are invaluable because they help us to recover something of 'the obstinate, irreducible individualism' of the reader.[101] Terms, such as 'the woman reader', or the 'typical reader', like 'the reader' of early reader-response criticism, tend to obscure 'the diversity of individual readers and the range of reading practices available at any one historical moment'.[102]

This book aims to expose the diversity and range of different reading practices available at a number of different 'historical moments' between 1695 and 1870. Although it often reveals the obstinate individualism of the reader, it does not suggest that all reading is inherently appropriative, anarchic or subversive. Reading cannot 'be deduced from the texts that it makes use of', but most of the readers examined here tend to 'obey rules, follow logical systems, imitate models', as Chartier suggests. Even if their own readings are as unpredictable and as eccentric as those explored by Scott-Warren, they are often part of a larger reading community with whom they shared texts; individual testimony often exposes collective rules. As Adrian Johns has argued, the history of the book has taught us that texts are 'unable to force concurrence', but this does not mean that we cannot describe how they were used in particular circumstances, by specific individuals or groups of people. In much the same way that Johns has looked at scientific experiments in the seventeenth century, I have attempted to reconstruct how texts were used 'by *these* people, *here*, in *these* circumstances, with *these* results'.[103] Each chapter looks at more than one reader in order to be able to suggest something about the range of different reading practices available at that moment.

The start and termination dates of this study are not entirely arbitrary. The year 1695 marks the abandonment of state censorship with the lapse of the Licensing Act of 1690 and is often taken to represent the point at which British society began to be dominated by print. Much recent work on the history of the book in Britain uses 1695 in this way whilst acknowledging that it oversimplifies a much more complex period of transition. It is not my intention to make a distinction between seventeenth- and eighteenth-century readers that would resurrect the grand narrative of a transition from intensive to extensive reading, but 1695 provides a useful boundary between the group of readers examined here and those documented in a range of recent studies summarised in the fourth volume of the *Cambridge History of the Book in Britain* which covers the period 1557–1695.[104] There was certainly a steady increase in print production as more presses became active after 1695, and most histories of British print culture have assumed that the eighteenth century saw a steady rise in reading for all classes. However, St Clair's recent revisionist work suggests that it was not until the last quarter of the century that the publishing industry looked beyond persuading the upper income groups to consume more books.[105] Chapters 2 and 3, which look at reading in the period 1695–1770 largely confirm St Clair's suggestion that new books were confined mainly to the wealthy, but by considering new readers of the 'middling sort', such as the excise officer John Dawson, I discover a range of varied reading practices and communities that studies based on the examination of print production can easily overlook. Chapters 4 and 5 look at reading in the new, more commercialised world of the Romantic period, paying particular attention to the institutions of reading that developed at this time, such as circulating libraries. Chapters 5 and 6 analyse the ways in which different communities consumed the most commonly reproduced print items of the early nineteenth century, including the new range of reprinted texts that became available after 1774.

My termination date of 1870 is perhaps more contentious. Chapter 6 concludes by looking at the reading of those objects identified by Eliot as the commonest products of a modern industrial society, the weekly newspaper and the advertising poster, in order to suggest that the kinds of autobiographical sources that I have used throughout this study are largely inadequate to deal with both the 'mass audience' and the new spaces for reading that appeared during the 1840s and 1850s. Spaces such as the railway bookstall and the advertising hoarding allowed new forms of disengaged reading to emerge that are particularly difficult to trace. Representations of these spaces produced during the 1850s and 1860s give some sense of how they were used, but as this chapter acknowledges they were often part of a complex discourse of reading that was anxious about the way in which print was proliferating. I do not share this anxiety, of course, but the vast range of different readerships that were being targeted by the publishing industry in the 1870s suggests that a different approach to that taken in this study will be needed to map the experience of reading during the late nineteenth century.[106]

Like the majority of historians of reading, I am reluctant to reproduce the grand narrative of reading that runs from intensive to extensive, but this does not mean that this study is not interested in describing historical change. By bringing together these case studies I hope to replace these opposed terms with a more nuanced account of the various practices available to readers in the eighteenth century and after.

2
Reworking the Word: Readers and their Manuscript Books, 1695–1730

Despite a widespread questioning of the suitability of the term 'extensive' as an accurate description of the reading practices of the late eighteenth century, the notion (derived from the work of Rolf Engelsing) that at 'sometime' during the eighteenth century reading changed from the 'intensive' study of a few texts to a new way of comprehending a broader print culture has remained largely unchallenged. For example, in *Samuel Johnson and the Life of Reading* (1997), Robert DeMaria proposes that 'a downward shift occurred' during the eighteenth century so that 'reading became more frequently a matter of mere reading and less often a matter of study'. Using Johnson's own terminology, DeMaria argues that his reading can be divided into four distinct types: 'study' (or 'hard reading'), 'perusal', 'mere reading' and 'curious reading'. The first two types are forms of 'intensive' reading, whereas 'mere' and 'curious' reading are 'extensive'. This account of Johnson's reading life is particularly useful because it demonstrates that an individual could engage in many different forms of reading, whilst at the same time arguing that some forms were better than others. In both private and public statements Johnson urged himself and others to study, whereas in practice he enjoyed 'mere reading' as a guilty pleasure. DeMaria's modified version of Engelsing's theory works well as a way of describing Johnson's conflicting attitudes towards the reading culture of the mid-eighteenth century, but the notion of a 'downward shift' from 'study' to 'mere reading' that he proposes as a general model for the history of reading during the long eighteenth century is problematic. Like Johnson, DeMaria prefers 'study' to other types of reading and this leads to his idealisation of a mode of 'intensive' reading that Engelsing's theory suggests would have been the norm for many people in the early eighteenth century. However, as DeMaria's is forced to acknowledge, there is a great deal of difference between Johnson's notion of 'study' and the compulsive rereading of the Bible, which left 'little time for reading much else', that many 'intensive' readers actually engaged in.[1]

My aim here is not just to suggest the dangers of idealising a particular type of reading practice, but to call attention to the way in which recent case studies of mid- to-late-eighteenth-century readers have tended to reinforce the notion that most early-eighteenth-century readers engaged in the close study of a relatively limited number of books. While it is true that a macro assessment of the impact of print during the long eighteenth century might well describe greater access to books for some – and hence the possibility of 'extensive' reading – this broad generalisation risks effacing the actual practices of readers at both ends of the period.[2] As recent studies of reading in seventeenth-century England have made abundantly clear, it is impossible to describe the many and varied reading practices of this period as 'intensive', even if much of the surviving evidence point towards a studious or scholarly attitude towards texts. Even readers of scurrilous satire and amusing jest books often diligently copied parts of these texts into their own manuscript books, but again this kind of close reading is quite different from the repeated reading of the Bible described in the 'intenisve' model. This is not to deny that some readers did indeed read intensively. William Coe (1662–1729), whose diary is examined in Chapter 3, refers to the same few religious texts throughout the thirty- odd years in which he kept notes on his spiritual life. But Coe, like Johnson, was on his guard against 'mere' reading, and he notes that he occasionally succumbed to the temptations of an 'idle jest book'.[3]

This chapter looks at three wealthy readers who were active in the early eighteenth century in order to investigate the different ways in which they used manuscript books to record their reading. The books produced by Charles Caesar (1636–1707) and Elizabeth Freke (1641–1714) suggest that a hybrid form of personal miscellany was common amongst gentry-class readers during the early eighteenth century. Caesar's book is a mixture of commonplace book, personal miscellany and reading diary that brings together a diverse body of texts that were then reworked to fit a new personal context, whereas Freke's 'Commonplace Book' contains extracts from a range of texts alongside a version of her diary-like autobiographical 'remembrances'. Both show evidence of having reworked printed texts into new contexts, but Freke's book also reveals how reading helped to refashion her sense of self and history in her autobiographical writings. Because the primary function of these books was to record extracts, they have very little to say about the way in which these transcription practices fitted into the broader reading life of the compiler. I conclude with a case study of Gertrude Savile (1697–1758), who produced both detailed reading journals and a commonplace book during the 1720s, which suggests that it was possible for some non-professional readers to engage in a complex range of different, sometimes conflicting, reading practices and styles that are in many ways similar to those described by DeMaria as typical of late-eighteenth-century readers.

Reworking the word – Charles Caesar (1636–1707) and Elizabeth Freke (1641–1714)

During the past decade, literary scholars and book historians have become increasingly interested in the relationship between print and manuscript in the early modern period. Consequently the triumph of print seems less assured than it once did, and historians are now less likely to treat manuscript production in the seventeenth and eighteenth centuries as a curious anachronism. Much of the early work in this area looked at the manuscript as a mode of publication, but Harold Love's study of the ways in which different texts were shared and read in various 'scribal communities' has led many scholars to adopt a reader (rather than author) centred approach to manuscript culture.[4] Indeed, as I suggested in Chapter 1, much of the most important work undertaken so far on the history of reading in the early modern period has paid particularly close attention to the way in which readers made use of commonplace books. Surviving copies of commonplace books are particularly important as evidence because, as Peter Beal has argued, they were the 'primary intellectual tool for organising knowledge and thought amongst the intelligentsia' during the early modern period.[5] The humanist commonplace book, as defined by Erasmus in the *De Copia Verborum* (1513), and reworked by many later authors, was used as a pedagogic tool in grammar schools, universities and inns of court throughout this period. Readers were encouraged to produce a series of headings under which extracts, known as *loci communes* (or commonplaces), were gathered.[6] These quotations provided scholars and lawyers with a store of borrowed similes, metaphors and maxims that they could use in their everyday lives, or rework into new texts. 'Early modern Englishmen', Robert Darnton has argued, did not read texts from beginning to end but 'in fits and starts' jumping 'from book to book'. They 'broke texts into fragments and assembled them into new patterns by transcribing them in different sections of their notebooks'.[7] Creating a 'repertory of "sententiae" ' (sententious or epigrammatic sayings) or exemplary passages was such a common practice during the Renaissance that some publishers facilitated the identification of suitable passages for transcription using typographical devices such as 'commas, inverted commas, asterisks, pointing fingers in the margin, or the printing of the text of the maxims and examples in a type different from the one used in the body of the text'.[8] Some historians of reading have examined the ways in which early-modern readers reacted to, or reproduced, these prompts. William Sherman has argued that Renaissance readers 'were rarely satisfied with the selections made by others'. The playwright Ben Jonson, for example, marked out additional choice passages to those highlighted by the editor of his copy of Chaucer.[9]

Both Peter Beal and Ann Moss have argued that as an intellectual tool the commonplace book must often have predetermined the way in which a text was read, as readers searched for examples and epigrams suitable to be placed under headings compiled mainly from pre-existing lists. However, as Moss has also noted, the 'open-ended acceptance of variety and self-contradiction' encouraged by the commonplace book tradition made each set of quotations into a unique object.[10] Recent work by Heidi Brayman Hackel and Kevin Sharpe on seventeenth-century readers supports the idea that commonplace books frequently expose very personal reading profiles. Sharpe argues that Sir William Drake used his commonplace books to construct an anti-humanist vision of the world, whereas Hackel notes that by the mid-seventeenth century some readers were choosing to include page references to the original text, rather than transcriptions, in their otherwise traditionally laid out commonplace books. In such instances the manuscript book was no longer a portable library of quotations, personalised and remade by the reader, but a guide to the original text.[11]

Such evidence suggests that readers were beginning to ignore the exact rules underlying the construction of the humanist commonplace book in order to create their own more informal, or as in Drake's case, more radical, compilations of quotations. As Moss notes, by the late seventeenth century it was not unusual to discover 'examples of manuscript notebooks carefully ruled up as commonplace books with the traditional run of mostly moral heads' that were nevertheless filled with extracts from a wide range of different genres that bore no relation to the original headings.[12] One anonymous manuscript book compiled between 1660 and 1690, now in the Beinecke collection, was originally given headings such as 'piety' and 'war', but it actually contains complete transcripts of poems by Edmund Waller and others on entirely unrelated topics.[13] Such books reveal an initial formal method of reading being overtaken by a new set of reading practices that valued texts in their entirety rather than in exemplary sections. That the typographic highlighting of passages suitable for transcription from printed books was also in decline in the late seventeenth century supports this conclusion.[14] That some of the manuscripts described by Moss even have 'a nicely calligraphed index and a few desultory entries' in the humanist style, however, suggests that the commonplace book tradition still exercised a powerful influence over the way in which readers approached texts.[15]

During the late seventeenth century, various forms of manuscript book compilation continued to underwrite reading as a specific cultural practice amongst the cultural elite, who were much more likely to have the combined skills of reading and writing than those further down the social scale, and as those examples of traditional commonplace books that have been transformed into more informal compilations of complete texts suggest, the commonplace book was still a popular pedagogic tool. By the end of the seventeenth century the traditional humanist commonplace book, with its moral headings, was beginning to disappear, but John Locke and other enlightenment scholars encouraged readers to keep a new kind of manuscript book that borrowed heavily from its Renaissance predecessors. Locke's 'New Method of Making Common-Place Books', first published as part of *Le Bibliotheque Universelle* in 1686, was frequently included in his collected works after it was translated into English in 1706.[16] That many surviving manuscript books are laid out in accordance with the complex system explained in this chapter are testament to its influence. Printed commonplace books based on Locke's system were still being published in the nineteenth century, and two of the Romantic readers examined later in this study completed books using his methodology.[17]

Locke's 'New Method' still encouraged readers to record extracts from their reading under headings, but these were now to emerge from their reading rather than dictate it. They were advised to make careful references to the source of the transcription, including the author's name, the text's title, date and place of publication and the size of the volume. Both the total number of pages in the book and the particular page from which the extract was taken were to be recorded in order that the same passage could be found in a different edition of the same title.[18] Despite the continued use of the term commonplace book, and the concomitant encouragement of readers to make careful notes on their reading under headings, Locke's methodology suggests an underlying change in the nature of scholarly reading practices, which were now much more likely to focus on understanding a text's argument than gathering an appropriate quotation for use in conversation or reworking as a new text.

Not all text compilations made during the seventeenth and eighteenth centuries were commonplace books. Harold Love has argued that it is important to 'maintain the distinction between the commonplace book and the personal miscellany' when describing manuscripts produced during this period. The personal miscellany was a manuscript book 'into which the compiler entered texts of varying lengths which were either complete units or substantial extracts'. Love suggests that many late-seventeenth-century personal miscellanies include transcripts from texts circulated in manuscript, such as the 'libertine and state poems' collected in several volumes by Dame Sarah Cowper (1644–1720), but they remain quite distinct from the professionally written miscellany or anthology produced for sale by scribal publishers during this period, which can usually be recognised by a combined neatness of hand and organisation. Although often the work of a single compiler, personal miscellanies were sometimes produced by groups acting in the service of an aristocratic owner who added the manuscript volume to his (or her) private collection when it was completed.[19]

Love has argued that 'there are no sources apart from personal letters and diaries that bring us closer to late seventeenth-century readers' than the personal miscellany, but much of his own work has tended to concentrate on those books that include transcripts of scribally published material (usually referred to as manuscript separates) because he is interested in the reading communities associated with the production and consumption of clandestine satire. He does acknowledge, however, that the copying of these texts into personal miscellanies was part of a much larger culture of transcription that encouraged readers to produce a range of manuscript compilations, including commonplace books.[20] The circulation of manuscript separates declined in the early eighteenth century as state censorship began to be reduced, and it may be that for some groups the need to compile manuscript books declined with it. However, outside the elite communities connected to the court and state examined by Love, many readers were already transcribing texts from both manuscript and printed sources into their miscellanies.[21] Such a book was 'personal' in the sense that the compiler created an original editorial arrangement of writings by an array of different authors that had originated in a range of different sources. These compilations reveal that their creators assumed the same right to 'recompose, reapply, add and reorder' printed texts as they did with manuscript materials.[22]

I now want to look at a series of manuscript books created by two gentry-class readers, Charles Caesar (1636–1707) and Elizabeth Freke (1641–1714), during the early years of the eighteenth century, which show this process of recomposition and reordering in action, in order to suggest that transcription remained an important part of reading culture in an age which is more commonly associated with the expansion of print culture and the fixity of print. Caesar compiled six manuscript books between 1704 and 1706, one of which has survived as part of the British Library's manuscript collection.[23] The British Library also holds the two volumes created by Freke between 1682 and 1714. Each of these manuscripts has been catalogued as a 'commonplace book', but they do not contain the formal headings and indexes associated with the Humanist commonplace book, or its Lockean descendent. Similarly, although both contain substantial reworkings of extracts from texts circulated in print and manuscript they do not fit the strict definition of the personal miscellany used by Love. Indeed, they have more in common with the hybrid collection of original maxims, extracts and table talk that he describes as associated with Sarah Cowper and the Duke of Buckingham, but both also include autobiographical material. As Love's investigation of the so-called 'Buckingham Commonplace Book' suggests, such hybrid forms of compilation (or personalised anthology) were relatively common amongst gentry-class readers at the beginning of the eighteenth century. These books were compiled using the reading techniques associated with the creation of commonplace books and miscellanies, but they also show reading being put to use in other ways.

Charles Caesar's 'The Second Volume 1705'

Charles Caesar (1636–1707) was the son of Sir Charles Caesar and grandson of Sir Julius Caesar, who had both held the office of Master of the Rolls. Little is known of his early life, but he spent time as a fellow-commoner at Jesus College Cambridge in the 1650s. An early family historian, who had access to his manuscript books, describes him as 'a loyal subject to his king' and a 'sincere member of the established church'.[24] The tone is perhaps a little defensive because his grandson, also Charles Caesar (1673–1741), was arrested as a Jacobite in 1717. Caesar gave his seat to his son in 1692 in order to retire to Stamford where the surviving manuscript book appears to have been compiled. Described on the cover in Caesar's own hand as 'The Second Volume 1705', this book is significant because it reveals the range of material that he felt was important enough to transcribe during a relatively short period of time. Although each entry is not formally dated, a frequently interrupted narrative of national and international events, including 'The Famous Campaign in Germany' (dated 2 April 1704), the 'Great Victory at Blenheim' (August 1704), and the marriage of 'Mary Churchill, Daughter of Marlborough' (February 1704/5), suggests that the book was compiled in less than a year. That a list of 'Victoryes obtained by English Valour 1704' has been updated to include a reference to 'Alacantra in Spain – 1706' and Catharine the Queen Dowager (who died in 1705) removed from a prayer for the royal family suggests that the book continued to be read and added to after it was completed in February 1704/5.[25]

It has not been possible to identify sources for all of the texts entered into its two hundred folio pages, but it begins with a series of short poems, epigrams and maxims, attributed to 'Herbert's Sacred Poems', including 'Advice against' drunkenness, swearing, and 'the telling of lyes' which have been abstracted from 'The Church Porch' section of Herbert's *The Temple* (f.1v).[26] That Caesar was able to reduce Herbert's text to a series of pithy statements in this way shows the influence of the commonplace book tradition, as do the various groups of 'Claudian's epigrams', 'excellent maximes' and 'choice sentences' that are scattered throughout the volume (ff.164r–165v, f.174r).

Caesar's transcripts do not only come from printed sources. The main body of the text includes ten sermons, three of which (delivered by Barnabas Oley at a church close to Caesar's home) never appeared in print. Many of the others, including *Upon the Most Lamented Death of King William Third* (1702), written by his father, were recently published (13r–130r).[27] A series of running titles (such as 'Sermons') appears across the top of the page throughout the manuscript, making texts relatively easy to locate despite the lack of an index (perhaps included in a now lost volume), and the generous margins are filled with notes that act as pointers or which summarise content. Notes such as 'After four Good sermons concerning the Excellency and Usefulness, of the Common Prayer or Liturgie … Be pleased to read a Copie of Verses Upon the Same Subject, Out of Mr Herbert's Sacred Poems' (f.63r) indicate not only that this was a public rather than a private document, but that Caesar wanted readers to make connections between the various texts transcribed.

Complete transcripts of three pamphlets first published in the 1650s follow the 'Sermons' sequence. No source is acknowledged for the story of 'An Appearance of an Holy Angel' in Stamford (ff.144r–46r) or 'The Merry Divel of Mascon in France' (ff.150v–158v), but the many differences between Caesar's versions and those published as *The Good Angel of Stamford* (1659) and *The Divill of Mascon* (1659) perhaps suggests that they were copied from later reprints. Caesar notes that his version of the Royalist *Seasonable Speech* (1659) is recorded as transcribed from an edition 'licensed to be printed in 1692' (ff.134v–144r). As a postscript at the end of this text declares, it had been republished in order to discourage any one who had a 'great Reverence' for Cromwell as 'a man of Piety, and a great Champion for the Liberties of the Nation'.[28] That Caesar altered the title of the text so that it described Cromwell as 'that Bloody Tyrant, and Unjust Usurper' indicates that he shared the text's opposition to those who idealised the Protector. Caesar's marginal pointer 'Monarchy the Best of Governments' and his end comment 'this Loyall and Learned Speech was the First Step to the Restoration of King Charles the Second' (neither of which appear in the original) suggest that he was reading the text as a loyal statement of obedience to the monarchy rather than as a commentary upon the Jacobite uprising of 1692, which may well have been the reason for its republication. The civil war theme is continued in 'A Miraculous Sight', an eyewitness account of the image of the King's execution appearing in the sky above Jersey in the 1670s, for which I have been unable to locate an original (ff.158r–59v).

The remainder of the volume is taken up with a long sequence headed 'Miscellanea' (ff.159r–190v). This section contains short poems, such as 'On a Papist' and 'On a Puritan, or a Presbyterian', which originally appeared as 'To Rhemus' and 'On Phares' in Francis Quarles's *Divine Fancies* (1632), and extracts from long works such as Martin Lister's *Journey to Paris in the Year 1698* (1699), from which a debate about the evils of drinking coffee is reworked (f.160r, f.168r). Two satirical texts are transcribed in full; Ned Ward's *All Men Mad: or, England All a Bedlam* (1704), which is described as 'an Ingenious Poem, Lately Printed' (ff.176v–185v) and the August 1682 issue of *Heraclitus Ridens; Or, A Dialogue Between Jest and Earnest* (ff.185r–187v).[29] Caesar added marginal notes to both in order to identify the real people disguised by fake names or initials ('Earnest' in *Heraclitus Ridens* is revealed as 'Sir Roger L'Estrange'), or to draw attention to particular passages (such as 'Fornication described' in *All Men Mad*). Both of these texts celebrate the anarchic nature of satire. The majority of texts included in this section were relatively short and cheap: the *Brief Character of The Protector* is an 8-page pamphlet; *All Men Mad* is just 503 lines long and the British Library copy is marked 6d.[30] Caesar may well have transcribed the former because it was a relatively rare object that passed through his hands, but it is important to note the way in which the process of transcription transformed the portable, ephemeral, printed text into a subsection of the much larger personal miscellany. Not all of the entries in Caesar's book were copied from manuscript or print, however. Notes on 'Two Prodigies, or Wonders of Nature Anno 1701, Exhibited at Stamford in Lincolnshire, 1701', for example, appears to be autobiographical, as Caesar notes that the 'Tall young man' was 'measured by my self, at seven foot, and three inches high' (f.171v). The volume concludes with an entry made on Caesar's birthday that records details of his birthplace and the names of his children and grandchildren similar to the kind of family history recorded in the end pages of a Bible (f.192v).

Such a collection, transcribed from both print and manuscript sources, suggests the anthologists delight in variety. It gives a sense both of what Caesar was reading in 1704/5, which included some much older material, and of the kind of texts that were shared by his reading community, or which he wanted them to share. Although it does not fit the restrictive definitions of the commonplace book or the personal miscellany offered at the start of this chapter, its hybrid form reveals the continuing importance of transcription to reading practices and text transmission during the early eighteenth century. Both Caesar and Freke's manuscript books suggest that this was a culture in which readers regularly returned printed texts to manuscript either for preservation or for further circulation.[31] This occurred, in part, because print was still a relatively expensive medium and print runs often quite short, but transcription was also a very natural part of the reading process for gentry-class readers, such as Caesar, who had been trained in the art of compiling commonplace books when they attended University or the Inns of Court.

The commonplace book tradition, with its insistence upon gathering together quotations for practical or studious purposes, was in decline from about 1650, but the survival of many personal anthologies similar to that created by Caesar proves that the connection between reading and transcription did not decay with it.[32] As Adam Smyth has argued, it is tempting to construct a narrative in which the form and meaning of a text becomes 'fixed' once printed, but as his work on seventeenth- and early-eighteenth-century readers of printed miscellanies makes clear, these readers often reworked printed materials (some of which they probably owned) into their manuscript collections. In many of these collections the form of an individual poem or piece of prose was often carefully reproduced so that the manuscript book mimicked the printed page. Smyth concludes that readers engaged in this process because the act of 'transfer rendered the poems the property of the compiler in a way that mere ownership of a printed book could never do'. Even if the text itself was traced from the original, the new arrangement of material in the volume was a sign of the reader's control over the printed text.[33] Many of Caesar's transcriptions are accurate reproductions of the formal contents of the printed original, but as with his copy of Ward's *All Men Mad* he tended to personalize the text by making it conform to the paratextual conventions, such as headings and marginal glosses, used throughout the manuscript. As is the case with his amplifying of the anti-Cromwellian message of the *A Brief Character*, these minor amendments provide vital clues about how these transcribed texts were interpreted.

In other instances this personalising process was more thorough, often remaking the text in the image of the reader. Caesar appropriated texts for his own use, whatever their source, sometimes creating a new title, as in his reworking of texts by Herbert and Quarles, or by combining quotations from different sources without acknowledgement. Many texts in his volume are reproduced without reference to their original author or source. For example, the version of 'A Fable on K. W.' included as the first text in the 'Miscellanea' sequence does not contain any reference to its author or the text from which it was derived.[34] A version of Aesop's tale of the man with two wives, this poem has been identified by modern editors as the work of Matthew Prior (1664–1721), but was first published in *Poems on Affairs of State* (1703) as 'written by the Lord J----------s' (Lord Jeffries).[35] This is the text as it appears in print.

A Fable

> In *Aesop's* Tales an honest Wretch we find,
> Whose Years and Comforts equally declin'd;
> He in two Wives had two domestick Ills,
> For different Age they had, and different Wills;
> One pluckt his black Hairs out, and one his Grey,
> The man for Quietness did both obey,
> Till all his Parish saw his Head quite bare,
> And thought he wanted Brains as well as Hair.

The Moral

> The Parties, hen-peckt W------m, are thy Wives,
> The Hairs they pluck are thy Prerogatives;
> Tories thy Person hate, the Whigs thy Power,
> Tho much thou yieldest, still they tug for more,
> Till this poor Man and thou alike are shown,
> He without Hair, and thou without a Crown.[36]

As the *Index of English Literary Manuscripts* records, several contemporary manuscript anthologies, including those produced by Sarah Cowper, contain versions of this poem. The 'Fable' probably circulated for a time as a separate and at least one of the copies referred to in the *Index* is part of a scribally published miscellany. Almost all of these books reproduce the poem as found on the printed page. The only transcript that differs significantly was probably created in 1724 or later.[37] By contrast, Caesar's version contains several differences from the printed edition.

One of Old Aesop's Fables

In Aesop's Tales An Honest Wretch We Find,
Whose Year's And Comforts Equally Declin'd;
Hee in Two Wives Had Two Domestic Ills
For They Had Different Age; And Different Wills;
One Pluckt His Black-Hairs Out; And One His Grey,
The Man for Quietness Sake; Did Both Obey;
Till the Whole Parish Saw His Head Quite Bare
And Said He Wanted Sense, As Well As Hair.

The Morall of This Old Fable
Applyed to King William the Third And
His Last Parliament; Which Began -1701

The Partyes Hen-Peck't William Are Thy Wives!
The Hair They Pluck Are Thy Prerogatives;
Tories Thy Person Hate; And Whigs Thy Power;
Tho' Much Thou Yieldst, Yet Still, They Cry For More;
Till Thou, And This Old-Man Alike Are Shown,
One Without Hair, and One Without A Crown. (f.159r)

The version in his book is headed 'One of Old Aesop's Fables', rather than 'A Fable', and in the second section of the text 'The Moral' has been expanded so that it reads 'Applyd to King William the Third and His Last Parliament, Which Began 1701', which suggests that if it was copied from a manuscript separate it occurred sometime after the King's death on 8 March 1702. Both punctuation and capitalisation are significantly different from the printed text and other minor differences include the appearance of the king's name in full; the reordering of line four; the addition of 'sake' to line six; the substitution of 'the whole' for 'all his' in line seven, of 'sense' for 'brains' in line eight, and of 'One' for 'He' and 'thou' in line 14. Prior's editors have argued that he probably wrote this poem as a comment on the resumption bill of April 1700, when King William gave in to Parliament's demands that land granted to his supporters in Ireland should be returned, but Caesar's reference to the parliament of the following year is supported by a copy in the hand of the King's private secretary which describes it as 'Esop's-Tale, 1701 par le Sr Prior'.[38]

Both the date of transcription and Caesar's fondness for reproducing texts 'lately printed' suggest that it was probably copied from the 1703 edition of *Poems on Affairs*, but whatever its source (and he could perhaps have seen both print and manuscript versions), Caesar's book demonstrates just how fluid the movement between various media could be in this period. Each new transcription of a text adds layers of meaning that we can use to help decode the way in which it was interpreted by the transcriber. The extension of the moral and the completion of the King's name draws attention to the fact that this is a poem critical of both monarch and parliament, but Caesar's invented marginal gloss ('King William and His Last Peevish Parliament Anno 1701') suggests that he interpreted the poem as a critique of parliament rather than crown.

As one of the *Poems on Affairs of State*, 'The Fable' was part of a volume that celebrated the art of satire by gathering together what the preface refers to as 'the poems of all Party's'.[39] In its published context the poem was surrounded by bawdy verse, such as the 'Epitaph on the Late King of Spain' (p. 240), which makes fun of the King's impotence, and other poetry critical of William's reign. If he was reworking this poem from *Poems on Affairs* Caesar chose to situate it in a new context. As the first poem in the 'Miscellanea' portion of the manuscript, it is part of a sequence containing several satirical texts, such as Ward's *All Men Mad*. This 'satiric' environment is similar to that of the printed volume. Ward's poem, for example, mocks the Whigs for their continued championing of the late King, but Caesar chose to follow the 'Fable' with two lines 'On King Charles, the Royal Martyr' – 'A Prince that Briefly to Characterise Him, / Did Only Want A People Fit to prize Him', – adapted from Francis Quarles's *The Shepheards Oracles* (1645) that appear designed to call attention to 'The Fable' as a loyalist text that exalts the status of the king above the battling parties of his 'Peevish Parliament'.[40] However, as Adam Smyth has argued 'reading the politics of a collection' is 'a delicate business', and we must be careful not to look for a stable political identity that never really existed, or which was not the primary concern of the reader as compiler.[41] That Caesar should recycle these lines from a Royalist text that had not appeared in print since 1646 suggests a particular concern with the reworking of civil war texts in new contexts. Wary as we must be about ascribing a politics to such collections, Caesar's frequent reproduction of allusions to the civil war suggests a commitment to preserving the constitution in church and state as it had been settled at the Revolution of 1688–1689. This was a reader picking over texts that could be used to emphasise that 'Monarchy' really was 'the Best of Governments', but he cannot be reduced to that one position.[42]

It is, of course, impossible to know exactly how Caesar read this poem, or how he intended later readers to interpret his transcriptions, but this example shows that historians of reading need to take account of both the way in which an individual text was reconfigured and the context in which it was reproduced. (It is not enough to simply look at which texts were reproduced and assume that they were interpreted in a way that directly corresponds to their original context.) Caesar's book is a 'personal miscellany' in the sense that it brings together a diverse body of texts (most of which were available in print) and reworks them to fit a new 'personal' context. As the volumes compiled by Cowper and others suggest this reworking of the word was a common practice amongst gentry-class readers in the early eighteenth century.

Harold Love has argued that miscellanies often reveal which texts it was acceptable to read in a given community. He provides evidence of some communities, for example, in which it was perfectly legitimate for a Godly poem to be interrupted by a pornographic ballad, and of others compiled by government officials or courtiers that feature lampoons against both the government and the crown. These mixed anthologies confirm that we should be cautious about using any single text included in an anthology as representative of the owner's true attitude towards the subject described.[43] Although it contains some unusual combinations of texts, Caesar's miscellany does not include any of the carnivalesque disjunctions associated with the volumes of clandestine satire examined by Love, or indeed of the sort reproduced in the original *Poems on the Affairs of State*. Caesar's book thus provides evidence of a reading community that is different to those examined by Love.

Elizabeth Freke (1641–1714) 'her book'

Elizabeth Freke (1641–1714) was the daughter of Ralph Freke a successful lawyer and landholder whose family were important members of the Dorset gentry. Her mother, Cicely Culpeper, died young, but the Culpepper family (noted for their support of the royalist cause during the civil war) played an important role in her upbringing. She married her cousin Percy Freke (1643?–1702) in 1672, without her father's permission, and although she often complained about a lack of financial security, the Norfolk manor of West Bilney, purchased by her husband in 1676, brought in a substantial rent, as did the Irish estate that she inherited on his death. Raymond Anselment has argued that the autobiographical sections of the two commonplace books that she created between 1684 and 1714 provide 'an unusually detailed account of a gentry woman's late seventeenth- and early eighteenth-century domestic world'.[44] The larger of the two volumes,

BL Add. MS 45718, bears the ownership inscription: 'Elizabeth Frek her book Given mee by my Cosen Sep. 1684'. It includes a series of autobiographical 'remembrances' that commence with her marriage in 1672. Begun in 1702, these diary-like entries were created retrospectively. Freke continued to add to this account of her life until 13 February 1714, although she also reworked many of the entries into the second, shorter volume (BL Add. MS 45719), begun in 1712.

Anselment's edition of Freke's autobiography (which reproduces both versions of the 'remembrances') reveals that she significantly 'refashioned' the story of her life as she reworked the entries for the second manuscript. The more sympathetic portrait of her 'deer Husband' which emerges in the revised entries, he suggests, is produced by 'omitting statements and actions that reflect the strained relationship' described in the earlier volume. At other times she makes significant alterations to the way in which events are told. The original account of the accidental shooting and death of her grandson is centred upon her own grief, but in the later version not only has her husband's sorrow become crucial to the narrative, 'this same shott' is said to have helped bring about his fatal illness. Anselment's conclusion that for Freke the reconstruction of the past was both 're-creative' and a form of recreation is particularly useful for thinking about her reading practices.[45] She must have spent a great deal of time rereading her own manuscripts in order to rework them. As many of the entries in the larger volume make clear her autobiographical writings were designed to be reread (they are described as 'convenyent for me to think on') in much the same way that a series of extracts from the Psalms entered into the same volume were intended to be regularly consulted.[46]

In an entry dated 3 November 1710, Freke records that her hair caught fire while she was 'sitting in my chamber all alone reading', but she makes little reference to reading or her possession of books elsewhere in the autobiography.[47] Most of what we can discover about Freke as a reader can only be recovered by examining the larger of her two manuscript volumes as a combination of autobiography *and* transcribed materials. These transcripts, taken from print, manuscript and oral sources reveal the various kinds of material that she thought were useful to preserve, but I also want to suggest that the autobiographical sections of the manuscript show the way in which Freke fashioned and refashioned her sense of self within a historical perspective derived from her reading of contemporary accounts of the recent past. Freke's reading supports Daniel Woolf's contention that this period saw a change in the way people read history. The older pattern of reading history for 'the example, the isolated episode, the portable anecdote' had, of course, not entirely disappeared, but Freke was one of a new breed of readers who used the historical past to give 'order and meaning to personal autobiography'.[48]

The first 120 folio pages of Freke's manuscript consists mainly of 'receipts' 'collected & abstracted' from a range of oral and printed sources, including John Gerard's *The Herball; or, General History of Plants* (1597) and Nicholas Culpepper's *School of Physick* (1659). These recipes were clearly intended for practical use, and in one instance she records that they were 'for my owne use and most of them experienced by mee'.[49] The structure of the manuscript also suggests that it was once divided into discrete sections in order to make individual entries easier to locate. For example, all of the notes on 'the history of Plants taken out of Gerard's Herball' are gathered into a numbered sequence and a blank page left to divide it from the next section, which contains nearly 200 entries on 'Trees, Shrubs, Bushes, Fruits, Resins and Gums' also taken from Gerard (ff.175v–158r). However, the blank page that once marked the end of this section has been filled with two poems, the 'Downefall of Charing Cross, by the Long Parliament in the Yeare 1648; After they had beheaded King Charls the First' and 'An Epytaff on K: Wm. the Third' (f.157v). Similarly, the poem 'A Song Made by my Husband's Father Captain Arthur Freke' occupies what was undoubtedly once a blank division, and is now followed immediately by additional entries to a sequence of 'short receits … for my use' (f.133r, f.140v). This section ends with another poem 'The French King's Cordiall: On 134', dated 1704 (f.125v). Much of the rest of the manuscript is taken up with transcripts of historical documents relating to the Bilney estate, but in the midst of this material is another poem 'The British Ambassador's Speech to the French Kinge 1713' (f.121v).

Neither the recipes nor the poems are reproduced in Anselment's edition of *The Remembrances* because of lack of space, but I want to suggest that these transcripts help to reveal the role played by reading in the construction of Freke's autobiography. A shorter version of the poem 'The Downefall of Charing Cross' appeared in *Sportive Wit*, a collection of 'a la mode lampoones', published, banned and burnt in 1656.[50] Texts from printed miscellanies were frequently reworked in both manuscript and print but the inclusion of a version almost identical to that produced by Freke in Percy's *Reliques* (1765), where it is described as 'often printed', suggests that she might have transcribed it from a later printed source.[51] 'The French King's Cordiall' was widely circulated in manuscript, but both it and the anonymous 'Epitaph on King William, 1702' were included in the four-volume edition of

The Poems on Affairs of State (1707) that Freke owned.[52] However, both the date 1704 and the significant number of differences between Freke's version of 'The Cordiall' and that which appeared in *The Poems* (where it is dated 1705) suggest that it was copied from an earlier manuscript separate. Her manuscript book thus reveals a reader who moved confidently between manuscript and print, preserving important texts as she went.

Freke made minor adjustments to the published version of 'The Epitaph on King William', a far less ambiguous poem on William III than that reworked by Caesar, in order to fit it into her manuscript collection. This is the printed original.

Epitaph on King WILLIAM, 1702

William the Third lies here, th' Almighty's Friend
A Scourge to *France*, a check t' Imperious *Rome*,
Who did our Rights and Liberties defend,
And rescu'd *England* from its threaten'd Doom;
Heav'n snatch'd him from us whom our Hearts caress'd
And now he's king in Heaven among the Blest,
Grief stops my Pen; Reader pray weep the rest.[53]

Freke changed the way in which the text was laid out on the page in order to fit it into the limited amount of space available next to 'The Downfall of Charing Cross', in the process making a minor adjustment to the title and altering the spelling throughout.

An Epytaff on K: Wm the Third

William the third lies heer, the almightys / friend /
A scourge to France,-
A check to imperious Roome:
Who did our Rights & Libertys Defend –
And Rescued England,
From its threatened Doome,
Heaven snatched him from us,
As whome our Harts carress'd,
And now hee's king,
In heaven Among the Blest,
Grief stops my pen
Reader pray weep the Rest. (f.157v)

We know that Freke owned the four-volume edition of *Poems on Affairs of State* (1707) because it was amongst the books 'putt into the deep deale box by the fireside in my own closett' when she left her estate to visit London in October 1711. This list, along with another inventory of books placed in 'the great chest in my upper closet', gives some indication of her reading repertoire during the period in which the 'remembrances' were being written. Many of the books that she owned were religious works, but a significant number of histories are also listed. These include 'i thick history of the wars of England, Scotland and Ireland' and '3 new books of the life and reigne of King William the Third of blessed memory'.[54]

Freke used these volumes of contemporary history to help construct the narrative of her autobiography and to place her own life in context. For example, the section of the manuscript in which she recalls being 'a deep sufferer with my deer husband, Percy Frek' because of the 'loss of all we had by King Jams and excominycated by him and outlawed for an absentee in 1689', probably written in the summer of 1710, uses several sources to help flesh out the account of the Irish wars, including George Story's *True and Impartial History* (1691), the narrative of which is sometimes followed quite closely.[55] Freke's account of the period 1689–1694 ends with a description of the death of 'good Queen Mary' in which she is said to have 'expired in the armes of a loveing husband' (p. 151). Her account of this period clearly combines information drawn from the '3 new books' on William III with her own and her husband's experience of these events, but whereas the King and Queen are idealised throughout, little mention is made of Percy Freke's active resistance to the Irish Jacobites. Freke's idealisation of William's 'corrage and conductt' during the battle of the Boyne may have something to do with the fact that his defeat of James II eventually led to the restoration of Percy Freke's Irish estates (p. 145). Whatever its cause, however, her description of 1689–1694 is one of a series of idealised accounts of the King that occurs in her manuscripts. A passage 'transcribed from The London Post Man September 2d, 1710' celebrating the repair of a 'statue in honour of King William the 3d of glorious memory … our late deliverer from popery', is, for example, given a prominent place in both versions of the 'remembrances' (p. 155). Throughout the autobiography 8 March is noted as the date 'remarkable for the death of our good King William' (p. 75), and both his death and that of Queen Mary appear to have had a particular importance for Freke.

Indeed, Freke seems to have drawn on the romanticised account of the death of Queen Mary for the modified version of the death of her own husband that appears in the revised 'remembrances'. In the first version

Freke reveals that she was 'nott able to hold' her husband at the moment of death, whereas in the revision he is described as dying 'in my armes', in much the same way as Mary is said to have 'expired in the armes of a loveing husband' in the account of the Queen's death (p. 251, p. 150). In such instances Freke appears to have drawn upon idealised accounts of the 'good' queen and her 'loveing husband' in order to re-imagine her own difficult relationship with Percy Freke in more positive terms.

In this context the undated transcript of William's 'Epitaph' can be considered a very personal text. By removing it from *Poems on the Affairs of State* she remade it in a new less ambiguous context that suited her idealised reading of the monarch. In the printed volume the 'Epitaph' is preceded by the bawdy seduction fantasy 'A Cure for the Green Sickness', which includes the lines 'At last I did by Dalliance raise the Pretty Nymph's Desire, / Our inclinations equal were, and mutual was our fire'. A number of other poems in the collection satirise the events of William's reign. In 'A Panegyrick on K. W.', for instance, the king's 'Loyal Slaves' 'beg the blessing of Eternal War' and in 'The Mourners' the reader is encouraged to 'mourn for the mighty mass of coin mis-spent' by William's government.[56] There are other positive assessments of William's reign within this volume, but Freke's reworking of the text as the 'Epytaff' – and her spelling is part of this personalising process – situates it within a new context, away from both satirical attack and bawdy innuendo. By placing it next to 'The Downefall of Charing Cross', which satirises the iconoclasm of the 1649 parliament as paranoia ('Since crosses you soe much disdain / Faith Iff I was as you / For fear the King should Rule Againe / I'd pull down Tyburn's Tree') Freke establishes an unambiguously Williamite context for reading. Given that these poems were reproduced alongside the extracts from Herbals and texts of 'physic' that were intended to be 'put to use', it seems certain that Freke transcribed the 'Epitaph' in order to reuse it as part of her autobiographical project, in much the same way that she reused the transcript from *The London Post Man*. Freke was a reader who transcribed texts for a number of different reasons. Her manuscript books were used to preserve texts (such as Captain Freke's song), which were an important part of her family's history, and to stockpile historical documents that could be used in legal disputes, as well as to record recipes for everyday use. Freke used her manuscript book to gather together material that would later be used in new contexts, and all of these various activities show her to have been a particularly active reader.

The manuscript books compiled by Caesar and Freke reveal active rather than passive readers. Both appear to have understood texts as malleable forms that could be removed from their original context in order to be reworked for various ends. Although both sometimes acknowledge that they are returning texts 'lately printed' to manuscript, reworking them in new contexts in the process, neither is particularly concerned with their original author or the context in which they originally appeared. Indeed, their transcription practices constantly blur the boundaries between author and reader, manuscript and print. Freke's autobiographical recreation of the period 1689–1694, for example, never acknowledges its debt to the historical works that it so closely follows.

These books, like all manuscript books, reveal the reader with pen in hand, involved in the close study of texts. The commonplace book and the personal miscellany are forms of 'hard reading' (to use De Maria's term), but the very nature of the source means that they tell us very little else about the reading life of the individual (or group of individuals) that created them.[57] Even Freke's autobiography, although it gives some insight into the way in which she interpreted history, has little to say about how she read the other texts that she owned. For example, she does not record the title of the text that she was reading whilst 'sitting in my chamber all alone' on the day her hair caught fire, and it is impossible to tell from the 'remembrances' whether reading alone by candlelight (with all of its potential dangers) was a regular part of her reading experience. Caesar's volume of transcripts is, of course, even less informative about the way in which the copying of texts fitted into the broader patterns of his reading. In order to move beyond a discussion of early eighteenth-century readers as studious yet creative, I now want to look at the evidence of another reader, Gertrude Savile (1697–1758), whose manuscript book and journals suggest some of the other ways of reading available during this period.

The reading practices of Gertrude Savile (1697–1758)

Gertrude Savile began to compile a daily 'journal' sometime before September 1721. She continued to make regular notes on her everyday existence throughout the rest of her life. Not all of her journals have survived, but those made between July 1727 and January 1730 often include details of visits to the theatre and reading, alongside sometimes coded accounts of her emotional life. A manuscript book into which she entered short extracts from texts has also survived. Although undated, it appears to have been compiled during the late 1720s and early 1730s. The journals reveal that although she never married, Savile was a relatively wealthy woman. During the late 1720s she lived in a house in Golden Square, London, that was paid for by her brother, George Savile,

Lord of Thornhill and Rufford, who also gave her a generous allowance of around £200 per year.[58] Her income puts her just above the 'middling ranks' described by Lorna Weatherill as those earning between £40 and £200 per year.[59] Taken together, Savile's journals and manuscript book provide an unusually detailed picture of the cultural life of an early eighteenth-century woman reader.

Savile and contemporary print culture

As the books compiled by Freke and Caesar demonstrate, text transmission via manuscript was still an important part of post-Restoration reading culture, but print was becoming more pervasive. James Raven has argued that 'after vigorous growth from the late 1690s, printed publication rates mushroomed between the late 1740s and the end of the century'. Between 1710 and 1719, nearly 23,000 separate titles were produced. The term catalogues issued by booksellers give some idea of what the market was like during the early years of the eighteenth century. Between 1700 and 1705 more than half of all new titles were works of 'divinity'. History, law, maths, classics and poetry were also popular. Reading and piety often went together, but as Raven makes clear, although the book trade was still dependent upon the production of religious books, by the 1720s publishers were experimenting with smaller and cheaper formats for secular texts, such as plays, as part of the 'courting and the creation' of new customers. The first octavo edition of Shakespeare appeared in 1709 and many other books, including religious works and novels, began to be produced in duodecimo during the first quarter of the eighteenth century.[60] However, whilst print culture was certainly expanding during this period, it is wrong to think that these were texts produced for a mass audience. Many plays and novels had an average print run of between 750 and 1,000 copies, and as Ros Ballaster has noted, even the 'comparatively cheap cost of one to three shillings a volume for a duodecimo novel in the early 1700s would have been prohibitive for the vast majority of working people ... who could command a wage of only seven to fifteen shillings a week'. Books in folio, which often sold at a guinea a volume, were only affordable by 'the aristocracy and upper bourgeoisie'.[61] London was the centre of the book trade, and with high literacy rates, especially amongst women, it also supplied many new readers. The expansion of the market for print during this period was thus largely based upon the repackaging of books for relatively wealthy readers such as Savile.[62]

Based in Golden Square, Gertrude Savile was well placed to benefit from the expansion of the London trade. However, despite providing many details of her everyday life in the journals, Savile has little to say about how she acquired her books. In July 1727 she recorded the impulsive purchase of '8s. worth of silly Books' from a bookseller next to the Half Moon Inn, Richmond where she had stopped with her mother for a few hours. She spent a further 15s on religious books during a shopping trip just ten days later.[63] A series of account books compiled during the late 1730s include references to hiring books at 1s for two weeks as well as regular purchases of newspapers and books, but changes in her family circumstances had made her a wealthier and more independent woman by that time.[64] It is possible that Savile rented books from booksellers during the 1720s, but the fact that she makes little mention of the process of buying or hiring texts suggests that she found them easy to acquire.

Of course, books do not have to be bought. On 21 July 1728 Savile borrowed Edward Young's *The Universal Passion* (1728) from the daughter of a family friend during a visit to their home. She read it rapidly, sending it back during the evening of 23 July, when she noted, ' 'tis exceeding seveer 'tis all satir but mighty pretty & too just – he is grown a favourite author of mine, I like it so well I am not content with once reading it but design to bye [sic] it'.[65] Unfortunately the 'catalogue of my books' that she created during the evening of 13 August 1728 has not survived, but as this reference to the intention to buy *The Universal Passion* suggests, Savile was able to purchase new books for repeated reading with relative ease (p. 128). Her journal records that she reread some of the 'silly' books purchased in July 1727 during the following year.

The only other book that she recorded borrowing in 1728 was George Stanhope's *Paraphrase and Comment on the Epistles* (1705–1726) that she was lent by another friend of the family one Sunday afternoon when it was too cold to attend church.[66] Savile regularly attended church on Sunday and often read religious texts at home on her return. During 1728 her Sunday reading included Samuel Clarke's, *A Demonstration of the Being and Attributes of God* (1705–1728) and 'a Book of Luther's'(p. 97).[67] Most of the texts that she read during the late 1720s were of a secular nature, but regular attendance at church (where she heard sermons by many leading divines), and the reading of religious books, must have framed her experience of reading plays, novels, pamphlets and newspapers.[68] That the experience of religious texts was more than a repeated weekly ritual is suggested by her description of reading a sermon by George Stanhope:

Deserv'd pitty of my mother, when a little of it wou'd have soften'd and calm'd me. I thought she might have bestow'd a little, but she

did not. Then I made myself undeserving of it. I threw myself on the
Bed; slept not, but had thoughts fit for Bedlam. At last I read an excellent sermon of Dr Stanhope's upon Christ's answer to the Young Man
'If thou wilt enter into Life, keep the Commandments'. It composed
me a little. (pp. 53–54)

As Robert DeMaria has noted, Samuel Johnson also often read to calm
his nerves.[69]

Including quotations, Savile read 63 texts during 1728. Her reading
supports William St Clair's contention that 'no historical reader, whatever his or her socio-economic or educational status, read printed texts
in the chronological order in which they were first published', but her
diaries reveal that she did consume a great deal of contemporary material.[70] Quotations from the Bible, Shakespeare and Beaumont and
Fletcher are included in the journal, but even after newspapers, periodicals and ephemera have been excluded, 18 of the texts that she recorded
reading in 1728 were printed for the first time between 1727 and 1729.
A further eight books were first published in the 1720s, and many of the
older texts, such as Nicholas Rowe's play, *The Ambitious Stepmother*
(1701), were available in recently published octavo or duodecimo editions.[71] That some texts still circulated in manuscript during this period
is confirmed by her reading of 'a New Tragidy in Maniscript that has not
been acted' (p. 137).

Reading in the context of theatrical performance

Savile's regular attendance at the theatre is one of the most important
contexts for her reading. During the early part of the eighteenth century
audience participation or additions by the actors often helped to change
the meaning of the text being performed. As John Brewer has argued,
'dramatic interpretation' was sometimes shaped as much 'by the play
between performers and audience in the theatre' as it was on the written
or printed page.[72] Savile certainly took the audience into account when
she and her aunt attended the first performance of John Gay's *The
Beggar's Opera* at Lincoln's Inn Fields on 29 January 1728. After noting
that the theatre was 'very full in great expectation from the odd Title',
she wrote an unusually lengthy description of the performance that suggests that this play challenged her own expectations about what could
be performed on the stage.

The top charicters were Highwaymen and Common Whores and very
exactly drawn and yet manag'd so as to be inofencive and very witty

(which one woud think impossible); full of Sater [satire] upon higher Charicters – indeed upon almost all Vices, with a little too much upon Polliticks. In the whole it was wonderfully entertaining and instructive, tho the Subject was so Low. (p. 100)

She saw the play again on 7 February, this time in the company of her mother, because it was rumoured that the King and Queen were to attend, and a few weeks later was turned away from a performance because the theatre was full. On this occasion she noted that that 'the Town' was 'stark mad' about the play (p. 109). She saw it for a third time on 26 March in the company of her sister-in-law and two other aristocratic ladies, but was disappointed that she didn't see anyone that she knew 'nor any of fashion', and again in July, when it was 'sorryly performed' by a new company at the Haymarket (p. 111, p. 127). The genuine excitement that Savile felt about the play's combination of high and low culture on the first night was obviously modified by seeing several performances under different circumstances, and by her knowledge that it was the most popular play in town. However, her attitude towards these performances must also have been altered by her own reading of the play, which she acquired soon after seeing it for a second time. The first edition of *The Beggar's Opera* which included 'the musick engrav'd on copper plates' was sold for 1s 6d by John Watts from his premises in Wild Court near to the theatre, and it was probably at this shop that Savile acquired a copy sometime before 15 February, when she read it 'in intervals before and after supper' to a group of friends gathered at the house in Golden Square (p. 103).[73]

As Savile's reading of part of *The Beggar's Opera* to this group demonstrates, she lived in a society where the oral performance of texts was a relatively common occurrence. During 1727 she acquired a new maid, Mary Stanwick, who's reading she described as 'tolerable' (p. 85). Frances Harris has noted that servants frequently read devotional works to their employers during this period, but Savile's reading to Mary was unusual.[74] On 4 July 1728 the pair took a trip across the Thames to Greenwich, where she read three acts of Richard Steele's play *The Conscious Lovers* (1722).[75] Both women may well have seen this comedy when it was performed at the Theatre Royal in Drury Lane. The octavo edition of 1723, which Savile probably read, includes a frontispiece depicting the actress who played Phillis in the original production, but the printed text was not simply a memorial of the play as it was performed. There is also a five-page preface by Steele that comments upon the difference between seeing a play in performance and reading it in 'the Closet, or any other circumstance of the Reader, whether alone or in Company'. By suggesting that 'the greatest Effect of a Play is to excite the Reader to go see it', Steele argues that it was written to be performed rather than read, but the preface is an attempt to persuade the *reader* to concentrate on the way in which it modifies comedy as a genre.[76] As Harold Love has argued, after the Interregnum, the reading of plays was increasingly done 'for its own sake rather than as a way of imagining or reimagining a performance', and authors often attempted to take control of reading in 'the Closet' by deploying persuasive prefaces and other paratextual devices.[77] Although it is impossible to tell whether Savile responded to Steele's attempts to persuade the reader to see the play as a new sort of comedy that also dealt with serious emotions, her journals suggest that it is difficult to separate the private reading of a play from its performance, either at the theatre, or in front of friends and servants. For Savile, as for anyone who regularly attended the theatre during this period, the interpretation of drama often involved seeing a performance before reading the printed text (with its additional materials), either alone in the 'Closet', or in company. These various kinds of performance must have influenced the way in which a text was interpreted.

As the reference to reading a new play in manuscript makes clear, Savile did not only read plays that she had seen in performance. For example, on 2 January 1728 she recorded reading *Double Falshood … Written Originally by William Shakespeare* (1728), which had been performed at Drury Lane in December 1727. Savile had not seen this play and her reaction, 'I think it is a poor one for his', demonstrates the good judgement of someone familiar with Shakespeare's work, as it was in fact written by James Shirley (p. 94). Similarly, on 9 Februray 1728 she recorded reading John Sturmy's *Sesostris* (1728), which she describes as 'a new tragydy; a so-so one' (p. 102).[78] Savile's regular attendance at the theatre and her reading of new plays in both print and manuscript meant that she was particularly well informed about contemporary drama. However, as her reaction to *Double Falshood* as 'a poor one for his' and to *Sesostris* as 'so-so' suggests, she didn't have a well-developed critical vocabulary. To Judge Savile's reaction to texts in this way is undoubtedly anachronistic, however. There was not yet a tradition of reviewing plays, and her journal entries were not intended as a close reading of the text. Indeed, we know exactly what she means when a play is described as 'so-so' or 'poor', because she is judging it against all of those other texts that she had read or seen in performance. That she rarely had anything more to say about these texts reveals just how impressive *The Beggar's Opera* must have been when she saw it for the first time.

Reading and transcription: Savile's manuscript book

The 1727–1730 sequence of the journal contains many extracts from the texts that Savile was reading. Despite her apparent disappointment with *Sesostris* and *Double Falshood*, she entered quotations from both plays into her journal. Why did Savile make extracts from texts that she judged to be mediocre, and what do these extracts tell us about her reading practices? The following quotations from *Sesostris* were added to the journal on the day before she recorded her dissatisfaction with the play.

> For every pain
>
> Relief is found. My wound admits no cure.
> Peace with her smiling Train has left my Breast
> Her wonted seat and visits me no more.
>
> Fancy gives us Pleasure, gives us Pain
> And Heav'n and Hell are seated in the mind.[79]

The chief subject of both is pain, but Savile does not appear to have intended these extracts to illuminate or comment upon her emotional state in the way that she sometimes used quotations in the journal. For example, an entry describing how she had talked unguardedly during a visit to a friend includes an appropriate quotation from the *Spectator* on passion as a 'short Madness' (p. 136). She also made use of extensive quotation at the end of each year when she summarised the major events of the past twelve months under a series of headings such as 'own' and 'state affairs'. The December 1727 summary of her 'own affairs' includes a note explaining that 'speeches' from three contemporary texts had been added because they 'have an application to some parts in it'.[80] In the case of the quotations from *Sesostris*, the journal was acting as a store for quotations that might be used in the entries or the 'heads' at the end of the year, but they clearly show that the process of extracting short maxims was very much a part of Savile's everyday reading experience.

As well as entering extracts into her journals, Savile also stored quotations in a manuscript book that was much closer in style to the Humanist commonplace book than either its Lockean descendent or the hybrid miscellanies constructed by Caesar and Freke. Listed on the verso of the front cover are 27 headings that run from 'Hope – Joy – Disappointment' through 'Happiness', 'Virtue and Vice' and on to 'Ruin', under which she entered short quotations similar to those on pain extracted from *Sesostris*.[81] These lines are not included in the section headed 'Comparison in Pain or

Grief', but extracts from Sturmy's tragedy are incorporated into the book under the headings 'Joy' and 'Love'. As in the classic commonplace book tradition, Savile mined this play for a series of maxims, and in doing so destroyed any sense of the integrity of the original text. Her manuscript book does not contain any references to the speaker or the section of the text from which a quotation was taken, or to the edition that she was reading, although a narrow margin on the left-hand side of the page has been used throughout to note either the text's author or title. The book contains more than 250 of these marginal references, some of which cover as many as 20 different quotations from the same author.

When removing these extracts from their original context Savile sometimes made significant changes to the text. For example, the following lines from Act II Scene V of Elijah Fenton's *Mariamne* (1723) were reworked when they were transferred into the 'Death-Life' section of the manuscript book.

> E'en life, that dear ennobling gift of heav'n,
> Which in the order of creation, ranks
> The palest glow-worms animated ray
> Above the brightest star, with me will lose
> Its boasted value when I lose my child.[82]

By removing any reference to its original context as part of a speech by Mariamne in which she talks about 'the strong emotions of a mother's woe', Savile transformed the original into a generic statement about life.

> ---- Life that dear ennobling gift of Heav'n
> Which in the order of Creation ranks
> The palest glow-worms animated ray,
> Above the Brightest Star.[83]

Mariamne was one of many plays staged in the 1720s that debated the nature of royal power. In Savile's version the capitalisation of 'Heav'n' and 'Creation' converts this section of the text, in which Mariamne stands up against the tyrannical power of her husband, the King, into a depoliticised statement about the munificence of God. During the early eighteenth century drama with a 'political theme' often used ancient settings, such as Greece or Rome, to explore 'modern predicaments'.[84] *Sesostris*, which is set in ancient Egypt, is a reworking of a favourite contemporary genre, the usurpation play. It ends with the death of the 'Tyrant' Omar, 'usurper of the crown of Egypt', and the restoration of the true King's son.[85] The parallels with British history are obvious, but all of the extracts that Savile made from this play ignore its political content. Harold Love has argued that many of the tragedies written between 1660 and 1740 are 'richly open' to modern 'Foucaultian readings' because they are so concerned with power.[86] There is a great deal of evidence to suggest that early-eighteenth-century audiences paid close attention to the way in which a text examined power structures and conveyed political meaning. Sections of the first audience of Addison's *Cato* (1713), for example, famously tried to make this deliberately ambiguous work toe the party line.[87] Savile's reworking of these texts, with their anxious treatment of the theme of usurpation, into sources for a range of general topics suggests that we need to recognise that not every early-eighteenth-century reader was a proto-Foucaultian concerned with politics and power. Even the most controversial text about the abuse of authority could be made conventional. The way in which Savile parcelled out extracts from these plays under various headings will repay an extended study of her manuscripts.

The art of making commonplaces is often associated with the (male) scholarly tradition of reading, where it is seen both as a way of disciplining the reader and of producing a stock of quotations that could be put to use in the compiler's professional or personal life. Savile's rewriting of texts to fit the headings chosen for her manuscript book, and her use of quotation in the journal, suggest that she followed this tradition by making these texts her own. Given the large number of entries included in her manuscript book, searching for extracts must have been a major part of her reading experience. None of the texts that she owned have survived, so it is impossible to know whether she underlined or marked passages before reworking them, but the transcription of short passages into the journal as she was reading suggests that cutting texts into chunks was something that she did automatically as part of the reading process. Unlike Caesar and Freke, she did not transfer entire texts into her book.

All texts, whatever their quality, could be subjected to this process. Savile's manuscript book contains extracts from dramatic works, conduct books, poetry, periodicals and even romances. The section on 'Love' is typical. It contains quotations from 20 texts. Although the most quoted text is Edward Young's, *A Vindication of Providence* (1728), this section is dominated by extracts from 13 plays. This is not surprising given the number of references to attending the theatre and reading drama recorded in the journals, but only four of these plays were first published in the period 1727–1730. Of the other nine, Addison's *Cato* (1713) and Nicholas Rowe's *Ulysses* (1706) were available in relatively recent editions and *The Winter's Tale* in Shakespeare's *Works*. Many of the others had not been in print (even as part of a collected works) since the late seventeenth century. These include Sedley's *The Mulberry Garden* (1675) and Rymer's *Edgar* (1678), which had not appeared since 1675 and 1693 respectively. Daniel's *Hymens Triumph* (1615), which is quoted several times (although not mentioned in the journals), appears to have been out of print for more than a 100 years.[88] The manuscript book thus helps us to recognise that Savile had access to older texts, perhaps via her brother's library or the second-hand trade, as well as the contemporary material that is referred to in the journal entries.

Novels and romances

The 'Love' section of the manuscript book also includes two quotations from *Clelia*, a romance by Madame de Scudery available in English translation from the 1650s.[89] That Savile reproduced further substantial sections of this text under the headings 'Obligation, or Provokation; Praise or Contempt; Gratitude or Resentment', 'Virtue and Vice', 'Jealousie, Distrust, Imagination, Fancy', and 'Indiscretion, Vanity, Reputation, [and] Shame' suggests that she took it just as seriously as the other texts that surround it in her manuscript book. However, this text was central to one of the most widely distributed attacks upon women's reading of the period. On his visit to a 'Lady's Library', Mr Spectator found a copy of *Clelia* 'which opened of it self in the Place that describes two Lovers in a Bower'. Throughout this essay, which first appeared in the *Spectator* on 12 April 1711, women's reading of novels and romances is connected to erotic pleasure.[90] Ros Ballaster has argued that this image of a lady's library, which contains many 'Counterfeit Books' that 'served only to fill up the number, like Faggots in the Muster of a Regiment', is used to expose women's reading as 'a form of conspicuous consumption' whilst at the same time establishing an 'ideological equivalence between fictionality and femininity'.[91] However, although Scudery's romances and Manley's satirical *New Atlantis* proto-novels are conspicuous amongst the contents of the library, this is not just an attack upon women as readers of novels. The lady is criticised for acquiring a mishmash of texts 'got together, either because she had heard them praised, or because she had seen the Authors of them'.[92] During the first quarter of the eighteenth century, both the female reader of romances and the 'learned woman' were frequently depicted in negative terms, especially in dramatic works by Steele, Colly Cibber and Congreve.[93] Savile was undoubtedly familiar with the 'Lady's Library' essay, as she was an enthusiastic reader of the

Spectator in volume form, and although it did not dissuade her from reading either *Clelia* or other fictional works, her journal entries do sometimes register conflicting feelings about her reading of novels.

During 1727–1728 Savile read novels by three women writers, Aphra Behn, Penelope Aubin and Eliza Haywood, who have been the subject of several recent revisionist studies.[94] Behn's novels had been available in collected editions since the 1690s, and Savile probably owned the duodecimo edition of *All the Histories and Novels of the Late Ingenious Mrs Behn* (1722).[95] She certainly read *Agnes de Castro, The Fair Jilt, Oroonoko* and *The Lucky Mistake*, all of which were contained in this edition, between 24 August and 4 September 1727, when she and her mother were renting part of a small house in Wandsworth whilst waiting for their Golden Square residence to be repainted.[96] During these few weeks away from home Savile had less access to books than normal and was forced to share a room with her maid. This meant that she had to retreat to the summerhouse in the garden in order to read privately, but she read at least one of these novels, *Agnes de Castro*, aloud to her mother. The portability of the duodecimo edition meant that it could be taken out with them on trips to Clapham Common and the park at Wimbledon, where she also read it aloud, probably within hearing of her maid.[97]

Ros Ballaster has argued that Behn's novels contain heroes or heroines that 'resist social or domestic tyranny' and represent 'virtuous merit', but in this instance Savile had nothing to say about the way in which she and her mother interpreted these texts. By contrast, Aubin's *The Strange Adventures of the Count de Vinevil* (1721), which she read alone in the summerhouse, is condemned with the single word 'silly' (p. 49) by which she presumably meant that it was an unsophisticated text. It is tempting to think that this novel was amongst the '8s. worth of silly Books' bought in Richmond just a few weeks earlier. That Savile owned the *Strange Adventures* is suggested by the fact that she mentions looking at it again in the following year when it was one of 12 novels that she read between 16 August and 22 October 1728.[98] Eliza Haywood's *The Perplex'd Dutchess* (1727) and her translation of *The Memoirs of the Baron de Brosse* were also read for a second time during this period. The journal entry for the first reading of *The Memoirs* clearly shows that she usually read this kind of book in the privacy of her own room.

Lay till 11. All day alone. Had nothing to do but indulg the depth of mellancholy which I think I am at present more hopelessly overwhelm'd in than ever. Din'd and sup'd alone. Lay on the bed as much as I coud. Read 2 books of the Life of the Baron Debross, an old story. After supper read some Spectators, the best things that ever were writt. They put me into a little composure. Bed 11. (p. 71)

That Savile saw no contradiction in moving from Haywood's translation to the *Spectator* suggests that the latter's satire against the female reader was less effective than some critics have assumed, although in some later entries Savile does condemn her own reading of 'silly' texts. Almost all Savile's references to novels suggest that the sociable reading of *Agnes de Castro* that took place in August 1727 was something of a one off. Most were enjoyed as a solitary pleasure 'after supper' in her own room, often by candlelight.

It is possible that these texts were read silently and alone because they included erotic scenes of seduction. William B. Warner has argued that Behn 'composed the first novels of amorous intrigue in Britain' by combining elements of British satire, French 'secret histories' and Spanish novellas, but it was Eliza Haywood who perfected the form of the seduction novel during the 1720s.[99] These texts often contain what Paula Backsheider and John Richetti have called a 'critical awareness of male tyranny' that goes hand in hand with scenes of 'erotic arousal' that explore female sexuality in ways not available elsewhere in the culture of the time.[100] This is certainly true of Haywood's short novel *The City Widow* (dated 1729 in *The English Short Title Catalogue*, but read by Savile in October 1728), the action of which is predicated upon female sexual desire. Several pages are given over to the widow's attempts to seduce a man whom she also hopes to marry.

She took his hand, and, on the pretence of letting him feel the palpitation of her heart, suffer'd it to rove as far as her *Twitcher* wou'd give it leave. Tho he had the most perfect love for her, and as great a share of modesty and virtue as any of his sex; yet here did his honour a little recede at the strength of the temptation, and *desire* getting somewhat the better of *respect*, he returned her caresses with a warmth he had never presum'd to discover till that time. The impulse of nature transporting him to actions more fit to be guess'd at than described.[101]

The sexual act does not occur because of a misunderstanding, thus saving both the widow and her lover from disgrace, but Haywood makes much of the widow's thwarted desire. Ballaster has argued that Haywood's work often calls upon 'the female reader to identify with the troubled heroine, yet paradoxically enjoin her to interpret the tale as moral admonition'.[102] In this instance, however, the banal warning that 'a woman of fortune' is always 'fit prey for avarice' (p. 30) is dispensed with in a few lines and is clearly of secondary concern to the 'actions more fit to be guess'd at than described'.

Between 5 and 19 September 1728 Savile read two novels by Haywood, *The Perplex'd Dutchess* (1727) and *The Arragonian Queen* (1724), as well as the anonymous *The Prude* (1724) and Segrais's *Three Novels*, all of which contain what might be termed 'amatory' material. During this time she neither went to the theatre nor read any plays, although she did continue to listen to her maid reading from *The Travels of Cyrus* (1727). Savile's reading of these texts appears to reinforce Warner's argument that 'novels of amorous intrigue', such as those by Haywood, 'support the pleasure-seeking reader sequestered in a more or less private act of reading'. For a short period during 1728, Savile became a serial reader of texts that structured reading 'according to the central imperative of the print market' which needed readers to return to indulge in the same pleasure time after time.[103] This serial indulgence may well have been encouraged by the fact that the same few publishers produced many of the novels that she read. Most were 'printed for D. Browne Jun at the Black Swan Without Temple Bar and S. Chapman at the Angel in Pall Mall', or 'for J. Roberts near the Oxford Arms, Warwick Lane', and tended to contain advertisements for other novels by the same publishers on their end pages. For example, surviving copies of *The Prude* include a list of books recently published by Browne and Chapman that features Haywood's *The Arragonian Queen*, which had originally been published by Roberts. Savile began to read this novel just a few days after completing *The Prude*. Her serial reading habit may also have been encouraged by the format of these books. After finishing the '3rd part' of *The Prude*, Savile moved straight on to 'The Beautiful Pyrate', the first of three self-contained stories included in Segrais's *Three Novels* (p. 134). The book was finished just three days later. She was able to acquire and read novels very rapidly because they were short, relatively cheap, and readily available from nearby shops. Haywood's *The British Recluse* sold at 1s 6d for 138 pages, whereas the second edition of the *Arragonian Queen* was advertised at 1s for 58 pages, and *The City Widow* (at least in the surviving 1729 version) was 6d for just 31 pages. Produced in octavo or duodecimo formats, these books were ideal for private reading because they were portable and easily concealed,

Savile's serial reading of novels came to a sudden end shortly after she acquired *The City Widow* and Bignon's *The Adventures of Abdalla* on

Saturday 19 October 1728. She completed reading Haywood's short novel 'after supper' and went to bed sometime after midnight having begun the second of the 'new books got tonight' (p. 144). Her journal entry after completing this text some three days later is remarkable for the way in which she compares her reading of novels to an addiction to alcohol.

> Made an end of 'The Adventures of Abdella'. I can find no morall or design in it. 'Tis a collection of silly but very entertaining Lyes, of Fairies, Enchantments etc. Such books I read as people take Drams, to support for an hour sinking Spirits, and alass! the more is taken, the more is nesessary. Read News- want another Dram. (p. 144)

The English Short Title Catalogue (ESTC) does not include any edition of *The Adventures of Abdalla* published in 1728, but given that it was bought on the same evening as another cheap text, *The City Widow*, it is likely that Savile was reading part of the version 'printed and sold by R. Newton' at 3d per volume, which the ESTC records as being published in 1729. Savile's search for, and failure to find, a 'morall or design' certainly seems to be a response to the introduction to this edition, which notes that 'some short Morals are added to the Whole, by way of Explanation, to render it useful as well as diverting'.[104] Several other novels that she read during this period, including those by Aubin, make similar claims about the novel as a source of moral instruction. The 'Preface to the Reader' of Aubin's *The Noble Slaves* (1722), which Savile read on 30 September 1728, argues that in an age which found 'Books of Devotion tedious' it was the job of the author of 'Novels and Stories' to 'expose vice' and 'encourage virtue'.[105] Her *Strange Adventures of the Count de Vinevil and his Family* (1721), which Savile read for the second time a few days later, condemns contemporary print culture while alluding to its own combination of 'delight and instruction'.[106] In this text 'Divine Providence' allows 'Christian innocence and purity' to triumph over 'Muslim treachery and lust', in what Richetti and Backscheider describe as 'crudely imagined representations of good and evil opposed'.[107] The *Adventures of Abdalla* uses a similar Orientalist setting, but the 'instruction' promised by the preface is reduced to a rather unconvincing set of 'remarks' at the end of each volume.[108]

Savile still clearly enjoyed this 'silly' text despite, or perhaps even because of, the fact that it lacked the crude moralisation of Aubin. However, the underlying assumption that a text should have a 'Morall' or instructive dimension clearly had something to do with her rejection of the *Adventures of Abdalla* and the subsequent reduction in the number of novels that she was reading. The next novel referred to in the journal is *Female Falshood* (1722), which she read 'after supper' on 25 November. The 'Advertisement' to this text, which argues that it exposes the 'ill conduct of coquets' in order to 'instruct' the reader, connects it to the 'amatory' tradition, but at more than 300 pages per volume this was certainly a more expansive and expensive text than those purchased earlier in the year.[109] If the nature of the instruction given in this text was still morally ambiguous, Le Sage's *The History and Adventures of Gil Blas* (1716), which she read between 23 and 28 December, was clearly opposed to the amatory novel. Its 'Address to the Reader', supposedly written by the novel's main protagonist, argues that if the 'Kind Reader' pays due 'regard' to the book's 'Moral Instructions' he or she will 'meet with the Utile and Dulce, according to the Rule of Horace'.[110]

As I have already noted, many of the other texts that Savile was reading in 1727–1728 depicted female readers of novels in a negative light. *The Spectator* associated novel reading with sexual fantasy, or daydreaming, as did many contemporary plays and even Behn and Haywood sometimes denigrated women readers of the genre in which they worked.[111] Given this context, it is quite possible that the anxieties that Savile expressed about her novel reading – particularly its association with the taking of 'drams' – are a response to this anti-novel discourse. Savile's journal entries show that she was clearly worried about texts (such as *The City Widow*) in which moral instruction came second to the depiction of pleasure, but it is not my intention here to suggest that Savile simply rejected reading 'amatory fiction' in favour of 'moral' texts such as *Gil Blas*. As her description of Bignon's 'very entertaining Lyes' (and of Aubin's work as 'silly') implies, Savile was struggling to articulate a response to the new kinds of text that were emerging during the 1720s.

Savile's journals reveal a reader who was able to combine many different styles of reading – from the regular weekly consumption of religious texts through to the rapid consumption of novels. Of course, she was able to enjoy this diverse range of texts because her privileged background and London location gave her easy access to print culture, including texts in performance. That she was frequently read to by her servants, and perused texts late into the night using expensive candlelight, should also caution us against thinking of her as a typical reader. Without a husband and with few family responsibilities, Savile had far more freedom to read than many of her female contemporaries.

Her manuscript books do however help to reveal something of the complex (and sometimes contradictory) nature of women's actual reading practices during this period. They afford a tantalising, if brief, glimpse into the reading lives of the other women with whom she read and from whom she borrowed books.

3
Diversities of Reading Practice, 1695–1770

This chapter attempts to recover something of the diversity of possible reading practices available during the first half of the eighteenth century by looking at three very different readers, William Coe (1662–1729), Dudley Ryder (1691–1756) and John Dawson (1692–1765). As James Raven has argued, the 'recovery of individual practices and perceptions demands reflective, careful engagement with available sources', and I use these three readers to reflect on the various sources, from journals and diaries, through to library catalogues and annotated books that make their reading experiences available to us.[1] Gertrude Savile's journals record not only what she read, but also how often, when, where and under what circumstances. As argued in the previous chapter, her reading notes suggest that journals and diaries will provide the vital evidence about the context of reading that is missing from most commonplace books and miscellanies. However, not all life writing being produced in the period 1695–1750 was as revealing about reading as that produced by Savile in the 1720s. For example, the very structure of the journal kept by William Coe, which records mercies received and sins committed, was based on his religious reading, but it also occasionally exposes another reading life, in which he enjoyed 'idle jest books' and newspapers, which remains otherwise hidden. By contrast, Ryder's diary, kept when he was a law student at the Middle Temple in 1715/1716, appears all-inclusive. Originally begun as an aid to study, with notes on books read, a careful reading shows that Ryder was part of an interpretive community that particularly valued the public discussion of texts. Evidence of John Dawson's reading is contained in a range of sources, including library catalogues, annotated books, a miscellany and an autobiography, each of which provides a new perspective on his reading practices.

Varieties of writing about the self – the 'diary' of William Coe (1662–1729)

According to Stuart Sherman, Daniel Defoe's *The Life and Strange Adventures of Robinson Crusoe* (1719) can be read as 'a condensed history' of writing about the self during the late seventeenth and early eighteenth centuries. After the shipwreck, Crusoe first draws up 'a two-column chart in which he reckons the "Good" and "Evil" ' in his situation before going on to create 'a journal of every day's employment'. Years later he writes his 'Life' which includes a reproduction of the chart and an edited version of the journal. The process, if not the novelistic end result, is similar to Elizabeth Freke's reworking of earlier autobiographical material to produce the later version of the 'remembrances' discussed in Chapter 2. Sherman notes that Crusoe's chart is similar to a shopkeeper's ledger or capitalist's account book because during the seventeenth century many people had begun 'to track self, health, soul, [and] salvation' as though they were 'questions of debt and credit'. Nonconformists in particular were encouraged to balance their spiritual account book by keeping an extended record of the self.[2] Early guides to diary keeping, such as John Beadle's *The Journal or Diary of a Thankful Christian* (1656), argued that it was good to keep a 'rich treasure of experience; every experiment of God's favour to us, being a good prop for our faith for the future'.[3] By the early eighteenth century the spiritual ledger book and the record of faith had, by and large, given way to the secular journal favoured by writers such as Gertrude Savile, but the Christian, nonconformist, roots of the diary are still sometimes visible. Savile's annual summaries of her 'own affairs', for example, are similar to those records of the soul made in a religious journal, as are those entries in which Freke records her gratefulness for 'Gods greatt mercy'.[4]

That the diurnal record of the self was rooted in nonconformity needs to be remembered when considering the diary or journal as a record of reading experience. For example, the account of the self published as the 'diary' of the East Anglian farmer William Coe (1662–1729) is much closer to the record of faith recommended by John Beadle, and other nonconformist divines, than it is to Savile's journal of life in London. Kept between 1693 and 1729, Coe's journal is not a diurnal but contains accounts of sins committed ('I often hear good sermons but seldome or never think of them after') and 'mercyes received' ('my grey horse fell down with me ... and I got no hurt'), which he appears to have recorded as and when they occurred throughout the year.[5] This record was designed to help Coe monitor his religious life so that he could repent from the sins that he had committed. It is modelled on the guide 'to Salvation' outlined in Samuel Cradock's *Knowledge and Practice* (1673), which he owned. In a passage that Coe referenced in the journal, Cradock encouraged his readers to 'read over the History of their life past' in order to discover 'matter enough of praise' to 'send up … thankful ejaculations' such as 'Blessed be the Lord, in all my life I never broke a bone' (p. 206).[6]

Quotations from *Knowledge and Practice* appear both on the first page of the diary and in a passage written in the autumn of 1721. That this and a few other religious texts are referred to regularly throughout the 37 year period of its construction suggests something of their significance to Coe and his family. Cradock, for example, was frequently consulted for guidance after having committed a sin. On 13 January 1714, Coe's admission that he could not conduct family prayers that morning because he had stayed up late talking with friends is followed by a note suggesting that 'chapter 19, page 89' of *Knowledge and Practice* was of 'great use to all persons who desire at any tyme more solemnly to humble themselves before the Lord' (p. 238). Family prayers were obviously an important ritual in the Coe household and a reference to Thomas Comber's *A Discourse Concerning the Daily Frequenting of Common Prayer* (1687) suggests that religious texts, such as the *Book of Common Prayer*, were consulted during both morning and evening prayers (p. 252).[7] Throughout the diary Coe contrasts conversation, imagined as 'wicked and profane discourse', with 'reading or other good exercise', but it is clear that reading religious texts together was part of a sociable process that marked the beginning and end of each day for his family (p. 206).

Given that Coe's journal is the record of someone attempting to achieve religious salvation it is not surprising to find that it provides substantial evidence of the context in which religious books, such as Cradock's *Knowledge and Practice*, were put to work, but it also contains two passing references to secular texts. On 6 May 1711 Coe committed the sin of spending a 'great part' of Ascension Day 'reading an idle jestbook' and on 24 May 1721 was grateful that a fall from his horse, while at 'a slow trott reading the Northampton news paper', didn't result in any broken bones (p. 230, p. 250). These entries suggest that Coe didn't just confine himself to the intensive and repeated study of religious works that are the main focus of the journal. That the reading of the newspaper (which was clearly not regarded as a sin) only appears by accident shows that, just like any other source, diaries and journals need to be treated with a certain amount of caution. Like all autobiographical sources they were constructed under particular circumstances and with particular aims in mind. Indeed, as Anne Kugler has noted, most recent research on diaries argues against the traditional notion that they reveal a picture of the self that is more 'true' than that disclosed by an autobiography. Both produce a version of the self that is fit for public consumption, even if the author conceived of the diary as a private document.[8] Coe's diary was kept as a record of his faith rather than his reading, so we need to be cautious about drawing any general conclusions about his own reading practices, or about reading in the early eighteenth century more generally, from its contents. It is unclear, for example, how often Coe read the relatively new phenomenon of the newspaper, or indeed how frequently he read to relieve the boredom of a familiar journey by horse. Although the diary emphasises that Coe saw religious reading as 'good exercise', and suggests that he regularly used books during family prayers and in the construction of the diary itself, it says little about the other texts that he read, the context in which reading took place (was he alone when he read the 'idle jest book'?), or the status of reading in his community.

Indeed, as Daniel Woolf has argued in his recent study of the 'contexts and purposes of history reading', 'diurnal notes of books borrowed or bought are not rare for the Augustan era'. What is 'less common' is the 'systematic' record of reading 'over an extended period' that gives detail of the context in which texts were read.[9] The diaries kept by the Durham minister, Christopher Parkes, between 1689 and 1700, and the Anglican deputy registrar, Henry Prescott, between 1704 and 1719, show that they consumed history in many different contexts. Prescott sometimes read texts intensively from beginning to end; at other times he merely 'turned' the pages in a casual manner. To mark significant days (such as the anniversary of the Restoration) he listened to his son reading the ' "proper parts" of Clarendon's *History of the Rebellion* over a pint and a meal'. Woolf makes much of these various contexts, including Prescott's frequent reading over a 'domestic pint', in concluding that by the eighteenth century 'the study of the past was already on the way to being a leisurely recreation rather than the highly focused study practised by Anthony Grafton and Lisa Jardine's Gabriel Harvey, or by William Sherman's John Dee, and by many other readers of a century earlier'.[10] Elizabeth Freke's 're-creative' use of history in the 'remembrances' supports this conclusion, but she appears to have been a solitary, rather than a sociable, reader and writer. For Coe and the readers of history examined by Woolf, reading was often part of a sociable process and I now want to look at the way in which the future Chief Justice of the King's Bench, Dudley Ryder (1691–1756), documented his interaction with other readers in his community when he was a student in London.

'Our conversation turned pretty much upon books' – reading and sociability in the diary of Dudley Ryder (1691–1756)

The diary compiled by Dudley Ryder between June 1715 and December 1716 gives a particularly vivid account of the relationship between reading and sociability. The son of a linen draper, Ryder was educated as a nonconformist at the dissenting academy in Hackney, north of the expanding city of London, before going on to study at the Universities of Edinburgh and Leiden. He was admitted to study law at the Middle Temple in London in June 1713. It was during his time as a law student that the diary was created.[11] The first entry sets out what he considered to be the 'many advantages' gained by this method 'of setting down whatever occurs to me':

> I intend particularly to observe my own temper and state of mind as to my fitness and disposition for study or the easiness or satisfaction it finds within itself and the particular cause of that or of the contrary uneasiness that often disturbs my mind. I will also take notice especially of what I read every day. This will be a means of helping my memory in what I read. I intend also to observe my own acts as to their goodness or badness.[12]

Like Gertrude Savile, Ryder was particularly concerned with his state of mind. His attention to the 'goodness or badness' of his own behaviour reflects the generic origins of the diary as a record of the state of the individual's soul. As this entry makes clear, however, Ryder also intended the diary to have an impact upon his studies by helping him to remember what he had been reading. As a result much of the diary is taken up with detailed summaries of texts. This entry is typical: 'Rose at 8. Read Boileau's reflections upon Longinus, wherein he particularly exposes Perrault for his unjust treatment of Homer, Virgil and all the best authors of antiquity. They are admirably well made and worth a second reading' (p. 30).

Such entries show Ryder to have been particularly interested in, and adept at, summarising a text's argument. Despite keeping a diary as an aid to memory, Ryder did not use it to record quotations and, unlike Savile, he does not appear to have recorded useful phrases or extracts in a manuscript miscellany. Indeed, Ryder criticised his friend Mr Whatley for sometimes quoting Greek and Latin authors as they walked together and advised him 'never to do it in company where he was not well known, because it would expose him as vain' (p. 201). Even when Ryder decided to reorganise the way in which he studied after reading *An Essay Upon Study* (1713), the 'little paper book' that he created was used to 'set down whatever remarks' occurred to him during his reading rather than to gather quotations for later use (p. 219).[13] Ryder's advice to Whatley suggests that he did not think of his reading as a source of quotations with which to interlard his conversation, as was the case in the common-place book tradition. Displays of learning, such as those entered into by Whatley, were clearly out of vogue amongst Ryder's friends, but the discussion of texts was still a very important part of their conversation.

Sociable reading and the public sphere

As a student at the Inns of Court, Ryder's reading went largely unsupervised. He divided his study between familiarising himself with the legal texts that were necessary for his professional life and reading for the purposes of self-cultivation or enjoyment. As one might expect, he often found the latter more attractive. For example, on 26 July 1715 he was unable to concentrate 'upon the law' and instead took up his copy of Boileau's 'tenth satire'. His 'remarks' on this text show that he thought rereading Boileau would help to cultivate 'a polite and natural way of thinking and writing' (pp. 62–63). Other texts were read 'to improve my style' (p. 38). Ryder particularly admired male writers who expressed themselves with so much 'freedom and ease' that it seemed as if they were 'talking to you' (p. 47), and often referred to reading as a way of improving his social skills: 'I think it is very useful to be acquainted with books that treat of characters. Nothing fits a man more for conversation' (p. 46).

As the diary attests, Ryder read a remarkable range of texts in a wide variety of contexts.[14] The Middle Temple, on the north bank of the Thames, south of Fleet Street, was particularly convenient for visiting London's many bookselling zones. As John Macky notes in his *A Journey Through England* (1714), 'Law, History and Plays' could be acquired from the booksellers 'about Temple Bar'. 'French-Booksellers' were found in the Strand, those for 'Antient [sic] Books in all languages ... in Little Britain and Pater-Noster-Row; those for Divinity and Classicks on the North Side of St Paul's Cathedral'.[15] All were within walking distance of the Middle Temple and Ryder sometimes records walking back to Hackney with a new book in his hand. On 16 August 1715 he noted that he and his brother had 'looked over the books' at John Clark's shop 'at the Bible and Crown in the Poultry, near Cheapside' before buying a translation of Horace (p. 77). He also bought a number of French books in Moorfields, which was the place to go for old and second-hand books during this period. As a law student Ryder was also familiar with Westminster Hall and its environs, which were famous for the sale of 'law books, newspapers and political pamphlets'.[16] Ryder's description of reading in Westminster Hall provides an important insight into the 'bookseller's shop' as reading space:

> As I stood at the bookseller's shop in the hall I read some part of *The Persian Tales*. They are very entertaining and apt to lead one on insensibly till it is not without a great deal of reluctance that one breaks off reading, the story being continued through a variety of other stories or episodes, if I may call them so, which continue one's expectation and make one a little uneasy to get to the end of the original one. (p. 130)

Given that most bookshops and stalls kept their stock on shelves behind a counter it is unlikely that this was a surreptitious reading. That the customer had to request to look at a book meant that shopping for texts was of necessity a sociable process. Contemporary illustrations of bookshops and stalls, including those in Westminster Hall, tend to depict conversation between customers and staff. Giles Mandelbrote refers to several late-seventeenth-century accounts in which well-to-do customers, such as Samuel Pepys, visited bookshops to sample books, exchange news and talk about the latest publications.[17] For Ryder, reading a portion of *The Persian Tales and the Turkish Tales* (1714) was presumably part of the same process of 'looking over' the books that took place when he visited Clark's shop with his brother a few months earlier.[18] On this occasion Ryder was merely killing time while he waited for a Sheriff to be chosen, and despite his reluctance to stop reading he did not buy the book.

Ryder's account of reading part of *The Persian Tales* in Westminster Hall shows that he was largely unfamiliar with fiction, but it is also emblematic of his consumption of texts in public places. On 21 June 1715, for example, he entered a coffee house and talked 'in strange company about the peace, the cessation of arms', before proceeding to read 'three or four Guardians' (p. 39). He visited at least 13 other similar venues during the time in which he kept the diary. One of the attractions of the coffee house for early-eighteenth-century customers was the fact that newspapers, periodicals, pamphlets, satires and lampoons were often available at the tables.[19] Habermas identified the coffee house as a key institution in the construction of the 'bourgeois public sphere' as a 'social space for public criticism of the state', which he argued 'arose first in Great Britain at the turn of the eighteenth century'. Several historians have disputed his time frame, by arguing that the coffee house provided the 'architecture' for the emergence of the public sphere during the Restoration, but Habermas's emphasis upon this space as important to the communal discussion of texts remains central to current debates about the dissemination of ideas during this period.[20] For example, Steve Pincus suggests that 'Restoration Britons flocked to the coffee houses in droves because it was there they could gather news or political gossip and criticise or celebrate the actions of the government'.[21] Ryder used the coffee house in exactly this way. On 25 July 1715, he spent part of the morning at John's Coffee House, where he and two friends talked about not being able to 'depend upon our English troops' because the 'common people are so poisoned with Jacobitism', before going on alone to the British Coffeehouse where he 'looked over many of the *Examiners*' (p. 61). Later that same day he tried to recreate the political conversation of the coffee house in a different location by talking to a 'waterman about the king'. That this conversation ended when he realised that 'the waterman seemed not to be of my mind' (p. 62) implies that the rules governing the coffee house as a space for reading and conversation were different to those that applied elsewhere. Throughout the diary Ryder appears much more confident in his opinions when talking about texts in the coffee house or tavern than he does in any other social situation.

Of course, the social experience of texts was not reserved for the bookshop or coffee house. Whilst staying at his aunt's house, Ryder spent 'all the day indoors' reading Burnet's *History of the Reformation* (1683) to his aunt and sister (p. 111).[22] This kind of reading for an audience of family and friends is similar to that undertaken by Savile when she read part of *The Beggar's Opera* aloud at her home in 1728, but Ryder also records that reading aloud occurred in the public space of the coffee house. On 5 October 1715, he listened to Mr Jackson 'reading some of *Tale of a Tub* to Mr Demodore' at John's Coffee House (p. 114). However, Ryder also describes another kind of shared reading during which texts were 'read together' as a couple that seems quite different to that performed by Jackson: 'Cousin John Ryder stayed at home with me. We walked in the garden together and read a sermon of Archbishop Tillotson together and talk[ed] about it, and what else it raised in our minds' (p. 209). This style of reading, although not done as a preparation for 'action', is similar to the shared reading of texts undertaken by Gabriel Harvey and other facilitators of knowledge in the previous century.[23] It is unclear how this practice worked (did they take it in turns to read aloud, or both peruse the text silently at the same time, discussing it afterwards?), but we do know that when he read *Hudibras* 'together' with his dancing master, Ryder acted as a guide to the text, explaining 'the difficult words or allusions in it' as they went along. The matter of fact way that this episode is introduced suggests that this kind of 'reading together' was a common event: 'Mr Fernly came to see me. He is a man of no manner of education. Happening to lay his hands upon *Hudibras* we read some of that together' (p. 261).

Ryder read in a wide range of contexts and styles, from private study in his closet, through 'reading together' with relatives and friends, and on to the communal consumption of texts in the coffee house. In all of these instances he had at least some direct contact with the text, either reading it himself, or hearing it being read aloud, after which he tended to enter into discussion with his friends or record his first impressions in his diary. In the case of George Berkeley's *Principles of Human Knowledge* (1710), however, Ryder took part in a number of private and public discussions about a text that he had never even seen.[24]

The *Principles* is first mentioned in the diary on 16 July 1715 when Ryder recorded that he and his friend Mr Smith discussed 'Berkeley's notion of abstract ideas' as they walked together from Smith's house to London Fields. Smith, who later became a dissenting minister at Hackney, owned a copy of the text and obviously went into some detail about the ideas laid out in the introduction, as Ryder noted that he didn't understand how Berkeley 'distinguishes general ideas, which he allows, from abstract ones' (p. 56). 'Mr Berkeley's notions concerning matter', which are set out in the main body of the book, were the subject of a conversation between Ryder and three friends, Messrs Jackson, Porter and Witnoom, in a tavern a few days later.[25] It is not clear whether any of these men had actually read *The Principles*, but Ryder recorded using Porter's argument against 'Mr Berkeley's notion of abstract ideas', which must have been put forward during this discussion, when he next talked to Smith in private. The topic was dropped because Smith was unable to defend Berkeley against Porter's critique, which suggested that abstract ideas were necessary for thinking about God and the self (p. 65). Several weeks later Porter reiterated his objection in a discussion with Ryder and three other friends at a coffee house. On this occasion, Ryder found the argument against Berkeley less convincing and he appears to have attempted to formulate an answer to Porter's objection even though he still hadn't read the book.[26] Ryder visited Smith the next day and they talked 'of Mr Berkeley', perhaps reading part of the *Principles* together, before taking the book home with him to complete. Such was his eagerness to get on with the text that he read part of it while walking home and finished it the next day (p. 95).

This evidence confirms that complex ideas, such as those outlined in Berkeley's *Principles* were circulating amongst Ryder's friends at the same time as they were discussing contemporary news and events in a wide range of public venues, such as the coffee house and tavern. This is not surprising, of course, given that the architecture of the public sphere was in place long before Ryder's birth, but the way in which he was able to gain a detailed knowledge of Berkeley's ideas before reading the *Principles* has important implications for the way in which we think about the history of reading. It suggests that although the coffee house and tavern were important sites for text distribution, they were also venues in which it was possible to participate in a public discussion about a text that only a few of those taking part in the debate had actually read. Given that during the eighteenth century 'reading was often a social occasion where people did not necessarily come into visual contact with the text and did not always follow the text very closely' it is perhaps not surprising that none of Ryder's friends seems to have objected to his talking about ideas derived from a book that he had not read.[27] Smith and Porter's different interpretations of Berkeley's ideas meant that Ryder decided he needed to read the text, but he and other participants may well have absorbed many other contemporary ideas circulating within this community without having any 'visual contact' with the text being discussed, or indeed without having any further need or desire to see the text itself. *The Spectator* notes how easy it was to gain access to 'those little Circular Audiences' that assembled for discussion at Will's and other London coffee houses during this period.[28]

Perhaps not surprisingly, when Ryder did eventually get to read Berkeley's *Principles* almost two months after he had first discussed it with Smith, his interpretation was informed by the discussion of 'Berkeley's notions' that had taken place amongst his friends:

> Came home and finished Mr Berkeley's book. I am mightily pleased with the greatest part of it, and though he has not yet fully convinced and made me see his notions in a very strong light yet they have gone a great way [to] clear up the objection against them that Mr Porter makes. I am in great hope thoroughly to conceive Mr Berkeley the next time of reading and that that difficulty will entirely disappear. (p. 95)

As this entry makes clear, Ryder's reading was to a great extent determined by Porter's objection to Berkeley's ideas and the two men later agreed to write short accounts of the text to further their discussion.[29] Ryder claimed to dislike conversations in which 'a man no sooner advances a new thing but somebody or other in the company without observing whether it be just or no is seeking for an answer against it', but many of the discussions of books that took place amongst his friends have something of this dialogic quality about them (p. 37). Several of the conversations that he recorded in the diary 'turned pretty much on books' in this way and he used his entries to rate his own performance (p. 57). On one occasion after talking about 'Mr Addison's genius' with his friends in the tavern, he noted that he was 'very well pleased with myself in the share I bore in this conversation' (p. 94). In December 1715 he 'resolved to be very conversant with Mr Locke's works' because he had been 'told' the Lord Chancellor had come by 'that clear, close way of talking' through the frequent reading of texts by Locke and Chillingsworth (p. 155).

In the case of Berkeley a chance conversation about the *Principles* turned (eventually) into a reading of the text itself which in turn lead on to further discussion. More often, however, Ryder read in order to make sure that he was never short of topics for conversation. *Hudibras*, he noted, was 'exceedingly full of the most comical wit' which could be used in 'conversations with the ladies' (p. 271). He often condemns others for being dull to talk to because they had not read enough. It was 'very difficult' for him 'to maintain a conversation' with his sister, for example, because 'not having been used to reading, her knowledge is confined within the compass of a very few things' (p. 81). In Ryder's world to be poorly read was to be excluded from conversation. However, the argument that Ryder's 'interest in reading in general, and history in particular, derived entirely from social concerns', put forward by Daniel Woolf, doesn't pay enough attention to the various ways in which he read.[30] Ryder certainly read in order to be able to impress in conversation, but he also enjoyed reading 'together' with friends and family, and often perused texts alone 'in his closet', either as part of his studies or for religious salvation.

'Remarkable' margins – The 'Exciseman and Staymaker' as library owner and annotator

Lorna Weatherill's study of will inventories has demonstrated that book ownership was expanding amongst the middling ranks of society in the late seventeenth century. This expansion was most rapid in London, which had the highest incidence of book ownership in the country by 1705, when 38 per cent of the inventories sampled by Weatherill contained books. By 1725 this had risen to 52 per cent.[31] Of course, London was the centre of the English book trade and, as the diaries of Gertrude

Savile and Dudley Ryder suggest, it was relatively easy for wealthy Londoners to acquire and discuss books within the city. This relative ease of access to printed matter needs to be taken into account when thinking about London readers, but as recent studies have demonstrated the book distribution system was quite efficient by the late seventeenth century. Provincial readers were able to order books relatively easily, and coffee house culture was widespread.[32] There is, however, a scarcity of documentary evidence for the reading of texts by these new, non-professional readers. I now want to look at one such reader, John Dawson (1692–1765), who did not enjoy either Savile's wealth, or Ryder's privileged access to University and the Inns of Court.

John Dawson left a particularly detailed record of his reading life. His surviving papers include an autobiography (in the form of a 'Life' similar to that created by Freke), two volumes of diaries, a personal miscellany and two library catalogues. Many of the books that he owned have also survived.[33] This section considers the importance of library catalogues and annotated books as sources for the history of reading. Dawson's 'Life' reveals that he was born in Leeds, Yorkshire, and that his father was a textile worker who later worked as an excise officer in Ireland. Dawson had many jobs, but eventually followed his father into the excise. After working in Penshurst, Kent, for a number of years he moved to London in 1727 to become part of the 'Fourth Division' of the London Brewery section of the excise.[34] In his own survey of the 'Liberty of Churchend and Hoxton', completed in November 1729, he describes himself as 'Exciseman and Staymaker'. He had married Phillecia Andrews, a widowed staymaker, earlier that year and they lived together in a house in Hoxton market place with an annual rent of £8.10s. During much of the 1730s Dawson's household included, his wife, a daughter from an earlier marriage and an apprentice. Because he had more than one occupation, and given that his daughter appears to have been apprenticed to another staymaker in Hoxton, the income of the entire household is difficult to calculate.[35] However, Dawson's annual 'salary' as an excise officer would probably have exceeded £80, placing him comfortably within the 'middling ranks' of society, who earned between £40 and £200 per year.[36] Both the size of Dawson's household and his purchase of books and other luxury goods, such as silverware, suggest that he was a fairly typical member of this social group.[37]

Dawson's library

Just before his death, Dawson left the 879 volumes of the library that he had compiled between 1710 and 1762 to the church of St Leonard, Shoreditch. 635 of these volumes have survived.[38] The bequest contained several manuscripts including a notebook of accounts that contains a 'catalogue of my books' created sometime in the 1730s.[39] This catalogue records details of 104 volumes, including five manuscript books, and is divided into five sections that organise the contents according to size. These sections, which range from 'Books in Folio' to 'Small Twelves' (duodecimos), are then subdivided into columns that record a shortened version of the title (sometimes including the author's name), the month and year in which a book was acquired ('first had'), and either its 'price' or 'value'. The dates of acquisition run from 1710 to 1739 and the catalogue itself appears to have been in use until 1742. An unusually detailed document, it provides a datable stratum of acquisition for books contained in the bequest to the Parish, and reveals much about how Dawson thought about and handled his books during the 1730s and 1740s.[40]

Because the catalogue records the date of acquisition, 'price' or 'value', and arranges the books by size it is possible to gain a crude impression of the development of the library between 1710 and 1739, the amount that was spent on books each year and the formats that Dawson favoured. The most expensive book listed is 'Stowes Survey with Strypes Addit, 2 vols', in folio, which is recorded as having a 'price' of £4 in 1733. The catalogue values the books that he bought in that year (which included another folio) at over £8, but most of the values listed range from 1s to 10s per item, for books either in octavo or duodecimo. It also records that while the library was expanding rapidly during the years 1729–1736, its development was uneven. For some years, such as 1734, no acquisitions were recorded. This suggests that books were still a luxury item for readers such as Dawson. Even in 1732, the busiest year of his book buying only 15 purchases were recorded, all in the cheaper formats of octavo and duodecimo. It is not clear whether the 'price' recorded in the catalogue represents what Dawson actually paid for any of the books listed, or what he thought they might be worth if sold (especially as both 'price' and 'value' are used in the list), but it is significant that a number of books are given a price lower than that recorded in contemporary guides such as the *Term Catalogues*. For example, Dawson records that he paid 4s for two volumes of Abel Boyer's, *History of the Reign of Queen Anne* in 1716, a book that was advertised in 1709/10 at 6s per volume.[41]

The catalogue shows that Dawson's library was dominated by texts published in London between 1678 and 1733.[42] Almost half were purchased within four years of their publication, and a small number were bought in the same year that the book was printed. Ownership inscriptions in the surviving books reveal that some of the older texts in the collection, such as the *Whole Duty of Man* (1670), were inherited from his father. That several books published much earlier, such as Gavin's *A Short History of Monastical Orders* (1693), are recorded as 'first had' in the 1720s and 1730s, suggests that Dawson (like Ryder) must have had access to the second-hand trade. There is not the space here for a full analysis of the different genres contained in the 1739 catalogue, but it included many books on history and religion as well as guides to work, education and conduct. The collection of history is particularly notable because of the number of texts, such as Thomas Salmon's *Chronological Historian* (1733), which include near contemporary events. The addition of Abel Boyer's *History of King William the Third* (1702–1703) to the library in January 1731 meant that it contained a complete chronology of events in Britain from 1688 until the late 1720s.[43]

Dawson's library, stocked with many contemporary texts mainly written in the vernacular and published in London, was far different from those created by 'serious' readers during the same period. Scholarly libraries were often much larger and contained books in a number of different languages, or printed in a number of different European cities. Even William Congreve's library, which as John Barnard notes was 'much more strongly biased towards English literature than most', contained many books produced on the Continent. Compiled in 1722, the inventory of the library of the Cambridge student, John Gibson, contained 216 volumes, many of which were in Latin, French, Greek and Hebrew.[44] David McKitterick has argued that 'Latinity' could be almost as important as literacy in determining the ways in which readers deployed their skills during this period.[45] The absence from Dawson's collection of books in languages other than English confirms that he is a reader from outside the scholarly tradition. The lack of fiction and poetry in the list is also remarkable, especially when compared with the catalogue of books bequeathed to the Parish in 1765, which contained large numbers of plays and novels. That many of the books listed as part of Dawson's library in the 1730s are not included in the 1765 bequest underlines the fact that we need to be cautious about using final catalogues and probate inventories as evidence of all the books owned and read during a reading lifetime.

The catalogue that Dawson compiled in the 1730s, like the majority of library catalogues, offers a picture of a library frozen at a particular moment in time. It only includes evidence of the books that he bought or inherited, not those that he borrowed or heard read. Unfortunately, his diaries make little mention of his reading, but they and the 'Life' confirm that his cultural diet also included newspapers. And his personal miscellany contains transcripts from a range of texts, including political pamphlets, which do not appear in the library.[46] The catalogue thus provides important evidence about the construction of a library by a non-professional reader of the 'middling-sort', and the availability and price of books in London during the early eighteenth century. What it cannot reveal, however, is the strategies that Dawson adopted for reading these texts.

'As different as seeing from blindness' – annotation strategies, 1700–1750

Some of the strategies that Dawson adopted when reading can be reconstructed using the surviving books. Much of the most compelling evidence for the history of reading thus far compiled has come from studies of the ways in which readers annotated the texts that they owned or borrowed. For example, the close examination of Gabriel Harvey's annotated Livy by Lisa Jardine and Anthony Grafton, and the work of William Sherman on John Dee, has led to the identification of a class of professional reader paid to transform reading as 'public performance' into political action during the late sixteenth century.[47] Recent work on seventeenth-century readers by Kevin Sharpe and Steven Zwicker has concentrated upon what the latter calls 'the ways in which readers shaped books'.[48] H. J. Jackson's two book-length studies, *Marginalia: Readers Writing in Books* (2001) and *Romantic Readers* (2005), examine discursive annotations produced between 1700 and the present day.[49] As Anthony Grafton has wittily argued, the history of reading might be best thought of as 'a marginal enterprise', but many historians remain sceptical about using marginalia to reconstruct reading practices.[50] Jackson notes that 'doubts focus on the privacy of the experience and the typicality of the surviving records'. And the question of whether annotations give any useful insight into the 'mental processes of reading' is often raised.[51] Anyone working in the margins is, of course, constrained by the amount of room available at the edge of the text, and may well be conscious that their marks are going to be interpreted by later readers, but Jackson argues convincingly that annotations 'stay about as close to the running mental discourse that accompanies reading as it is possible to be' (p. 256). This concern with 'mental process' is something of a chimera, however. Annotations made during the Romantic period frequently disclose evidence of reading as a social process. They were made with other readers in mind, and in order to work in this way, often reproduce typical patterns of reading. As Jackson says of Hester Piozzi's annotations, 'she read both as a particular reader under special circumstances and as a typical reader of her time, governed and constrained by deep structures common to all' (p. 257). Recent studies of marginalia (and other forms of annotation) have begun to help us to recover an important *material* dimension of reading that historians concerned with mental processes tend to ignore.[52]

Jackson's survey of annotations made during the Romantic period includes those created by non-professional or 'common' readers, but studies of the first half of the eighteenth century have tended to concentrate on the marginalia created by professional readers, such as authors, antiquarians and scholars, or the reception of canonical texts.[53] Dawson's annotated books are important because they shed light on the way in which a non-professional reader engaged with texts during this period. Before looking at some of them in detail, however, I want to give a brief overview of the range of annotation practices used by readers during the first half of the eighteenth century as revealed by a sample of books and pamphlets printed between 1690 and 1750, now in the British Library's rare book collections.[54] These annotations expose the varied and active practices of readers in this period, but they also show some common patterns, which suggest that the individualism of the reader was usually expressed within certain codes, and that readers frequently responded to the physical structure of the printed object by mimicking its language, or by exposing faults in its production.

By far the most common form of annotation is the mark of ownership, usually in the form of a signature, but other similar marks unrelated to contents also reveal important evidence about the ways in which books were used. Many texts from this period were used to store personal information, such as dates of birth, or to record financial transactions. Also common were amendments to printers' errors, such as spelling mistakes and erratic pagination. Of course, many texts printed in the early eighteenth century were less than perfect. As David McKitterick has argued, the printed word 'had merely reached the most textually advanced stage that was practical under a certain set of circumstances', and consequently, either the print-shop or the reader needed to make final adjustments.[55] Other signs of the reader's activity usually accompany such corrections. For example, Joseph Griffith amended several mistakes in his copy of John Flavel's *Sacramental Meditations Upon Divers Select Places of Scripture* (1700), but he also added a range of signs in the margin, including a manicule, or pointing finger, and the phrase 'Note Them', in order to draw attention to important passages. A number of dated annotations show that Griffith read this text several times between 1734 and 1756. During these readings he made notes between chapters reminding himself about which passages were 'deserving of a Remark' and which should be 'viewed over again'.[56] Such marks suggest a practice in which the search for 'remarkable' passages was an integral part of the reading experience, as was the need to reread.

Many eighteenth-century readers made major alterations to the critical apparatus of the texts that they read, including the addition of personalised tables of contents, new footnotes and systems of cross-reference. The annotator of a copy of the second edition of Thomas Salmon's, *A Review of the History of England in Two Volumes* (1724), corrected mistakes, placed cross-references to alternative sources in the margins and added thematic headings to the index.[57] Several cross-references to much earlier texts suggest that this was a scholarly reader with access to a large library, but volumes of history and practical texts are often annotated in this way. This style of annotation reveals readers who put their texts to regular and continued use, often building up layer-upon-layer of annotations that both added to the contents of the text and made it easier to use.

Several of the books listed in the finding aids as containing annotations are in fact bound together with manuscripts to form an anthology of similar material. For example, the text of Robert Samber's *On the Passion of Our Blessed Saviour* (1708) is unmarked, but the owner had it bound into a volume of sermons transcribed in 'December 1732'.[58] Such volumes provide further evidence that manuscript and print coexisted throughout the eighteenth century. To write in the margins or to bind together manuscript and print was natural to eighteenth-century readers. These readers frequently customised their books by adding additional manuscript pages in order to store information on the same subject. The owner of Edward Laurence's, *The Duty and Office of a Land-Steward* (1731) used this volume to store information about land management by both tipping and pasting in extracts from other texts as well as adding notes in the margins from *The Court Keeper's Companion* (1717) and other earlier books. This volume was bound together with a later notebook that seamlessly continued the pagination of the printed text.[59]

Of course, some early-eighteenth-century authors wanted their texts to be annotated. Verse satire features disproportionately in the record of annotations because it encouraged readers to take up the pen in order to fill the blank, or partially obscured names of those being attacked. Some readers used printed 'keys' to complete these texts, but the reader of the British Library's copy of *Law is a Bottomless Pit* (1712) added a key that does not correspond to that published later in the same year.[60] Such texts suggest one of the ways in which satire actively engaged the reader, but as John Feather's survey of production figures reveals, there were more sermons than satires in the hands of readers during the first half of the eighteenth century.[61] The content of these texts was often controversially sectarian, political, or both, and many readers felt compelled to record their disagreements in adversarial comments in the margin. The annotator of *An Essay in Favour of the Ancient Practice of Giving the Eucharist to Children* (1728) produced an extreme version of this practice in which every claim of the author is met with a rebuke. For example, when the text argues that the ancients saw 'no difference' between the communion of adults and children, the annotator has entered the damning response, 'as different as seeing from blindness' in the margin.[62] Robert DeMaria has noted that Jonathan Swift often engaged in this kind of adversarial discourse in the margins of his books.[63]

These annotations reveal only glimpses of readers at work. The British Library collection probably favours the scholarly reader, and between the guessing games played with the missing names of satire and the use of the text as a repository of information, there are undoubtedly many practices that have been lost to the record. That readers regularly customised their books by adding ownership marks, constructing new scholarly apparatus, inserting manuscript pages and engaging in discursive marginalia (although rarely all at the same time) does at least provide a context for Dawson as annotator. David McKitterick has noted that the autobiographical records that help to make sense of annotated books rarely survive so that we are forced to rely solely on the often difficult to interpret marks on the page in order to reconstruct the owner's reading practices.[64] What is most remarkable about the Dawson collection is the fact that it contains a diverse range of sources, including catalogues, autobiographical writings, notebooks and accounts that help us to see the role that annotation, amendment and addition played in his broader reading life.

Dawson's 'remarkable' annotations

All of Dawson's books include marks of ownership. For example, the copy of John Holwell's *A Sure Guide to the Practical Surveyor* (1678) that he inherited from his father contains his signature and the date 'February 14th 1709/10'on the verso of the title page as well as the marks of ownership of the older man.[65] He also often added a shelf mark, such as 'No. 52: Case 1. app: 8; No. in app: 6', that identified where the book was stored in the library, although in this case it is missing.[66] Dawson was the kind of reader who tended to customise his books by creating new indexes and adding extra pages rather than making discursive comments, although he did sometimes add marginalia. The *Sure Guide* does not include any marginal notes, but Dawson added page numbers where they were missing, an index to 'The Tables' and 'The Plates in this Book', and a table of additional information gathered from other sources. Indexes and additional pages for storing information are a common feature of his books. This may well be because his library included many practical texts, such as Echard's *Newsman's Interpreter* (1704), which needed to be updated if they were to remain useful. His copy of *The Merchant and Tradesman's Daily Companion* (1729) contains a manuscript 'Table of contents' created using shortened versions of the text's own headings which, like the guide to 'The Tables' in the *Sure Guide*, must have made it easier to access information needed on a regular basis.[67] The way in which Dawson annotated these practical books suggests that he was a reader determined to put his texts to work, and like many of the readers whose traces can be found in the British Library's collections, he customised his books by making them into a hybrid of manuscript and print.

Dawson's history books contain many more examples of writing in the margins than any of the other texts that he owned. Daniel Woolf's work on British probate inventories and private catalogues has shown that by the early eighteenth century works of history were often found in the private libraries of readers of Dawson's social status.[68] His library was thus part of a growing trend for collecting secular books amongst the 'middling sort', but Woolf's findings suggest that the sheer number of histories that Dawson owned was unusual. Of the 39 octavo volumes recorded in the 1739 catalogue, 29 were histories (74 per cent). These were relatively cheap books, ranging in 'price' from 3s to 6s, but his ownership of a number of expensive folio volumes, such as Isaacson's *Historica Chronologica* (1633), Echard's *History of England* (1707) and Camden's *Britannia* (1722) (valued together at more than £5), suggests that he was prepared to invest heavily in this area.[69] Woolf's survey suggests that by 1700, many small private libraries included significant numbers of historical works, but that 10 to 15 per cent was typical, and more than 40 per cent very unusual indeed.[70]

The surviving volumes of Dawson's history books provide important evidence about the ways in which he understood and made use of their contents throughout the rest of his life. His copy of the second volume of *The Peerage of England* (1711) includes a number of features that are typical. This volume contains corrections to errors in dating and cross-references to passages in volume one, but there are no scholarly references to competing accounts of the sort found in the British Library's copy of Salmon's *Review of the History of England*.[71] As with his other books, Dawson created extra pages for his histories. The *Peerage*, for example, includes two manuscript indexes that list each peerage by place and each peer by name. Such additions were clearly intended to make the book easier to use, but they are also the product of a close and time consuming reading practice.[72] In some volumes, such as Puffendorf's *An Introduction to the History of the Principal Kingdoms and States of Europe* (1728) with its unfinished index to 'The Kingdoms & States in this Book', this long process was never completed.[73]

Dawson's copy of the *Atlas Geographus* (1711) is one of the most thoroughly worked over texts in the collection, with each new section preceded by a manuscript 'table' of contents. For example, 'A Perticular Table No 3', which is placed before a section of the text on the history of France, was constructed by copying each printed side heading from the text itself. This extension of the volume's printed apparatus is followed by a series of headings and references that are part personal index, part commonplace book. Notes under headings such as 'Batles [sic] in France' make reference to unusual events such as 'a batle fought by women in men's cloaths', which provide rare evidence of Dawson as a curious reader, picking over his histories for interesting narratives.[74] They are a striking contrast to the carefully constructed indexes, chronologies and annals that make-up most of the additions to these volumes.

Woolf has noted that despite being overtaken in terms of production and reputation by new forms of historical writing, annals continued to flourish as a way of interpreting history in the first half of the eighteenth century.[75] As already noted, Dawson's library included an unusually large number of chronologies, but he also added his own manuscript annals to the histories that he owned. This process is best illustrated by his copy of the second edition of Salmon's *Chronological Historian*, bought soon after it was published in 1733, which contains several layers of addition. Dawson abstracted the major events from this volume to create a series of annals bound into the end papers, including a chronological table of the 'Kings of England' from 828–1727, and a list of the Parliaments that met during each reign.[76] Both were created using information contained in the text itself, which concludes with the death of George I in 1727. The fact that Dawson did not add any supplementary information in order to expand the book's contents beyond this date means that he was not using it as a store of information on the same subject, as was the case with many of his practical texts. This evidence suggests that the process of abstraction, of creating contents lists and chronologies, was particularly important to the way in which he read history. Indeed, it suggests that he needed to engage with volumes of history on this level, and had to turn their contents into annals, or other forms of his own writing, if he wanted to make sense of them.

Dawson's copy of Salmon's *The Chronological Historian* is marked throughout with coded marginalia. As a manuscript table of 'The Signification of the Marks in this Book' (Figure 3.1) makes clear these annotations were used to compile the series of annals and tables bound into its back pages. Passages marked PM, PP, Pa and PD for 'Parliament Meet', 'prorogued', 'adjourn'd' and 'Dissolved', for example, were used to supply information for the table of parliaments. In using code, Dawson was drawing upon a technique for reading history that had been available since the Renaissance. Gabriel Harvey used astrological symbols to call attention to interesting historical lessons in his books, and Dawson's use of capital letters mimics the form, if not the purpose, of Bodin's *Methodus* (1566), in which the author encouraged readers to

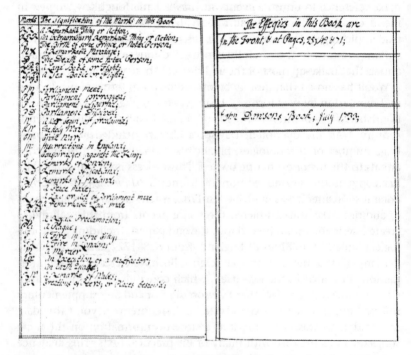

Figure 3.1 'The Signification of the Marks in this Book' taken from Dawson's copy of *The Chronological Historian* (1733)

place the letters 'C H' in the margin next to an example of the *'consilium honestum'* of a government.[77] Dawson's use of 'R R' for 'a Remarkable Thing or Action', and 'R R R' for 'an Extraordinary Remarkable Thing or Action', are direct descendents of this method, and although there is something slightly comic about his terminology (how does one distinguish between the merely 'remarkable' and the 'extraordinary remarkable'?) both the structure of this code, and its distribution in the margins, tells us something about the active nature of his reading.

After Salmon's final entry for the year 1647, Dawson ruled a line across the page and then continued to add to the margins as the 'remarkable' events of the English Civil War unfolded. Next to the passage for 30 January, 'The king being ordered to be put to Death this Day', he left a sign that indicated that this was a 'remarkable' event ('R R'), but he does not seem to have responded to Salmon's obvious sympathy for the monarch, or to his opposition to Cromwell, and after the words 'he submitted to the block and his head was severed' he wrote 'Ex' in the margin – the code for the 'execution of a malefactor'.[78] Given the nature of Dawson's marginalia, however, it is not at all clear whether he intended this marginal 'Ex' as a challenge to the authority of the text. He certainly never engaged in the sort of adversarial marginalia deployed by other readers during this period.

That so many of Dawson's histories include tables filled with facts gleaned from their pages suggests that this was simply the way in which he read, chopping up history into digestible chunks, and transforming major events into annals for easy reference as he went. This technique was, however, also clearly put to use in the construction of his autobiographical journal, 'The Life of John Dawson; Officer of Excise', which he probably began in 1720. This volume contains a series of diary-like entries from the year of his birth through to 1764. The years 1701–1728 contain detailed notes on national and international affairs that have clearly been derived from the manuscript tables that he created whilst reading history.[79] Additional information for this project was stored in the books themselves. Several of the volumes of Boyer's, *The History of the Reign of Queen Anne Digested into Annals* that he owned contain autobiographical notes on the end pages which correspond to the years covered by that volume.[80] The margins of *The Chronological Historian* are even more densely covered with markings from the year of his birth onwards and he obviously used this text to supply much of the historical framework for the 'Life'. Notes about when parliaments met or were dissolved are, for example, frequently noted in this volume, as are royal proclamations and 'remarkable' laws.[81]

National events that were of autobiographical significance were marked 'R R R' in his copy of the *Chronological Historian*. For example, this 'mark' appears next to a paragraph in the section that describes the issuing of a reward of £1000 'to any Person who should discover the Author ... of a Libel, intitled [sic] *English Advice to the Freeholders of England*' in January 1715.[82] Why should this event be more remarkable than the execution of the English monarch, what makes it worth that additional 'R'? This event was 'extraordinary remarkable' because as Dawson notes in the 'Life' he had acquired a copy of this pamphlet 'at the Lord Downs's' as he was making his way to sea to rejoin the excise in January 1715, and was subsequently 'committed to Hull Gaol about the advice to the Freeholders of England' where he remained for three months.[83] Published anonymously by Francis Atterbury (who Daniel Defoe accused of Jacobite sympathies), this pamphlet was a Tory 'libel' upon the Whig government that fell foul of the law because it included a personal attack upon George I.[84] That Dawson was imprisoned for possessing a copy of this text shows that despite the emergence of spaces in which private citizens could publicly 'criticise or celebrate the actions of the government', as Dudley Ryder was doing in London in the same year, reading could still be a dangerous act in a period dominated by partisan strife and Jacobite dissent. Given these circumstances, it is hardly surprising that Dawson should have used his marginalia to draw attention to an event that was of such importance in his own life.

This evidence suggests that when Dawson read contemporary history he tended to take it personally, searching out evidence of proceedings in which he had been involved and reconstructing the accounts of these, and other contemporary events as part of his autobiographical project. Annotating his books was thus part of a purposive reading strategy, the end result of which was the production of a complex autobiography that aimed to place the individual 'life' within the context of contemporary European history. Like Elizabeth Freke, Dawson was a reader particularly attuned to the act of writing, but his reading of history cannot simply be reduced to the purpose of producing an autobiography. As his annotation of the Civil War section of Salmon, and his chronological list of the 'Kings of England' from 828–1727 demonstrate, Dawson habitually read with the pen in hand, enjoying the process of abstraction and addition as he went. As already noted, Woolf has argued that for many eighteenth-century readers the study of the past was 'a leisurely recreation' rather than the 'highly focussed study' practiced a century earlier, but readers like Dawson appear to have combined recreation and study as they worked on putting their own lives in context.[85]

Dawson's annotation strategies were obviously a very important part of his reading experience, but his library catalogues, diaries and miscellany suggest that he engaged in a variety of different kinds of reading. As this and the previous chapter have demonstrated, by bringing together various case studies from the period 1695–1770 we can gain a sense not only of the diversity of reading practices undertaken by different readers in different social circumstances, but of the range of strategies devised by individual readers.

4
The Circulating Library, Book Club and Subscription Library: Readers and Reading Communities, 1770–1800

The *English Short Title Catalogue* (ESTC) gives some sense of the increase in book production that occurred during the eighteenth century. For example, between 1710 and 1719 nearly 23,000 separate titles were produced. By the 1790s this figure rose to nearly 68,000. Of course, as James Raven and others have noted, these figures take no account of survival rates or edition sizes, and to take them at face value is to ignore the importance of second-hand and imported books to the practices of actual readers.[1] In some accounts of cultural change in the long eighteenth century this increase in production is tied into a teleological model of progress in which a flourishing print culture combines with the march of literacy to produce a new enlightened and democratic culture. However, recent work by book historians suggests that this is an overly optimistic view. William St Clair argues that the 'censorship of price' excluded many from reading new books.[2] Even the somewhat more optimistic Raven, concludes that the 'commercial take-off in book production' during the late eighteenth century 'resulted not only from an increase in the number of purchasers, but also from greater purchasing by those already buying books'. Both acknowledge that commercial and institutional libraries were particularly important to this 'take-off'. The relationship between novel production and circulating libraries is well known, but the fashion for books to be displayed as part of a country house library also stimulated production. Both kinds of library had potential for the 'stacking of unread books' that were as much 'totems of faith, respectability or solidarity' as items to be read.[3]

Tied into the teleological model of expanding numbers of readers and readerships are a number of ideas about dominant reading practices. Elizabeth Long and William B. Warner have noted that the iconography of reading that emerged during the eighteenth century tended to depict reading as a solitary pleasure. Images of women reading alone are particularly common from the 1750s onwards, and as Warner argues, these can either be positive portrayals of a woman's absorbed concentration, as in Joshua Reynold's portrait *Theophilia Palmer Reading 'Clarissa'* (1753), or a visual representation of the anti-novel discourse that warned against 'the explicitly erotic dangers of novel reading', as in Jean-Baptiste Greuze's *Lady Reading the Letters of Heloise and Abelard* (1758–1759).[4] Although neither pays enough attention to the audience(s) for whom these images were produced, Long's argument that the solitary reader has become an iconic image of reading in the modern world is particularly useful, especially as she also suggests that such images have contributed to the 'historical invisibility of reading groups'.[5] Such groups are certainly under represented in the commonly adopted version of the 'reading revolution', which ties 'extensive' reading together with solitary reading for pleasure in a way that echoes many of these usually negative representations of women reading. In positive accounts of the expansion of print culture reading aloud tends to be figured as a group activity practiced only by working-class readers, but as Jacqueline Pearson has argued, diaries, letters and fiction attest to the fact that the ability to read aloud was considered a very important social skill amongst middle-class families during the late eighteenth century.[6] Such evidence suggests that historians need to take more account of reading as a social rather than a solitary activity. This chapter looks at the way in which two common forms of text distribution, the circulating library and the subscription library, encouraged sociable reading during the period 1770–1800.

The circulating library, book club and subscription library

During this period the circulating library was frequently the target of satirists who saw it as the source of new and indiscriminate reading practices centred on the novel. It is often invoked as a source of immorality during discussions of women's reading in novels and conduct books.[7] Frequently conceived of as a 'female space', 'satire on circulating libraries virtually always depicts library use as a practice where gender is a dominant factor'.[8] For example, Isaac Cruikshank's engraving *The Circulating Library* (*c*.1800–1815) depicts a fawning library proprietor in a shop full of women who have nearly emptied the shelves of novels and romances whilst leaving those filled with sermons untouched.[9] Many negative representations of female novel readers created during the 1780s and 1790s imply that they were in even more danger of succumbing to immorality if the book had been borrowed from a circulating library. However, these images produced by conservative critics of women's reading did not go uncontested. As Pearson argues, many respectable families, including the Austens and the Larpents, risked entry into the ambiguous space of the library in order to gain access to books.[10] In *Mansfield Park* (1814), Austen celebrates the circulating library in her depiction of Fanny Price's elation at becoming 'a renter, a chuser of books'.[11]

The libraries that real readers visited were of two main types: those that charged for each book borrowed and those that demanded a subscription. Libraries with a small stock of books were often an adjunct to bookselling or another business, such as hairdressing, and tended to charge on a nightly or weekly basis. Three pence per book per week was common in the last quarter of the eighteenth century, but some establishments asked as much as tuppence per book per night.[12] The circulating library run by Samuel Clay in Warwick during the early 1770s was of this sort. It lent books at 2d each per week, but as Jan Fergus's examination of the surviving records suggests, even this fee was beyond the means of a large number of people. Regular borrowing from Clay's library was restricted to three classes – the gentry, the professions and tradesmen.[13] Circulating libraries that charged annual, six-monthly or quarterly rates tended to have a larger stock. By the end of the century a number of large commercial libraries existed to cater for those attending fashionable resorts such as Bath, Margate and Brighton, some of which offered subscription rates for 'the season'. During the 1770s and 1780s, 16s was a common annual rate at these larger libraries, but during the 1790s many began to charge a guinea. All of the libraries in Bath, for example, raised their fees to a guinea in 1797.[14]

The commercial circulating library was, however, only one of several different kinds of library that became available to readers during the second half of the eighteenth century. The widespread association of the circulating library with trivial or immoral reading actively encouraged the development of subscription libraries, reading societies and book clubs.[15] For example, the members of the Lewes Literary Society claimed that it was founded in 1786 because they were 'disgusted at the usual trash of the circulating libraries'.[16] As such statements suggest, these societies and clubs tended to impose strict restrictions upon both what could be read and who could become a member. Substantial entry fees and large fines for overdue books were just part of what William St Clair has described as an 'array of instruments which ensured exclusivity of access'. Members of subscription libraries may well have been 'the first generation in their families to have had regular access to new books', but such institutions tended to widen 'the amount of reading among the upper social groups' rather than to spread it downwards as has sometimes been suggested.[17] Mechanics Institutes, which often catered for both middle- and working-class readers, did not become common until the 1820s.

Evidence of how these various institutions of reading operated has been preserved in a number of sources that challenge stereotypical notions of the circulating library as the preserve of the female novel reader and the subscription library as a male environment in which serious weighty tomes or pamphlets were discussed. During the 1790s most of the members of James Marshall's circulating library in Bath were men; the catalogue of the Sheffield Subscription Library published in 1798 contained 248 volumes in the 'Novels' section, including recent titles by Ann Radcliffe and multiple copies of Burney's *Cecilia* (1782).[18] During the 1770s and 1780s the most frequently borrowed books at the Bristol Subscription Library came from the 'history, travel and geography' section of the catalogue, but 'belles-lettres' (a category which included some recent novels) was also popular. Some book clubs and reading societies included substantial numbers of women members whilst others limited the number of women who could apply.[19] Although these records show that many of these institutions shared common methods of organisation (usually enforced by a set of printed 'rules') no uniform picture of the circulating or subscription library reader emerges. This suggests that each institution reflected the needs and demands of a specific reading community.

Representing the resort library and its customers

Library advertisements and other forms of public representation reveal much about the 'library space' in which reading sometimes took place. James Raven has argued that to recover 'a sense of the internal arrangements of these libraries' is 'to gain more clues about the cultural significance of reading' and the importance of reading in public. Images of the circulating library produced in the 1740s and 1750s suggest imposing 'boundaries' that limited access to a refined clientele. Although undoubtedly idealised, trade card and catalogue engravings from this period sometimes show subscribers in an 'almost domestic setting', attended by the Library's proprietor (or his assistant) who is providing sage advice about which books to read.[20] Similar images produced to promote the large commercial circulating libraries that came into existence to serve readers in seaside resorts and spa towns during the 1780s and 90s give some sense of changes in the cultural significance of the library during this period. The well-known etching of *Hall's Library at Margate* (1789) depicts a magnificent interior (42 feet square by 17 feet high), which is quite different to the 'domestic setting' used to promote earlier libraries. Both the print and description of the library that appeared in a guide to Margate published by Hall in the following year represent the library as 'elegant' and 'ornamented'.[21] In the image, reading is relegated to the margins of the room. Two well-dressed gentlemen are reading newspapers by the light of the windows to the left of the picture, whilst on the far right a fashionable looking woman takes down a volume from the shelves. At the centre of the image is a family group (complete with dog) who are engaged in conversation rather than reading.[22]

This idea of the library as a space for walking and socialising with other stylish holidaymakers was central to the promotion of these new libraries. *The New Margate and Ramsgate Guide* (c.1790) depicts the Church Field area in which Hall's Library was located as a leisure zone filled with new buildings, including two other libraries, a theatre, meeting house and assembly rooms. Both Champion's Library and Silver's Library are described in terms of their impressive architecture. Champion's is of 'grand appearance' with a 'piazza before it', and both are said to provide subscribers with access to 'good gardens'. Hall's Library was simply a more 'magnificent' version of these libraries. Surrounded by a 'noble piazza with seats for the use of the company' the main hall was said to be able to 'contain between three and four hundred people'. These descriptions promote the library as a 'truly brilliant spectacle', a site for visitors to see and in which to be seen. That they also contained 'suitable accommodation as well as ample matter for reading' appears to be something of an afterthought for the author of the *New Guide*. These promotional works show that this sort of library was usually found in the new commercial districts that sprang up in resort towns during this period to provide entertainment for those spending the season. As the *Guide* also makes clear, these new libraries frequently included shops that sold 'curious trinkets, pocket books and nicknacks', but not books.[23] Hall's main building was divided in two by a set of Corinthian columns that separated the library section from a shop in which silverware, toys and other goods were sold. As Lee Erickson has noted, the etching promotes *Hall's Library* as a place in which 'several kinds of merchandise' were available, but both toys and books are represented as 'minor attractions compared to the patrons themselves', who are depicted 'enjoying one another's company'.[24] Such images suggest that the new resort library was promoted first and foremost as a sociable space in which it was safe for well-to-do families to congregate, chat, play with their children, buy toys and trinkets, and perhaps peruse the newspapers or borrow books. The 5s subscription fee that each person was charged 'for the season' was as much for the privileged occupation of this space as for the borrowing of books. By combining the renting of books and newspapers with the sale of luxury goods and the provision of entertainment, which some-times included dancing and gambling, the circulating library helped to reinvent reading as a part of the leisure industry.

The resort library as 'Raffle Shop' – Charlotte Francis (1786–1870) and the 'Excursion to Brighton'

Despite much recent interest in the representation and contents of com-mercial libraries, the ways in which they are described in the autobio-graphical writings of their customers has been little explored. Charlotte Francis, later Barrett (1786–1870), is perhaps best known as the editor of the diaries and letters of her aunt, Fanny Burney, published in 1842, but her 'Journal of what passed in an excursion to Brighton' includes detailed information about the way in which she and her family and friends used the various libraries available in the resort.[25] Compiled between 16 August and 23 September 1799, when she was just 13 years old, it records that she regularly visited Fisher's Circulating Library and Donaldson's Marine Library.[26] The majority of entries refer to these libraries as sociable spaces rather than places from which texts were bor-rowed, or in which reading took place. Her first mention of Fisher's, for example, refers to the library's subscription book being used as a direc-tory of who was in town: 'if you pay a crown [i.e. 5s] you may write your name in the book & your address & your friends find you'. On this occa-sion they used 'the book' to find out the address of an 'acquaintance of Mamma's' staying in town, who they called on later that night.[27] In this instance it is telling that, although the 5s fee would have entitled the family to borrow books, Francis describes it as a payment for the use of the subscription book. Lee Erickson has noted that the narrator of Burney's *Camilla* (1796) 'acidly comments' on the fact that for some resort readers this was the only book they ever read.[28]

When not using the library to check who was in town, the Francis fam-ily went there to buy 'trifles' or to take part in raffles (f.14r). Charlotte refers to 'the rafle [sic] shop Donaldsons, or as he calls it the Marine Library' (f.25r) in a way that suggests that she thought that gambling was in fact its primary function. As the *New Guide* to Margate and several other sources make clear, raffles were a popular form of entertainment in circulating libraries during the 1790s. Customers bought tickets 'from one shilling, to ten shillings and six-pence per person' for goods previously displayed in the library's shop. More than 60 people sometimes competed in 'one raffle'.[29] On the evening of Saturday 20 August 1799, Donaldson's 'raffle shop' was 'so full' that Francis and her family could not get in and instead moved on to Fisher's where they met two friends. Here, Francis 'put into the rafle [sic] with Mr Broome's choice but lost' (f.18v). These entries indicate that for many subscribers the circulating library may well have performed a social function that was in many ways entirely separate from its role in the dissemination of books.[30]

Such entries appear to support the assumptions of contemporary satirists who argued that almost anything went on in the circulating library except reading, but the fact that Francis represents these libraries as central to her experience of being on holiday in Brighton is a useful reminder that during the late eighteenth century the expansion of library provision was part of the broader commercialisation of pleasure. Francis spent her days in Brighton 'shopping of a morning' and going to 'rafles[sic] in the evening', and even though she sometimes found the repetitiveness of this lifestyle tedious, on the whole, the diaries give the impression that she thoroughly enjoyed using the library as a social space and that her family approved of and encouraged her gambling. Robert Bisset's anti-Jacobin novel, *Modern Literature* (1804), also records that gambling was rife in the Brighton libraries and the difference in tone between the two accounts is very revealing. Francis's spirited enjoyment of the pleasures of the library and Bisset's outright condemnation of the library as 'shop' are at the opposite ends of the representational spectrum of their age.[31] When looked at in conjunction with the material produced to promote resort libraries, Francis's diaries help to recover a sense of them as thrilling places. Brightly illuminated and packed with people, they were full of exciting 'trifles' as well as books.

Despite this apparent lack of concern with the library as a lending institution, Francis's diaries do contain some hard evidence about borrowing, reading and the use of library space. She borrowed 'a volume of Voltaire's plays in French' from Fisher's in order to practice her language skills, and later read part of this volume aloud to her mother in their lodgings (f.11v).[32] Contemporary guidebooks suggest that, like Hall's in Margate, the Brighton libraries included tables at which newspapers could be read, but Francis does not appear to have used the library itself as a reading venue. She does note, however, that some of her friends made illegitimate use of this communal reading space.[33]

> Nobody goes to the libraries without subscribing but Mrs and Miss Middleton spend all their mornings there reading the newspapers & looking at all the things & yet neither of them subscribe & they excuse their meanness by saying that as Dr Hooper forbade Miss M. to be out in the night air, & as she does not want to read there is no occasion. (ff.43r–43v)

This entry reveals that both libraries included spaces for reading the newspapers similar to those depicted in the illustration of *Hall's Library at Margate*, and that it was possible to enter library space to read texts taken from the open shelves, or put on open display, without having to prove that you were a subscriber. As Francis's outraged tone suggests, however, to do so was to transgress the social codes of a membership community and, as in this case, must have risked embarrassing exposure. *A Guide to All the Watering and Sea Bathing Places* declared that 'no amusement is so cheap at Brighton as is reading', but this form of illegitimate entry was probably not what the author had in mind.[34]

Charlotte Francis's account of her 'excursion to Brighton' is important because it helps to draw attention to those who, although they did 'not want to read', nevertheless spent a great deal of time in the new-style commercial libraries, whether gambling, shopping or just 'looking at the things'. Perhaps not surprisingly, historians of reading have been reluctant to deal with those readers who appear to confirm so many stereotypes about the 'desultory' nature of reading in the circulating library, but the history of reading needs to account for reluctant readers too.[35] Although Miss Middleton and her mother are an illegitimate presence within the library and they did 'not want to read' in the sense that they were not interested in books, they were regular readers of newspapers. Many other legitimate customers must have used the resort libraries in exactly this fashion. The libraries in Margate and Brighton were all promoted primarily as places where people met to be entertained rather than as reading venues. By the early nineteenth century a centrally located library was an important part of what Erickson has called 'a resort's organization of pleasure'. In a competitive world libraries needed to add more and more non-reading attractions in order to appeal to subscribers. By the early nineteenth century many libraries included rooms for dancing or for playing billiards and other games.[36]

Francis's diaries provide a glimpse into the sociable world of the resort library, but many other urban readers combined various commercial and non-commercial institutions of reading in order to read extensively. I now want to look at one such reader, Joseph Hunter, whose experience of reading in Sheffield during the late 1790s reveals the limits of community, the power of the institution, to exclude as well as include.

Joseph Hunter and the Sheffield Subscription Library

The diaries of Joseph Hunter (1783–1861)

Born in February 1783 in Sheffield, Yorkshire, Joseph Hunter (1783–1861) was the son of a local cutlery manufacturer. His mother died when he was an infant and he spent most of his youth at the home of his guardian, the Presbyterian minister Joseph Evans, who preached at the town's Upper Chapel. Hunter was apprenticed to his father's trade at 14 and between August 1797 and March 1799 he worked in the shop and warehouse of the merchant and manufacturer Robert Hadfield. His career path changed in 1805 when he was sent to York to train as a Presbyterian minister. He became assistant keeper of the public record in 1838 after the publication of a number of antiquarian works had brought him to the attention of the commissioners of public records.[37] The set of diaries that he kept (with some long gaps) between March 1797 and July 1799 provide a particularly detailed record of his reading. This section of the chapter concentrates on the only complete section of the diary, which runs from 14 May to 18 November 1798, when he was an apprentice at Hadfield's warehouse.[38]

Hunter recorded his reasons for keeping a diary on 27 March 1797: 'I intend to set down all & everything which occurs to me during this year & likewise an account of the books which I read'.[39] Amongst the details of his everyday life he recorded his attendance at Chapel and visits to lectures, the theatre, a fair and waxworks, but the diary is dominated by references to books and periodicals. He noted the date on which he acquired a text, the library, individual, or shop from which it was borrowed or bought, and, in the majority of cases, whether he completed the text in its entirety. The following entry, made on 9 June 1798, is typical: 'I took Radcliffe's Tour to the Library; I was not so much entertained with it as I expected, tho her descriptions are very fine. Bought the 1st Vol of Lodge's Illustrations of British History, Biography & Manners'.[40] Despite occasional references to 'the reader' in some early entries, it appears to have been a private document.[41] As a record of the borrowing and consumption of texts it provides hard evidence about the use of commercial libraries and bookshops of the kind that we usually have to guess at, but it is not an ideal source. Hunter often had little to say about his methods and modes of reading.

Despite these limitations, Hunter's diary bears comparison with the records kept during the 1790s by Anna Larpent and Otto Van Eck that have been investigated by John Brewer and Arianne Baggerman, respectively.[42] Both Larpent, the professional reader living in London, and Van Eck, the beneficiary of a reading programme organised by his parents, rarely refer to the text as an object or commodity. By contrast, Hunter is almost always concerned with the text as a material object to be 'procured' from the library or bookshop. The 1798 sequence of his diary provides the 'reliable personal witness' to the use of a subscription library that Paul Kaufman sought in order to test the hypothetical reader he had constructed from the borrowing records at Bristol. Hunter's use of many different libraries reveals the limitations of concentrating upon the records of a single library in isolation and of constructing an idea of the reader based upon his or her association with one institution. His diaries suggest some of the limitations in talking about the 'circulating library reader' and the 'subscription library reader' as though there was never any overlap between these reading constituencies.[43]

Procuring texts

During the 1790s Sheffield was a rapidly expanding industrial town with a population that had reached 29,000 by the middle of the decade. That a commercial directory of 1797 reveals that this population had access to three circulating libraries, eight booksellers, one binder and three printers is evidence of the growing commercialisation of reading throughout the nation in the 1780s and 1790s.[44] During 1798 Hunter 'procured' books, periodicals, newspapers and pamphlets from many of these shops and commercial libraries as well as from 'Book John', who ran a stall in the marketplace, and two subscription libraries. Each lay within walking distance of his home in Norfolk Street and he used them in conjunction with the private libraries of family and friends to read widely. Figure 4.1 provides a breakdown, by volume, of the texts that Hunter acquired from these various venues during 1798.[45] The subscription library, known as the Sheffield Book Society, and referred to in the diaries as the 'Surrey Street Library', dominated Hunter's borrowing and reading experience with 38 texts borrowed and 33 read. This was the kind of reading institution that vetted its members, charged a substantial annual fee and allowed members to nominate texts for inclusion at a monthly meeting.[46] However, several references to reading texts in situ,

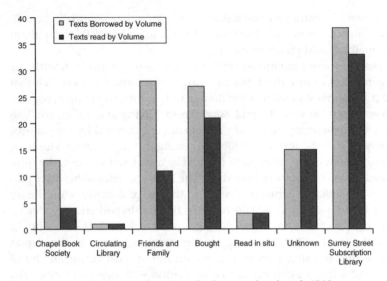

Figure 4.1   Joseph Hunter – Texts bought, borrowed and read, 1798

such as a print exhibited in a shop window, or a book displayed for sale in the marketplace, suggest the extent to which texts were available to be appropriated or consumed without payment within the urban environment. Hunter also describes his reading of the advertisements in ephemeral publications, such as newspapers, and of the packaging that came with commemorative coins.[47] Despite this apparent inclusiveness there is a hierarchy of texts within the diary. Books borrowed from the libraries are given the most space and the times at which they were borrowed and returned are central to its structure.

During the six months recorded in the 1798 sequence of the diary, Hunter purchased only two new books, George Smith's *Sermon to the Odd-Fellows*, and James Montgomery's *The Whisperer*, both of which were the work of local authors.[48] His purchase and reading of Montgomery's text provides important evidence of the way in which he selected and bought texts. Hunter first discovered that it had been published from a note contained in the *Iris*, a local newspaper edited by the author, which he read on 25 May 1798 (f.16v). The book was bought by his guardian for £1 2s 6d on July 15, probably from the bookshop belonging to Ann and Elizabeth Gales located near to Montgomery's print-shop, and given to Hunter who completed reading it on 9 August (f.22r, 25v).[49] In this instance the newspaper, which had featured material from the book in 1795, was central to the act of consumption. This process suggests something of the complex relationship between the newspaper as a source of information and the other cultural institutions located within the town that benefited from the spread of news about publications and cultural events. The newspaper encouraged the purchase of this text in the same way that it encouraged Hunter to attend lectures also advertised in its pages (f.10r). The delay of nearly two months between reading the advertisement and acquiring the text indicates that Hunter did not have the freedom to purchase new books with his own money and that he had to come to an agreement with Evans about the value of this text.

By far the greatest number of new texts purchased by Evans and Hunter were periodicals and newspapers. Evans bought the *Iris* on a weekly basis throughout the first year of the diary, but in July 1798 he began to share the cost with Mr Meanley and Miss Haynes, both of whom regularly supplied Hunter with texts (f.21v). Hunter's inclusion of this text as lunchtime reading in the hourly breakdown of his everyday life, entered into the diary on 10 August 1798, suggests that he probably read it more often than is apparent from the rest of the diary (f.25v). Its very ubiquity as part of the fabric of everyday family life may have prevented its being mentioned on a weekly basis, but several entries recording the transcription of passages from the paper suggest that it was not simply regarded as an ephemeral publication. He also regularly read a number of periodicals that Jon Klancher has argued had distinctly different ways of addressing their audiences, including the recently founded *Oeconomist* (1798), *Monthly Magazine* (1796), and the *Analytical Review* (1788), as well as the long established *Gentleman's Magazine* and the *Monthly Review*.[50]

During 1797 Hunter bought a number of second-hand books, pamphlets and handbills from 'Book John,' who is described as 'a person who stands in the Market place and sells books' (f.30v). Evans persuaded him not to make any further purchases in this manner, however, after he bought a *Petition to the House of Commons* for 6d in September of that year.[51] Evans disapproved of this purchase because he thought Hunter would not 'read much' of it (f.8v). As a consequence, during the following year Evans bought a number of second-hand texts that were to be regularly consulted. These included 18 volumes of the *Encyclopaedia Britannica* acquired for £8 8s, which, Hunter noted with disdain, 'had never been opened' by their previous owner (f.15v). New and second-hand books were clearly easily available in Sheffield in the late 1790s, but Hunter and his family bought mainly periodicals and newspapers.[52] These texts were central to their local reading community, and the fact that even this solidly middle-class family purchased newspapers collectively, indicates that regular access to new texts came at a cost that was still beyond the means of the majority of readers. The collective purchase of the *Iris* offers a good example of the way in which texts were shared amongst friends and family. Hunter borrowed a number of books from friends during 1798, but the majority of shared texts were copies of the *Monthly Magazine* and the *Monthly Review*. These periodicals were at the centre of his reading experience and their significance is underlined by their frequent transformation into book form through binding.[53]

Hunter also acquired texts from the 'Vestry' or 'Chapel' book society and a commercial circulating library. He was connected to the book society by his attendance at the Presbyterian chapel and must have become a subscriber during the early months of 1798, but it played a significant role in his reading only after June 24, when he noted: 'The Vestry Library has lately been new-modelled, they take in any kind of books whereas, previously they had only divinity. There are at present about 70 vols and 22 subscribers' (f.20r). By patronising several libraries he was able to access a number of new texts each week and to assess them at home in order to decide which he was going to complete. On 4 November 1798 he borrowed Anthony Robinson's *A View of the Causes and Consequences of English Wars* (1798) from the Vestry, but after having 'looked at' it he decided to continue reading a volume of Gibbon's *Decline and Fall of the Roman Empire*, borrowed from Surrey Street (f.41r).[54] Kaufman has noted that the main problem with library borrowing records is determining whether readers actually completed the texts that they had borrowed. By contrast to these inert sources, Hunter's diary gives a real sense of the variety of different strategies that could be applied to the books that he borrowed, including rapid scanning.[55]

As an alternative source of reading to Surrey Street, the Vestry performed a function partially fulfilled in the previous year by the library of Thomas Lindley, who is described as 'a hairdresser and owner of a circulating library' in a local trade directory.[56] Hunter did not subscribe to Lindley's library but paid to borrow fiction at the rate of 1d for '2 days & 1 night' (f.10r). He used Lindley's library only once during 1798, and recorded his disappointment with a novel, *The Castle of Mowbray* (1788), borrowed because its title echoed that of Walpole's *The Castle of Otranto* (1765) (f.17v).[57] This evidence suggests that John Brewer is correct in assuming that subscription library users increased their access to fiction by visiting circulating libraries, but in this case that use was infrequent, and does not significantly alter the pattern of reading revealed by the diaries.[58] As Figure 4.2 demonstrates, Hunter did not need to rely on the circulating library for fiction because Surrey Street had a large selection of contemporary novels as well as works by Richardson, Swift and Fielding that were included in the 'Moral and Miscellaneous' section of the catalogue. This particular instance of borrowing occurred because Evans lent Walpole's novel to a friend before Hunter had completed it. He must therefore have searched Lindley's catalogue for the same title and, unable to find it, chosen another which promised the same Gothic locale. His disappointment with *The Castle of Mowbray* demonstrates one of the perils of choosing a novel from the catalogue by title. Hunter also used this circulating library to complete a novel borrowed from Surrey Street: 'The 1st volume being lost at our library I got it at Lindley's Library in Church Lane' (f.9v). This evidence underlines Hunter's ability to move with ease between different libraries, but it also suggests that the notion of the subscription library as an institution dominated by texts concerned with the 'civic preoccupations and commercial interests of their members' needs to be modified.[59] The Sheffield Library was well stocked with fiction and in Hunter's experience circulating and subscription libraries often complemented one another.

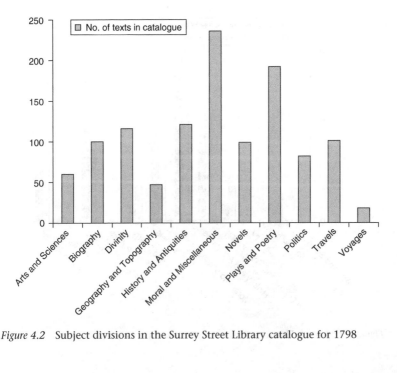

Figure 4.2 Subject divisions in the Surrey Street Library catalogue for 1798

The Sheffield Book Society or Surrey Street Library was an important institution. Founded in 1771, shortly after the inauguration of a subscription library at Leeds, it regularly published its catalogue and regulations. There were 117 members in 1798 including significant numbers of manufacturers (19), clergymen (13), solicitors (7), doctors (7) and merchants (5). As Sara Joynes has noted, Sheffield included fewer members of the gentry (3 in 1798) than most contemporary subscription libraries. That it included a mixture of both Anglican and Dissenting clergy and a significant number of women (13) also suggests that it was a somewhat unusual institution.[60] Membership was not open to everyone, however. Members had first to be nominated, and once this nomination was approved by at least two-thirds of the existing members, he or she had to pay three guineas as an admission fee and a further ten shillings annually. Joseph Evans was president several times during its early years and he undoubtedly encouraged Hunter to use this institution.[61] The catalogue that he purchased in May 1798 was one of the most important texts in Hunter's reading life (f.16v). Figures 4.2 and 4.3, reconstruct his borrowing during 1798 using the subject divisions of the

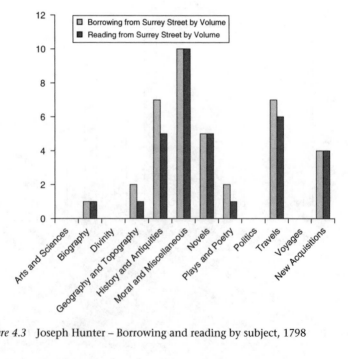

Figure 4.3 Joseph Hunter – Borrowing and reading by subject, 1798

1798 catalogue. It is immediately apparent that Hunter did not borrow any texts from certain subject areas within the catalogue (Arts and Sciences, Divinity, Politics and Voyages) and that his reading was dominated by texts from the imprecise category 'Moral and Miscellaneous'.[62] This contained any prose fiction that could not be included in the 'Novels' section of the catalogue and the majority of monthly periodicals. Of the items borrowed from this category three can be reclassified as fiction, but the majority were current issues of periodicals such as the *European Magazine*. Figure 4.4 redistributes texts from the 'Miscellaneous' category into their nearest modern equivalents (Periodicals and Fiction), but it is important to remember that their original categorisation may have played an important role in Hunter's selection process. In this modified picture of Hunter's borrowing and reading from Surrey Street the balance is more even, with an almost equal spread of texts among 'Travels', 'History', 'Periodicals' and 'Fiction'. The figures for the last category are boosted by the four volumes of Ann Radcliffe's *The Mysteries of Udolpho* (1794), which he read for a second time between 13 August and 3 September 1798 (ff.26r–30r).[63]

Kaufman found that the texts most frequently borrowed at Bristol came from the subject division 'History, Antiquities and Geography' which included texts listed under 'Travels' and 'Voyages' in the Surrey Street catalogue. The dominance of these subjects is reflected in Hunter's borrowing record, which includes 16 texts that fall into these areas, but the record does not simply confirm Kaufman's picture. The fifth most

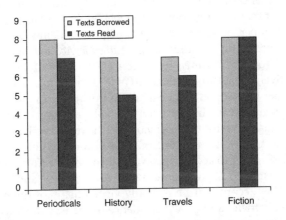

Figure 4.4 Joseph Hunter – Borrowing and reading from the Surrey Street Library (adjusted by subject)

popular category at Bristol, 'Theology,' does not feature at all in Hunter's borrowing.[64] Presumably Hunter did not need to borrow theological works because he had access to them from amongst the 700 books in his guardian's library.[65] Given this background, it is perhaps not surprising that he chose to use the subscription library as a source of travel, history and fiction, but it is significant that throughout 1798 he recorded only five instances of the private reading of religious texts. Two of these instances refer to 'Sunday reading' and suggest that he treated religious texts as significantly different from those that he consumed during the week (f.37r). His main mode of access to religious material came via the pulpit rather than from print. Hunter attended the chapel to hear sermons at least once each week, but the diary is at best vague about how he reacted to them. He occasionally noted the chapter and verse from which the subject of the sermon was taken, but, in the majority of instances, he recorded only the name of the speaker.[66] His very lack of response to these texts suggests that they were perceived as part of a mechanistic, ritual practice, in which interpretation was the work of the speaker rather than the listener.

Although it is not surprising that Hunter should restrict his borrowing from Surrey Street to texts not available from other informal sources, the amount of contemporary material that he borrowed is remarkable. Of the 39 texts borrowed in 1798, 31 were first published in the 1790s, with 23 of these published in 1797–1799. Texts found in the Geography – History – Travels area of the subject divide, which Hunter most frequently used, were notoriously expensive. Thus, in common with many readers, Hunter could afford to borrow but not to buy these texts, and it is significant that his only source for travel books was Surrey Street with its large number of subscribers who helped to defray the cost. The advertised prices for Staunton's, *An Authentic Account of an Embassy* (1797) and Townson's *Travels in Hungary* (1797) were £1 13s 6d, and £4 4s, respectively. That Hunter read both of these texts during a single week in September 1798 shows that he used this institution to supply new and expensive secular texts that were not available from any other source.[67]

Hunter's diaries reveal the interaction of the reader with available networks of distribution, and confirm that it was possible for a young middle-class reader to access texts with apparent ease from a number of different institutions, including both subscription and circulating libraries. They record that he regularly visited many of the booksellers located in Sheffield, and provide evidence of the way in which he used different institutions to supply different sorts of text. The reading life that they describe is far more complex than that which would be revealed by a study of either the borrowing records of one of the libraries to which he belonged, should they be discovered, or of the contents of his family library.

Consuming texts

Figure 4.1 revealed that Hunter borrowed or was given more texts than he actually read. Figure 4.5 breaks this reading down by subject.[68] It confirms that his reading was dominated by texts and genres available from the various libraries to which he belonged and underlines the importance of periodicals to his reading community. These figures demonstrate something of the complexity of Hunter's reading life, but the diary is also important because it reveals the various modes of consumption that he applied to these texts.

Hunter's reading experience was in part determined by the material conditions under which texts were borrowed. After going through the process of becoming a member and the payment of fees, books could be acquired from Surrey Street under a set of strictly applied rules. Up to two texts could be borrowed at any one time, as long as one of them was a play or periodical, and the size of the text and the date of its acquisition by the library determined the date on which it needed to be returned. A periodical could be kept for just two nights and a quarto a month,

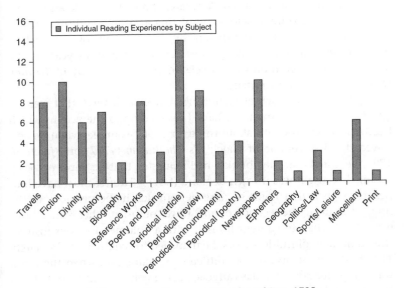

Figure 4.5   Joseph Hunter – Reading experience by subject, 1798

but this time was halved if the book had been purchased within the last six months, as many of those that Hunter read were. Fines were imposed for late returns and the volume had to remain in the library for at least one day before the same reader could borrow it again.[69]

Because titles were borrowed by the volume rather than in their entirety the completion of a work could be a long and fragmented process entailing several visits to the library. This meant that Hunter sometimes read the volumes of a text in a different order than was intended by the author, and that on occasion he had to wait for the relevant volume to be returned by another reader in order to complete a title.[70] For example, he borrowed the second volume of Helen Maria Williams's *A Tour in Switzerland* (1798) on 22 October along with a copy of the *Gentleman's Magazine*, which needed to be returned after two nights. After making notes from the *Tour* he returned it to the library on 24 October and replaced it with the first volume, which he kept until 5 November. To complete the entire text took just over two weeks, and during that time he also read a number of periodicals via the two-night loan system (f.38v, f.41r).[71] Some texts, such as Staunton's *An Authentic Account of an Embassy* (1797), which Hunter described as 'in universal demand', were more difficult to complete. He returned volume one of this text after noting in the diary that he intended to read the second, but he had to content himself with Townson's *Travels in Hungary* (1797), until it became available a few days later (f.30v, f.31v). He also sometimes returned a volume before completing a reading and then had to wait until another reader returned it. By contrast, texts owned, such as the *Encyclopaedia*, were regularly consulted throughout the year, and he took a considerable number of weeks to complete a copy of *Tristram Shandy* borrowed from a friend.

Acquiring books, such as Staunton's *Authentic Account*, that were in 'great call at the Library' must have impacted upon the way in which Hunter read and thought about these texts. For example, when he borrowed the first volume of Radcliffe's *The Italian* (1797) on March 20 1797, he noted that the librarian had requested that he 'must not keep it long' because it was in such demand (f.3v).[72] Hunter must have hurried through it that night because he returned it the next day in the hope of securing the second volume. It was out to another reader, however, and he had to content himself with a volume of travels instead. After a number of fruitless visits, he managed to acquire it on 24 March. The third volume also proved difficult to secure, and when the novel was completed some ten days after acquiring volume one, he noted that he found it disappointing (f.4v). Hunter's experience of this text, rushing through it to get to the end so that it could be returned to the library, was in part a response to the material conditions under which it was borrowed, but both his eagerness to get hold of the text (and his eventual disappointment) suggests something of what it must have been like to read a newly published text that was in demand by many other readers of the same reading community. It also indicates that this communal enthusiasm for a text could be spread rapidly amongst the library's members via the librarian who let everyone know which texts were most in demand.

Hunter's visits to Surrey Street were sociable events. He was often accompanied by friends and frequently engaged the librarian in conversation about which books were out to other readers. Sociability was also built into the rules of the Library. It operated via a monthly meeting at which the members were invited to nominate texts. If these texts met with the approval of a majority of members they were then bought and housed within the library. This process encouraged the public discussion of texts and the importance of periodicals in the decision-making process is revealed by a regulation that entitled members of the committee to have 'one monthly review delivered to them ... during the first month of its publication'.[73] Hunter mirrored this process by deciding which texts he wanted to nominate by reading reviews in a number of periodicals.

> The Monthly Magazine contains an account of the publication of that long expected work by Mr Conder of Ipswich, 'an Arrangement of Provincial Coins, Tokens and Medalets Issued in Great Britain, Ireland and the Colonies, Within the Last Twenty Years, from the Farthing to the Penny Size'. Price 7s 6d in Boards. I intend to get this proposed at the Surry Street Library. (f.35v)[74]

Each number of the *Monthly* contained 'a correct list of new publications' which gave full details about the size, price and publisher of a text just published and, on occasion, a brief sketch of its contents. Full reviews of texts only appeared in the 'half-yearly retrospect of domestic literature' printed in January and July. The *Monthly Review*, as its title suggests, provided full reviews of recently published texts. In this instance the *Monthly Magazine* kept Hunter informed about a subject that he was already interested in, but the diaries also reveal that reading the periodicals stimulated his desire to read new expensive texts.

> Brought also the European Magazine for June '98 [from Surrey Street], & the Monthly Review for Aug '98 from Miss Haynes. Took the 2 vols

of Monthly Magazines to Miss Haynes's & brought 5 other numbers. The Reviews and Magazines are full of Walpole's works in 5 vols 4to L10 10s. It appears to contain very curious things from what I have seen in the Reviews & c. If their funds should allow it I wish they should get it into the Surry Street Library. (fol.30r)

The committee did not buy Walpole's *Works* because they were too expensive, but Hunter's description of the periodicals as 'full' of reviews of this text is very accurate.[75] A serialised review appeared in the *Monthly Review* between July and October 1798, and Hunter's description of the size and price of the text directly echoes the announcement of its publication in the *Monthly Magazine* for May 1798, which also contained four pages of 'Walpoliana'.[76] The diaries thus provide important evidence about the way in which periodical reviews stimulated Hunter's desire to see a particular text or to read a particular author. Unable or unwilling to buy these texts he either put them forward for nomination, or hoped that another member of the subscription library would nominate them.

Through the process of nominating texts for inclusion, the subscription library encouraged the public discussion of texts and the use of the periodicals as a measure of the quality, or indication of the contents, of a text. The system of nominations was democratic, but its purpose was to negotiate difference. It is this process of meeting and selection that constitutes the subscription library as a reading community. The committee prevented the entry of books that did not meet majority approval. However, as the diaries reveal, Hunter did not always see this process as a benign force for good and he sometimes felt marginalised or excluded from the library as reading community because the kinds of texts that he wanted to see were being voted against. During the autumn of 1798 he noted that many books and periodicals considered 'jacobinical' were not being added to the Library: 'Brought "Anecdotes of the Founders of the French Revolution" ... A second volume has since appeared but they have not voted it into the library, as they have probably found the 1st volume to be too "jacobinical" for them to digest' (f.34v).[77]

Heather Jackson has noted that the removal of Jacobin texts was part of the temper of the time. In May 1798 a general meeting of subscribers at the Shrewsbury Library decided to remove 'politically sensitive' works by Rousseau, Godwin, Wollstonecraft and others that were part of what William St Clair has called 'the radical canon of the age'. Such exclusions may have been 'an act of calculated caution' rather than 'conservative reactionism', as Jackson suggests, but the exclusion of periodicals that were regularly read by members must have had an immediate impact upon their reading experience.[78] Both Shrewsbury and Sheffield chose to exclude the *Analytical Review*, which conservative writers viewed as an important source of opposition to the war against France. This periodical was a favourite with Hunter, who made notes on its contents and read texts, such as Robinson's *Causes and Consequences of English Wars*, reviewed in its pages. The diaries register its being 'turned out' as a particularly shocking event.

> Brought the 2[n]d number of the Anti-Jacobin Review & Magazine, which is got into the Surry Street Library instead of the Analytical which they have turned out. It is a most virulent attack upon all the friends of liberty or jacobins, as they are pleased to stile them; it is ornamented with caricature prints. (f.40v)

James Gilray's cartoon, *The New Morality*, which appeared in the inaugural issue of the *Anti-Jacobin Review* published in August 1798, depicts a number of texts (including Robinson's *Causes*) spewing forth from a 'cornucopia of ignorance' inscribed with the titles of three reviews, the *Analytical*, the *Monthly* and the *Critical*.[79] Given that there was a noisy celebration of Nelson's famous victory on the Nile in Sheffield in early October, the library committee may well have excluded the *Analytical* because they wanted to disassociate themselves from opposition to the war against France, but the effect of replacing it with the *Anti-Jacobin* was to make Hunter aware of his own position as a member of an audience that was now under attack.[80] He is referring to himself as one of 'the friends of liberty' in this passage from the diary, and it is from this position of identification with 'jacobinism' that he completed the resisting reading of the *Anti-Jacobin* as a 'virulent' text recorded in the diary.

This is not simply a reaction to the removal of the *Analytical*. Hunter's membership of both Surrey Street and the Vestry Library meant that he was particularly well read in the radical canon. Indeed his interest in the Vestry was stimulated by its expansion into subjects and genres other than 'divinity' in June 1798. During the next few months he borrowed 13 volumes, including radical texts such as Mary Wollstonecraft's *Origin and Progress of the French Revolution* (1794) and Robinson's *Causes and Consequences*. Although he sometimes made little progress with these texts once he returned home with them, he read Wollstonecraft in full, and borrowed it a second time for Miss Haynes to read. Several other books procured from this institution were borrowed for friends and family rather than for his own consumption. After taking

Mary Wollstonecraft's ' "Letters from Norway & c" back to the vestry library' he noted 'I did not read them but Mr E. said they were very entertaining and instructive' (f.20v).[81] With just 22 members, the Vestry was much smaller than the Surrey Street Library and may well have brought together a group of people with similar political beliefs. Radical texts were available from Surrey Street, at least until October 1798, as his reading of the first volume of the *Anecdotes of the Founders* (1797) attests, but the Vestry had a cheaper annual subscription (six rather than ten shillings) and it seems unlikely that all of its members also belonged to Surrey Street. One of the drawbacks of a smaller subscription library was, of course, that they could not afford to order many books. On 2 September 1798 Hunter complained that only one new book had been added to the Vestry at the monthly meeting. This was *The Spirit of the Public Journals* (1798), published by Richard Philips who had been imprisoned for selling Paine's *Rights of Man* in 1794. Despite the editor's 'advertisement', which claims that although much of its contents were 'of an anti-ministerial tendency' it was intended to gratify 'all parties', this was clearly a radical text.[82] Recent work on 'Romantic sociability' has suggested the importance of dissenting communities in the construction of an alternative politicised 'public sphere' during the 1790s, and the evidence of Hunter's borrowing seems to suggest that the Vestry Library provided a necessary alternative space to Surrey Street for the dissemination and discussion of radical texts during a period in which what was coming to be known as 'Jacobin' culture was under threat.[83] An entry made in the diary in September 1798, in which Hunter condemns *The Times* as 'a violent ministerial newspaper', suggests a familiarity with radical discourse (f.34v).

As Richard Cronin has argued, 1798 was the year that the rhetoric of the *Anti-Jacobin* triumphed. By presenting itself as 'the spokesman of sentiments held in common by an overwhelming majority of the nation', and defining Jacobinism as a force which 'rejects all habits, all wisdom of former times', the *Anti-Jacobin* forced many of its opponents to compromise.[84] For Hunter, reading in the autumn of 1798, however, this rhetoric appears to have helped him to construct a sense of his own reading practices as 'jacobinical'. In looking at the various institutions of reading available in the Romantic period, St Clair suggests that subscription libraries, reading societies and book clubs were essentially conservative because of the rapid removal of Paine's *Rights of Man* from their shelves in 1794, which helped to leave Burke's *Reflections* 'triumphant in the field'.[85] By contrast, Hunter's diaries suggest that some subscription libraries continued to take radical material until 1798, when what

Cronin describes as a mixture of 'government repression', anti-Jacobin propaganda, and the 'potent allure of the traditional for a nation at war and under threat of invasion', stopped the sympathetic reading of what now became classified as 'Jacobin' writing.[86] More importantly, perhaps, Hunter's account of the removal of the *Analytical Review* and other radical texts demonstrates that it was possible for those readers still sympathetic to the radical cause to read the Library's new acquisitions against the grain. All of this evidence suggests that the members of small reading communities, such as Surrey Street, did not necessarily share a common set of beliefs. The political crisis of 1798 reveals an underlying sense of conflict about what it was appropriate for a specific reading community to be seen to be reading.

The authority of the reviews

There has been much recent work on the 'reading patterns informing reviews and literary essays in popular periodicals'. James Machor has argued that such studies are valuable because they reveal attempts to direct and refine the reading practices of the audience that consumed them. He makes it clear that not all historical readers obeyed these directions – which were often inconsistent – but his insistence that 'the interpretive strategies that reviewers exercised' did have some influence over these readers is important.[87] As already noted, Hunter used periodicals as a source of information about new texts, but they also clearly influenced the way in which he selected and interpreted texts already held by the library. For example, on 11 October 1798 he borrowed Samuel Pratt's *Gleanings Through Wales* (1795) because 'the Reviewers gave it a very good character' (f.36v). Many of the other texts that he read in 1798 had received extensive critical attention in the *Monthly Review*, which was also associated with the cornucopia of ignorance in Gilray's *The New Morality*.[88] Of course, they were not his only guides to selection and he recorded the opinion of other readers on works of history and travel, but he was often deferent to the authority of the magazines and reviews on the subject of fiction.

> Took the 'Castle of Otranto' to the [Surrey Street] Library. It is one of the most entertaining novels I ever read – There is a note of his in [the] Monthly Magazine for May under the article Walpoliana, written in the year 1784, wherein he says he thinks that a romance may be formed wherein every incident shall appear supernatural & yet turn out natural at last. In this manner the romances of Mrs Radcliffe are formed. Brought from thence Mrs Radcliffe's Tour in Holland, Germany & to the lakes in England. (f.17v)[89]

In this instance, the reading of the novel and the periodical interacted, although it is hard to distinguish whether the magazine was read in the context of the novel or the novel in the context of the magazine. Nevertheless, Hunter applied Walpole's 'new idea of a novel' to a series of texts that he had already completed – the novels of Ann Radcliffe. It was the recognition of the applicability of Walpole's definition of the Gothic to these texts that influenced his decision to borrow Radcliffe's *A Journey Made in the Summer of 1794* (1795).[90]

Hunter's deference to the cultural authority of *The Monthly Review*, and the influence of the interpretative strategies deployed by its reviewers, can be seen in his reading of the anonymously authored *Fragments; in the Manner of Sterne* (1797):

> Mr E[vans] brought 'Fragments in the Manner of Sterne' '1797' from the library. The Monthly Review says it is the best imitation of Sterne that has ever appeared. I finished it that night & was very pleased with it; I think I will read 'Tristram Shandy' ... Wrote out of Fragments the piece upon war. (f.19r)[91]

It is significant that Hunter refers to the opinion of the periodical reviewer rather than his guardian and, as his reference to what 'the Monthly Review says' suggests, he appears to have read the review and text in tandem. That the review had some influence over the way in which this text was interpreted is confirmed by the fact that he transcribed the same 'piece upon war' that was central to the reviewer's deliberately ambiguous 'party' or 'political' reading of the text. That Hunter transcribed the section of the text dealing with what the review hints is a radical account of 'the cruelty of war' is perhaps further evidence of Hunter's 'jacobinical' reading strategies.[92] In this instance, however, the combined enjoyment of text and review also lead him to read *Tristram Shandy*. Hunter's reading of Sterne's novel between 8 July and 7 August 1798 illustrates the way in which the various sources of texts combined and interacted. Hunter came across the imitation of Sterne by chance when his guardian brought it from the Surrey Street Library and he immediately placed it within the critical discourse of the *Monthly Review*. He acquired the novel itself from a friend, and when entering notes about it into the diary situated it within the discourse of current critical opinion: 'It has of late become the fashion to cry down Sterne as the greatest plagiarist but if he made free with other peoples writings, we may excuse him, for he has put them into such beautiful language that they are hardly known' (f.25v). This passage uses the language of Ferrier's

'Comments on Sterne,' available in the library in a periodical cited by Hunter, and reflects the liberal critical stance taken towards 'plagiarism' by the *Monthly Magazine* in the article 'Poetical or Prose Imitations and Similarities,' included in the May 1798 issue.[93]

This evidence suggests that the critical strategies and reviews of texts available via the periodical press helped Hunter to make sense of texts, in much the same way that Machor suggests readers in antebellum America used reviews to aid their interpretation of fiction, but he approached each of his own reviews of fiction with a confident independent voice. Hunter's reading constantly acknowledges the importance of the periodical reviews, and there are several examples in the diary of him paying special attention to passages highlighted by the reviewers, but they did not enforce a particular reading, and he sometimes explicitly disagreed with them.[94] In his reading of Radcliffe's novel, *The Italian* (1797), Hunter referred to the same passage highlighted in the *Monthly Review*, but disagreed with the reviewer's opinion that this was the best of her novels (f.5r).[95] That some of the diary entries mimic the structure of reviews by including a summary of a text followed by an extract or discussion of a particular scene, suggests that they were important in forming the way in which he approached texts and contributed to his sense of self as a reader. His summary of the *Mysteries of Udolpho* (1794), provides a balanced account of the 'merits' and defects of the work, and he confidently describes himself as 'one of that class of readers who delight in the Marvellous' (f.30r). Unlike Anna Larpent, who was 25 years his senior, Hunter did not express a censorious view of novels and enjoyed them to the full without placing them within a purposive reading programme.[96] Hunter's reading strategies were clearly influenced both by the interpretative strategies of the periodical reviewers and by his face-to-face meetings with those who shared the texts that he was reading.

Consuming travels

Hunter read all four volumes of the *Mysteries of Udolpho*, in order, before producing his summary of the text. This procedure is typical of his reading of fiction, but he often applied a number of different reading strategies to texts from other genres. For example, he treated texts selected from the 'Travels' section of the Surrey Street catalogue in a number of different ways. He read part of Campbell's *Journey Overland to India* (1795) aloud on the day that it was borrowed and later transcribed a large section of it into the diary, where he noted that it contained both humorous and affecting narratives (ff.23r–25v). By contrast, he did not read any of the text of Pennant's *Outlines of the Globe: The View of Hindoostan* (1798), but noted that 'there are some beautiful plates in it' (f.26r)[97] Hunter often recorded his response to the non-verbal elements of texts and the copying of illustrations is an important feature of his reading of travel literature. For example, he copied the illustration of Strawberry Hill contained in Ireland's *Picturesque Views on the River Thames* (1792) on the day that he borrowed this book, but he did not proceed to read the text until several days later (f.22v). This reading focused on the image of Walpole's home because he was a fan of his work and he also seems to have chosen to read Radcliffe's *A Journey made in the Summer of 1794* (1795) because of his enthusiasm for her fictional works. Both of the entries that record his reaction to this text suggest that he focused on 'her descriptions' of landscape in order to produce an experience that was close to his reading of the novels.[98] However, as with most genres, if he was not 'entertained' with a volume of travels he stopped reading it: 'I have read part of Townson [*Travels in Hungary* (1797)], but I think I shall read no more as it consists of nothing else but mineralogical & botanical remarks' (f.31v). Hunter often read volumes of travels in part, or plundered them for illustrations. Like the majority of readers in this study he rarely dealt with the text as an organic whole. A volume such as Helen Maria Williams's *A Tour in Switzerland* (1798) was even mined for 'remarks' that supported his conception of himself as a radical reader: 'Thought the following remarks in Miss Williams was exceeding applicable to the manufacturers of Sheffield: "There is a spirit in that class, in all countries, more favourable to inquiry & consequently more hostile to unconditional submission" Vol 2 p.227' (f.38v).

Reading spaces; reading modes

Unfortunately, Hunter was more concerned with recording provenance than either the place or mode that characterised his reading, but it is possible to draw some tentative conclusions about these aspects of his reading experience. The 'account of how I spent the day hour by hour', entered into the diary on 10 August 1798, was designed to represent a typical working day. He rose at 7:00 a.m., 'drew part of a Landscape', wrote in his diary and 'read a little in' the *Encyclopaedia Britannica*, before walking to work at 9:00 a.m. He read 'part of the Iris' while eating his lunch at home between 1:00 and 2:00 p.m., and after returning from the warehouse at 5:00 p.m., spent nearly three hours reading 'in the Encyclopaedia' before retiring to bed at 10:15 p.m. (f.25v). Each of these readings took place at home from a text that he owned, but he does not record whether he read in company or alone, in his own room or with the family, in silence or aloud. That home was the most common venue for his reading is suggested by the fact that he often notes when reading took place in an unusual venue such as his workplace.[99] The type of reading, like the location, was too much a part of the fabric of everyday life to have received much comment in the diary, but there is enough evidence to suggest that he and his family sometimes read aloud to each other within the home. In April 1797, Hunter was unable to summarise the plot of Macklin's *Man of the World* (1785) because he had 'neither heard, nor read it all' (f.7r), and in July 1798 he noted that his reading aloud from Campbell's *Journey Overland to India* (1795) had confirmed the 'high character' of the book, although he does not mention who was in the audience for this reading (f.23r).[100] That Hunter rarely mentions such instances suggests that he mainly read in silence. The public performance of texts was certainly less significant to Hunter than it was for Anna Larpent, whose family regularly read aloud together, but as I have already suggested, discussion of texts with his family and friends was an important feature of his reading experience and the sociability that surrounded these discussions appears occasionally to have included reading aloud.

Silent reading was the dominant rather than the only reading practice in which Hunter engaged. The theory of the 'reading revolution' ties 'silent' and 'extensive' reading together into a teleological model but, as other studies of reading in the 1790s have demonstrated, the reader who consumed a large number of texts from a wide range of genres could participate in diverse modes of reading, and did not necessarily pass from one text to another without close study.[101] Hunter read at least 88 texts during the six months in which he kept the 1798 sequence of the diary and many of these were read rapidly, or in part, before being returned to the library or friend from whom they were borrowed.[102] He rarely returned to a text that he had borrowed before.[103] That Hunter left such a detailed record of his reading, however, demonstrates that he was a far from passive reader, and the diary was only one of the several manuscript books into which he transcribed extracts. Entries in the diary describe his use of a commonplace book, a notebook (for recording the plots of novels) and a number of volumes in which material relating to the history of Sheffield was stored. That summary and transcription were an important part of Hunter's reading is also suggested by the large number of entries in the diary that contain the phrases 'copied', 'wrote out of', and 'began to write into my common place book'.[104]

The extracts that Hunter copied into his commonplace book were often quite long. On 31 August 1798 he transcribed the entire first chapter of Zimmerman's *On Solitude* (1797), and on several other occasions he copied complete poems from the magazines and Reviews (f.29r).[105] As was the case with *On Solitude*, this process sometimes took place before he had completed reading a text in its entirety. Transcription suggests an interrogative reading practice and the desire to reread chunks from texts that had been returned to the library. Unlike Anna Larpent, Hunter did not return repeatedly to texts that included favourite passages, or intensely scrutinise sacred texts. His wide reading programme did not exclude the close study of texts, but it is difficult to characterise this reading as 'intensive' without emptying this term of much of its meaning. Hunter did not reread texts in order to confirm his religious faith or sense of self, as Brewer suggests Larpent did.[106]

The diary emphasises both the mobility of texts in Hunter's immediate circle – they move between the library and home and are exchanged by friends – and the modernity of his reading. Hunter's reading life was filled with contemporary books and periodicals. This evidence appears to confirm Brewer's assertion that a 'diversity of reading practices' existed at the end of the eighteenth century.[107] However, because Larpent lived in a household where books were unusually common and she sometimes acted as a professional reader he is reluctant to move towards a general theory of reading using just the evidence from her diaries. Hunter's diversity of practice was also founded upon a privileged access to a wide range of texts. The various commercial libraries and book clubs that he used, with their range of renting costs and subscription fees, came at a price that many other readers would have been unable to afford. Indeed, Larpent, Otto Van Eck, Charlotte Francis and Hunter all shared a similarly privileged access to texts and it is important to note that any modification to theories of reading put forward by these studies rests upon the testimony of only a handful of middle-class readers. In the late eighteenth century 'extensive' reading (without its pejorative meaning of simply passing from text to text) was a possibility for bourgeois readers such as Larpent and Hunter, but the number of texts that they regularly acquired would have amazed many of their contemporaries. It is perhaps best to think of these readers as in the avant-garde of a new and emerging set of reading practices rather than as representing the norm.

Hunter's diaries are important because they provide valuable evidence about the social distribution of texts, the importance of libraries to the urban middle-class and the influence of new critical discourses upon interpretation. The interpretative strategies learnt from the Reviews were particularly important to his reading, but whereas critics like Machor are content to suggest how such Reviews provided a range of strategies that readers could follow or reject, Hunter gives concrete evidence of the historical reader's ability to bring these strategies into play within the material context of a reading community that encouraged the perusal of reviews as the first stage in the acquisition of a book. Hunter's reading experience thus provides valuable evidence about the rules governing a series of different reading communities during the 1790s (reading as a member of the Vestry was different than reading as a member of Surrey Street), and of the way in which these communities fitted into the broader, national, interpretive community that supported the Reviews. However, as his identification of himself as a 'jacobinical' reader suggests, we should be wary of thinking of reading communities as united or harmonious organisations. Institutions like the Surrey Street Library had the power to limit membership and to exclude books that some of their members wanted to see. Hunter's dedicated compilation of a reading diary could not be more different from Charlotte Francis's record of the time that she spent in Brighton. Taken together they suggest something of the range of uses to which the new libraries of the late eighteenth century could be shaped.

5
Communal Practice and Individual Response: Reading in the Late Romantic Period

The turn to history in Romantic studies has tended to displace ideas about the rise of the individual and the importance of the artist as genius that were once associated with this period. The influence of Jerome McGann's work on the social text can be seen in those accounts of Romanticism that focus upon publication as a collaborative process involving author, editor and publisher. Zachary Leader's analysis of poems by Keats and Clare, for example, focuses on the close involvement of the editor- publisher John Taylor in the creative process. Other work has concentrated on the communal networks that helped to produce texts. Sonnet-writing contests and communal dining were important as forms of sociability to groups, such as the Hunt circle and the writers associated with the *London Magazine*, but they also led to the creation of texts that are best described as collaborative productions.[1] Work on this kind of collaboration has tended to focus on those groups that included famous authors, such as Keats, Clare and Hunt. By contrast, this chapter focuses on reception as a collaborative process by looking at examples of small groups of non-professional readers that came together to form book clubs and reading societies, or who contributed to the collectively owned manuscript books, known as albums.

Because reading societies often consisted of less than 20 members, and the family and friends of the owner usually helped in the compilation of an album, they are an important source for recovering the otherwise lost history of small communities of readers. Evidence from a range of groups operating across the period 1800–1850 suggests something of the way in which these reading communities operated at a local level. The various traces that they left throw new light upon how the group dynamic affected reading in a particular community, but a range of common assumptions about reading as a sociable practice can also be seen. Many reading societies formally discussed the texts that they bought; albums record that reading and the act of transcription could sometimes be transformed into a form of public performance, a social skill that could be done well or badly, much like reading aloud. I conclude by examining the reading practices of Anne Lister (1791–1840). Like many of the readers who compiled albums, Lister copied extracts from texts borrowed from the local subscription library into a series of manuscript volumes. However, her journals and letters reveal that she often used her reading to resist notions of a normative femininity.

Reading societies and communal practice

The communal reading of news described by Joseph Hunter in the late 1790s remained a common experience for many readers until at least the 1840s, when the price of newspapers began to fall. For example, in 1821 *The Monthly Magazine* noted the continued cultural importance of newspaper and magazine societies that usually consisted of 10 or 12 members paying a weekly or annual fee to share texts.[2] Reading societies and book clubs also remained popular during the late Romantic period. Using the figures contained in the *Monthly*, which notes that there were about 600 book clubs in 1821, William St Clair has argued that clubs, reading societies and 'permanent libraries' served around 80,000 families, or 360,000 readers, during the 1820s, a small but significant proportion of the national population.[3] As suggested in the previous chapter, the high cost of an annual membership tended to restrict such clubs to the upper social groups. Surviving copies of the rules devised to govern meetings and the circulation of texts indicate that these groups tended to bring together like-minded individuals from the same social class. For example, the 'rules and regulations' issued by the Hackney Reading Society in July 1824 show that new members had to pass the test of being voted into the society by a majority of the members before paying both the annual fee of one guinea and an entry fee of 'Half-a-Guinea to the Fund'. Just two anonymous votes against meant that an applicant was rejected. That the social aspect of meetings was particularly important is suggested both by this process of selecting only those members who suited the group dynamic and by the fact that members could be fined for non-attendance at social events, such as the annual dinner. At Hackney, the membership was also restricted along gender lines. No more than three women were allowed to join the group, which was capped at a maximum of 20 members. Perhaps, not surprisingly, given this policy, there were only 15 members during the 1830s, all of them male.[4]

Like most book clubs, Hackney did not have a permanent library. Instead texts were sold to the members at sales that took place every six months. The rules stipulated that any member nominating a text at one of the meetings had to be prepared to buy it at one of these sales for half the purchase price if it was to be included in the library. This process meant that members were able to buy books at a reduced price, but it restricted active membership to those who could afford to buy. Some reading societies, including the Eclectic Book Society in the City of London, to which William St Clair refers, bought all of their books at a discount from a single bookseller.[5] This does not seem to have been the case at Hackney, however, where a sub-committee was set up to investigate whether texts could be acquired more cheaply by buying ex-circulating library stock.[6] During the period in which the books were being circulated other costs might also be incurred. The number of days that a member was allowed to keep a text was strictly limited according to its size and a fine of sixpence per day was imposed for books kept too long. Each book was passed in turn to each member, who was expected to note the date on which it was received and 'the day forwarded' on the inside cover, or again face a fine. Those members who did not want, or had not the time to read a particular title, were given a second opportunity before it was sold. That members could pass on a text without reading suggests that in this instance the group's social activities did not include the formal discussion of texts.[7] Other more sociable groups held monthly meetings at which either the books or the topics of the day were discussed. In the 1810s the Eclectic held monthly meetings at the homes of its members that included time for the 'discussion of questions'.[8] When the Walworth Book Society met at each other's houses in the 1830s, one of the members who had given notice 'of a subject for discussion' at the previous meeting, was expected 'to introduce it verbally or by a written essay'. At Walworth these discussions were not always directly related to the texts in circulation and some members took more than one meeting to talk about their favourite topic. It is clear from the minutes of their meetings that although they officially met to decide which texts to buy, this group had a range of other social and educative functions that must have engendered a sense of collective identity.[9]

St Clair has argued that those who belonged to reading clubs and societies that circulated books to each of the members in turn benefited from seeing texts that they would not otherwise have considered. He gives the example of those members of the Eclectic who, although they had ordered Byron for their own reading pleasure, also ended up reading 'regular sermons on the serious risks they were running'.[10] In order to make the cost of entry worthwhile most members would undoubtedly have read what other members had proposed, as St Clair suggests, and where books were discussed at the meetings they were compelled to do so. However, many small book clubs, like the Hackney Reading Society, were not as eclectic in their tastes as the Eclectic. The books nominated at Hackney during 1836 are mainly reviews and magazines, with some travel writing, biography and a little fiction that included new writing such as *Sketches by Boz*.[11] A record of the sale of books to the members gives some sense of individual reading patterns. Mr Ord bought mainly Reviews, for example, whereas Mr Dicken was fond of literary biography, but most members took texts from all genres and had a similar purchasing profile.[12] Groups of this sort clearly brought together people who wanted to read the same kinds of texts, even if, in this instance, they did not feel the need to discuss them at their meetings.

Other groups felt compelled to comment upon their tastes in public. In December 1813 the Members of the Eclectic paid for an announcement to be placed in *The Times* and three other newspapers announcing that the *Monthly Magazine* had been 'expelled' from the Society. This public statement was the result of a 'special meeting' called by 8 of the 12 members who were opposed to the *Magazine's* 'prejudiced statements, and flagrant misrepresentations, of the late splendid victories achieved by the British Army'. Their proposal that it be 'discontinued' was carried unanimously and they decided to show the Society's dedication 'to the cause of truth and liberty' by announcing it publicly. That they felt compelled to make this declaration of their politics suggests that although these groups usually met in the domestic space of the home they thought of themselves as publicly accountable for their actions. As Leonore Davidoff and Catherine Hall have argued, during the period 1780–1850 clubs, lodges and reading societies helped to provide a platform for 'the middle classes to speak effectively' in public without aristocratic patronage and Paul Kaufman has argued that typical book clubs 'consisted of the upper middle class', including professionals such as clergymen and physicians. This is true of most of the groups examined here although both Hackney and the Eclectic included many more shop owners and manufacturers than doctors.[13] In this instance, the group used the mouthpiece of *The Times* to voice their opinion about what was appropriate reading matter for all right-thinking 'Englishmen' (like Hackney, this group had no female members). As their advertisement makes clear, all periodicals taken by reading groups should be of the 'greatest respectability' and reflect 'the support due from Englishmen to the Government of their country' by opposing the 'outrageous villainy of the Tyrant, who now sits on the Throne of France'.[14] To be a member of this group in December 1813 was to be part of a collaborative reading process that produced a shared consensus about some texts. Of course, this statement was produced under specific political circumstances, similar to those that led to the expulsion of 'Jacobin' texts from the Sheffield Subscription Library in 1798, but it suggests one of the ways in which the 'collective' reading practices of these groups must have impacted upon the reading of individual members. To read as a member of the Eclectic during this period was to be alive to a text's political ideology.[15]

The reader as scribe or, the art of the manuscript book, 1790–1850

This section examines the various forms of the non-commercial replication of texts in manuscript that existed in the early nineteenth century in order to assess the role played by manuscript books in both text dissemination and the structuring of group reading practices. Despite the emergence of many important studies of both the contents and the contexts of the production of early-modern commonplace books and verse miscellanies, little attention has yet been paid to the way in which they evolved after 1750. Indeed, it is often assumed that later anthologies were used less creatively because texts were more widely available in print.[16] During the early nineteenth century readers kept notes on their reading and transcriptions of texts in a variety of different sorts of manuscript book, from commonplace books that followed (or ignored) Locke's instructions on organisation, through to albums compiled by groups of friends as part of a sociable reading process.

The evidence presented here comes from a survey of 92 manuscript books produced between 1790 and 1850. It also draws on a number of autobiographical sources that describe the compilation and use of such books.[17] Manuscript books from this period are relatively easy to locate in research libraries and local record offices, where they are usually catalogued as 'commonplace books'. This description can be somewhat misleading, however. The commonplace book proper encouraged the compiler to make notes on their reading under a series of headings that were then recorded in the book's index in order to make information retrieval easy. Despite the continued production of printed commonplace books throughout the Romantic period, usually based on Locke's indexing system, readers rarely used them as they were intended. For example, the British Library's copy of *A New Commonplace Book* (1799), which is described as 'an improvement on that recommended by Mr Locke', contains only two entries, neither of which appears in the book's index.[18]

Of course, some readers continued to keep indexed volumes of extracts as aids to study during this period. Joseph Hunter (1783–1861) decided to keep a commonplace book after reading Locke's 'New Method of a Commonplace Book' in 1797 and Anne Lister (1791–1840) quoted approvingly from Benjamin Franklin's advice 'to read with your pen in hand, and enter in a little book' as she began a new volume of 'extracts' in August 1817.[19] Well into the nineteenth century Hannah More and other conservative writers continued to recommend that readers (especially female readers) memorised 'one select passage, one weighty sentence, one striking precept', usually from a list of recommended books.[20] Many early-nineteenth-century manuscript books contain select passages and striking precepts from the poets that reflect these recommendations, but this mode of reading does not dominate their construction. Women's reading was, of course, a particularly contested field during this period. Jane Austen was just one of the authors critical of the way in which female readers were expected to make extracts from outdated texts. In *Northanger Abbey* (1817) Catherine Morland's early reading consists of compiling quotations from Pope, Gray, James Thomson and Shakespeare in order to supply her memory 'with those quotations that are so serviceable and so soothing in the vicissitudes' of a heroine's life. Austen also condemns printed compilations of extracts from the canonical poets and the *Spectator* because they 'no longer concern any one living'. It is no surprise to find that in *Pride and Prejudice* (1813) the most ineffective of the Bennett sisters, Mary, spends all of her time making extracts.[21] The majority of manuscript books surveyed for this chapter are on the side of Austen rather than More, but volumes, such as those constructed by Hunter and Lister, show that these books remained important tools in the self-fashioning of some readers. Despite these important examples, however, the term 'commonplace book' fails to do justice to the diversity of forms produced during the early part of the nineteenth century.

Albums

The compilers of manuscript books rarely described the volumes that they created as commonplace books. Their own titles include, 'Poems', 'Beauties', 'Rhymes' 'Poems and Anecdotes', 'Gleanings', 'Extracts', 'Excerpta', 'Miscellanies' and 'Scraps', as well as 'M. S. Book' and 'Scrap Book'. Others remained untitled, but by the mid-1820s 'Album' appears to have been the compilers favoured term. Of the 92 volumes surveyed for this study some 34 included the word 'Album' in their title. These volumes consist mainly of transcripts from contemporary poets, with perhaps a few concise extracts from novels or travel writing, and some short prose aphorisms, often taken from Blair, Paley and other widely available moral writers. A few have illustrations either pasted in or created by the compiler(s). As I shall demonstrate the majority of books were collaborative productions compiled by groups of friends or family members.

All of the titles listed here are taken from anthologies or miscellanies compiled over a number of years, but not all early-nineteenth-century manuscript books were created for the same purpose, or from the same sorts of material. A number of the books in the sample were handed down as family heirlooms and contain layers of contributions gathered over generations, but others were made as gifts for a specific individual or occasion. For example, a volume with the title 'Excerpta; or, An Album' contains an inscription from the 'donor' dated March 1825: 'To Emma Garland, from her father; as an affectionate token of respect for her talents and esteem of her character:- A Collection of pieces made at various periods (chiefly modern) from writers of acknowledged excellence, but whose books are diffuse and expensive'.[22]

In this instance, it is the father rather than the daughter who is the primary reader, and the texts that he copied and created for this anthology attempt to impose his definition of 'excellence' upon the recipient. Such evidence reveals that even in the nineteenth century manuscript anthologies could be a form of publication and that the creator of such a book might have a specific audience in mind when the volume was being brought together.

Such gift books are often neatly copied and finely bound, and many early-nineteenth-century manuscript books appear to have been created in order to display publicly the taste and artistic ability of their creators. For example, the volume created by John Radford in the mid-1820s was designed to show off his use of the pen and his transcriptions of Byron's poetry are far more elaborately decorated than the printed originals. Other volumes mimic the style and content of print anthologies, but the majority of manuscript books from this period are far less formal. Of course, by the beginning of the nineteenth century it was possible to construct an anthology without the use of a pen, but 'Scrapbooks' made entirely from printed material were still relatively rare before 1860. Newspapers remained expensive items until the 1850s and the fact that groups often shared them must have limited the opportunities for gathering scraps. However, many of the books described as albums contain both extracts copied by hand and cut from magazines, newspapers and other printed sources. The 'album' compiled by Devereux Bowly and family during the 1830s is dominated by transcriptions of contemporary poetry, but it also contains texts cut from newspapers and has pasted in engravings.

Such hybrids are relatively common, but most compilers preferred to transform print into manuscript. For example, the book compiled by Emma Knight and friends, *c*.1817–1830, includes an unfinished copy of 'The Moslem Bridal Song' by Samuel Rogers. Knight must have been interrupted while transcribing this text from a local newspaper as the clipping that she was using as a source is tipped into the volume. This suggests that some compilers preferred to transcribe rather than paste, but it seems unlikely that Knight chose to do this simply because she wanted to make the volume into a uniformly handwritten text. For readers in the early nineteenth century, as in the early modern period, redrafting the poem to fit into a new context was an important part of the reading process itself.[23]

Transcription practices

Why did readers keep these volumes and what role did they play in the dissemination of texts? Unfortunately, the majority of manuscript books do not record whether the text transcribed was borrowed or owned and they have often been removed from the context of their creation so that we do not have any of the autobiographical papers that would help to make sense of their compilation. Joseph Hunter's 'Commonplace Book' has not survived, but as noted in the previous chapter, his diary records that he used it to preserve short passages from texts borrowed from a number of collective reading institutions, including subscription libraries, book clubs and commercial circulating libraries. James Nesbitt of Berwick, who kept what he describes as a commonplace book throughout the 1820 and 1830s, rather playfully suggests that its contents were designed to 'satisfy the devourer of newspaper paragraphs and circulating libraries', and it is clear that many 'library goers' (as James Raven calls them) transcribed passages from the books that they borrowed from these institutions for later rereading.[24] By the early nineteenth century those members of the middle class who believed in self-improvement and could afford to participate in the growing commercialised library sector had many opportunities to make notes from a wide range of texts.

Manuscript books also provide important evidence of the way in which texts were transmitted via more informal systems of exchange. The manuscript miscellany compiled by John Seller is bound with a volume of locally published poetry that lists him as a subscriber. On the end pages of this volume are two manuscript texts – 'Lines Occasioned by borrowing of Books and not returning them' and 'Advice how to use Books', which reveal the way in which book owners exchanged both manuscript and printed texts: 'If thou art borrowed by a friend, / Right welcome shall he be, / To read, to copy, not to lend, / But to return to me'. The combination of reading and copying is natural to Seller, and the ubiquity of the informal exchange of texts is also reflected in the 'Advice' which requests the borrower to, 'Read slowly pause frequently / Think seriously / Keep cleanly, return duly, / With the corners of the leaves not turned down'. Such methods of exchange are the glue that binds together any community of readers operating within a culture in which books are too expensive to be bought regularly.

Texts were also transmitted from one manuscript volume to another. For example, the book compiled by Charles Feist and friends contains a version of Joseph Cottle's poem 'The Affectionate Heart' which declares that it was 'Copied from G. Fisher's Common Place Book' rather than from a printed source.[25] Similarly, the 'M. S. Book' shared by various members of the Carey and Maingay families during the 1830s, contains several poems that are described as being 'taken from Fanny Maingay's Book'. This evidence suggests that manuscript books played an important role in text transmission, but it is also a useful reminder that home-made books were frequently read by others. As James Nesbitt noted, one of his favourite pastimes was 'to wade through the pages of a common-place-book' in order to find out more about the tastes of its compiler. Borrowing and copying clearly helped to create and cement friendships between compilers of manuscript books, even if Seller seems somewhat nervous about the way in which his books might be treated once out of his sight.

Transcription could also be an important resource for working-class readers who had little access to either new books or libraries. During the 1820s the farmhand Robert White relied upon his father's landlord to supply him with reading materials.

> Among other books, he supplied me with some of Sir Walter Scott's poems with which I was delighted. I retained 'The Lady of the Lake' above a month, and never read it consecutively, but got paper and made a copy of all the poetry which I still preserve. I rose at five o'clock in the spring mornings, that I might have an hour to drive my pen. I had another hour at dinner, and after six in the evening. I wrote while day lasted. Having no money to buy the book, for its cost in 1824 would be about 14 shillings.[26]

There is something exact about this recollection of copying 'all the poetry' that suggests that it is more than mere nostalgia. Scott's work was a challenge to any scribe. The 1819 edition contained 290 pages of poetry and an additional 143 pages of prose notes. The transcription of an entire text in this way is rare – although some scribally produced editions of banned texts were in circulation at this time – but many manuscript books compiled in the early nineteenth century do contain long passages from recently published works. For example the book compiled by the Feist group contains 35 pages taken from Letitia Landon's *The Improvisatrice* (1824), including the advertisement.

As Emma Garland's father noted in March 1825, the volume that he was presenting to his daughter had been compiled 'from writers … whose works are diffuse and expensive'. As an agricultural labourer, White could not have afforded to spend 14s on a volume by Scott, but even Garland, who arranged for his gift to be elegantly bound, did not have enough money to own the range of texts covered by this volume. Indeed, he had to admit that some of the transcripts were inaccurate, perhaps because they had come via other manuscript sources, rather than the original printed texts. As William St Clair has demonstrated, the new books of the early nineteenth century 'were expensive luxuries which could be bought, if at all, only by the richest groups in society'.[27] The quarto edition of *The Lady of the Lake* (1810) cost 42*s* and only dropped to 12*s* in the second octavo edition. Even Hunter, who was relatively well off, tended to visit the bookseller in order to buy pens, paper and ink, rather than to purchase new books. This perhaps explains why very few manuscript volumes contain long extracts from texts available in cheap editions.

Transmission via manuscript book offered readers a way of acquiring new and expensive texts, but few had White's patience, and the majority chose to reduce the Romantic epic into smaller chunks. These chunks provide important evidence about what these readers wanted from these texts. Many of the best-selling books of the period enjoyed a large audience in manuscript. As St Clair has argued, 'the larger the sales … the more frequently a book was also rented', and we might add that the more copies it sold and the more times it was rented, the greater the number of opportunities there were for the book to be borrowed and for transcription to take place.[28] In other words, the biggest-selling volumes of the period were, undoubtedly, also the most frequently transcribed.

A good example of this is the way in which compilers of albums frequently reproduced poems from the annuals. Given as gifts at Christmas time, these anthologies of original verse, prose and engravings were hugely successful. Titles such as *The Keepsake* regularly sold more than 10,000 copies per season during the 1820s and 1830s, which meant that they were amongst the best-sellers of the age. Although they did not cost as much to buy as most new volumes of poetry (and they came ready bound), such books were still relatively expensive (the *Keepsake* cost one guinea). The album compiled by a group of friends connected to a woman identified throughout by the initials 'M. A. B.' contains transcripts of several poems from the annuals, including John Clare's 'Crowland Abbey', which first appeared in *The Literary Souvenir* for 1828. This poem was later republished as part of Clare's *The Rural Muse* (1835), but M. A. B.'s transcription reproduces the distinctive punctuation of the annual version.[29] Because *The Rural Muse* sold relatively few copies, most critical accounts of Clare's poetry tend to assume that his work went largely unread during the 1830s, but as this transcript reveals, by being available as part of one of the most successful publishing ventures of the age, his poetry was not only read but reproduced for a new audience in manuscript.[30]

This suggests that much of the most popular verse of the period was reworked in new contexts by the compilers of manuscript books. In M. A. B's album poems, such as 'Crowland Abbey', are surrounding by the work of Thomas Moore, Byron and Scott, which rarely appeared in the annuals. The way in which poems are juxtaposed can often be revealing, and both the kinds of texts selected and the mode of their display is important. Reading Clare, Landon or Hemans (whose work was also often reproduced in the annuals) alongside the work of canonical writers, such as Scott, helps to underline what is most distinctive about their work. However, as the page torn from a newspaper tipped into Emma Knight's manuscript volume reveals, transcribers did not just copy from expensive books. During the early nineteenth century short poems and extracts from longer works were frequently included in newspapers and magazines. For example, Mary Groom's 'Common Place Book', brings together several poems by Landon and Hemans that first appeared in *The New Monthly Magazine* and the *Literary Gazette*. Such manuscript volumes suggest a reading practice that involved picking over both print and manuscript culture for enjoyable texts which could then be added to the compiler's collection and swapped with others.

Where these transcripts include traces of their original context, it is possible to say something about the kinds of texts consumed by the compiler(s) over the period in which the book was being constructed. However, the unfinished version of 'The Moslem Bridal Song' included in Knight's book shows just how difficult it can be to establish the source of a text without a note from the compiler. It is only because Knight left the original in her book that we know that she was copying this poem from a local newspaper rather than from the *Literary Gazette* in which it originally appeared. Nineteenth-century texts and their readers were often enmeshed in a complex web of textuality, and the manuscript book does not provide an easy route for historians of reading to get back to the text with which the reader(s) actually engaged. For example, Mary Groom recorded 15 of Byron's poems during the mid-1820s, including the unauthorised version of 'Fare Thee Well', rather than that, which appeared in Byron's works. Because this poem was also reproduced in the newspapers and as a pamphlet, it is impossible to tell which form of the text Groom actually read.[31]

The process of transcription could also radically alter the form of the text that was being reproduced. If new forms produce new meanings, as Roger Chartier and D. F. McKenzie contend, historians of nineteenth-century print culture will need to take greater account of the transforming powers of the pen, of the reader as scribe's ability to transform a text.[32] Texts in manuscript are always 'malleable', as Arthur Marotti suggests, and very few compilations contain exact transcripts.[33] The reader as scribe was free to retitle, and re-punctuate, and invariably ignored paratextual devices, such as footnotes. Robert White, very wisely, chose not to transcribe the extensive prose notes from the volume of Scott that he had borrowed, but in doing so he produced a manuscript version of the text that was very different in both appearance and meaning to the printed original. In much the same way that Marotti has argued that the revised and supplemented versions of Walter Ralegh's poems which appeared in the seventeenth-century miscellany 'were *historically* more important' than the 'purest' authorial versions, I wish to suggest that the transcripts included in nineteenth-century manuscript books need to be taken seriously.[34] Until the middle of the nineteenth century, many readers would have read and reread texts in forms dictated by the reader as scribe rather than by the collaborative team of author, publisher and printer that has been the subject of the recent, less author centred, approach to this period. The fragments of Scott and Byron included in these books must often have been more familiar to readers than the hot-pressed pages of the 'pure' authorial original. In June 1818 Anne Lister, who we know regularly reread her own volumes of extracts, noted that she had made 'an extract or 2 from Lord Byron's *Childe Harold* and the lyrics at the end of the book' before taking it back to the library.[35]

Early-nineteenth-century readers did not supplement and emend in the same manner as early-modern readers, but the texts that they produced are important because they reveal a variety of reading strategies. For example, Devereaux Bowly and his family only occasionally noted that Byron was the author of many of the poems scattered throughout the volume that they compiled in the early 1830s, whereas Mary Groom produced complex sequences of his work that suggests she was interested in him as an author. William St Clair has argued that by chopping up Byron's epic texts into beautiful passages, as Lister did, manuscript book compilers were able to defuse what was most radical about his work.[36] Some of these readers rewrote Byron's texts in their own image, whilst others remade themselves in the image of Byron. James Nesbitt refers to those compilers of manuscript books who chose to wear their shirts 'with the collar turned down a-la Byron'. Images of both Byron and Scott are sometimes pasted in alongside the verse. Lister chose to make extracts from both *Childe Harold* and the shorter verse contained in the same volume, but the evidence from the majority of these books suggests that most readers would have known Byron as the author of short poems, such as 'To Thyrza' and 'On A Cornelian Heart Which Was Broken' which were much more easily adapted to the manuscript tradition, rather than the epic poems for which he is now more famous.

The evidence presented here reveals that during the early nineteenth century the expensive nature of new books and the concomitant dominance of institutions of reading (such as subscription libraries) encouraged readers to compile manuscript books that brought together a disparate range of texts. These books were then reread by the compiler (or compilers), who also lent them to friends, who might again rework the text as part of their own compilation of extracts. However, the fact that in many books transcripts of literary texts are frequently interrupted by what one contributor to M. A. B.'s album refers to as 'words transposed, enigmas rare / Charades composed with puzzling care / Riddles for those who like them best / And questions to amuse the rest', suggests that we also need to pay attention to the ways in which the communities that compiled these volumes were taking part in a process that celebrated reading as a communal, rather than solitary, activity. They help us to recognise that reading in the late Romantic period was not just a serious act of acculturation. Reading as transcription was often part of a game played for fun.

The album as reading community

Although some manuscript books created during the early nineteenth century were clearly produced by individuals as private documents, the majority of 'albums' were group or family productions. It was common for visitors and friends to be asked to contribute to an album that was put on display as a public document. Adding to the manuscript was seen as an important ritual of friendship:

> Push the Album about, like the goblet it cheers us,
> 'Tis to friendship we fill as we scribble along:

> The mingling of taste to each other endears us,
> As, glowing, the pen writes a tale or a song.[37]

The manuscript book that emerges from this process is a product of the group, even if the album itself was declared to be the property of an individual. For example, the verso of the title page of the album belonging to 'M. A. B' contains four short pieces of verse in three different hands. The first is by M. A. B herself as the owner of the manuscript:

> My Album's open come and see!
> What! Won't you waste a thought on me?
> Write but a word, a word or two
> And make me love to think on you.
> M.A.B.

The rest are the work of contributors who describe the volume as containing something for everyone:

> Life's a medley all agree,
> This book's a medley you will see.
> Sometimes serious often gay
> Showering like an April day;
> Sunshine for the youthful mind
> And serious thoughts for those inclined.

This method of compilation was so common by the 1830s that it was satirised in Miss Porter's 'A Vision'.[38] In the version of this poem included in M. A. B's album a different contributor completed each of the five stanzas, and in a cruel joke upon the owner, the final quatrain reveals that the 'night mare' figure haunting the poem is in fact:

> ... M. A. B. with a grey goose quill,
> And an Album- sight of sorrow!
> Get up, she cried, and a whole page fill;
> For I want this back to morrow.

In this instance the public process that governed the construction of this form of the manuscript book is held up to ridicule, but the reproduction of this verse in several albums shows just how important this kind of manuscript book was to early-nineteenth-century reading practices. Such books helped to construct and maintain a network of readers based upon the sociable exchange (or creation) of texts. In this instance the album brought together a small group of friends who shared the communal space of the manuscript book. M. A. B. was at the centre of a group of readers who both read and produced texts with her album in mind. She and her friends were part of a social ritual, and their reworking of 'A Vision' is a dramatic example of the way in which reading and transcription were often public acts during this period.

M. A. B.'s friends produced a playful reworking of Porter's original poem, but even as they gently mocked her desire to fill the page, they were reinforcing the rules of their reading community. These volumes sometimes contain mild parodies of canonical works, and the occasional slightly risqué pun, but on the whole the boundaries of the text and of respectability are preserved. The liberty of the reader as scribe is constrained by a number of organising structures, such as the reproduction of short aphorisms, the gathering of texts into thematic sequences, and the use of poems dedicated to the owner of the volume. The majority of albums include contributions from both male and female readers, but as a form it appears to have been regarded as a 'female' or 'family' space. Those who contributed to such books were thus allowed to take certain liberties with the text, but they were also bound by the context in which it needed to be reproduced. The album demanded that contributors gave a kind of public performance that was similar in many ways to the disciplined nature of reading aloud. This means that we should be wary of considering these books as representative of what was being read. They are a public record of those texts that it was legitimate to share in public.

This element of public performance is clearly displayed in the 'M. S. Book' compiled by the Carey-Maingay group during the early 1830s. This book contains transcripts in a number of hands including those of Julia Burney, Edward Carey (1807–1849), and both Fanny and Margaret Maingay. It is structured much like the other books of the period, with short prose aphorisms taken from Blair, Paley and others, and poems dedicated to, or transcribed by, various members of the group. There are many transcripts of poems by the now little known Thomas Haynes Bayly, as well as pieces by Landon, Byron and Scott. As Byron's 'Written in an Album' makes clear, some contributions to albums were designed as tokens of romantic love. In this instance however, it appears as though the book was used to encode the break down of the relationship between Carey and Fanny Maingay.[39]

Extracts from Byron appear on 14 separate occasions in this book and Maingay and Carey seem to have used his work to establish their relationship. For example, one of Byron's most popular poems, 'On A

Cornelian Heart' has been retitled 'On A Gold Heart' by Maingay, and the gender of the speaker altered so that the reworked version of the poem reads, 'Since she who wears thee, feels thou art / A fitter emblem of her heart'. Similarly, the first two lines from his 'Well! Thou Art Happy' are used as the starting point for an original poem on 'The Love that I dare not reveal'. To rewrite Byron is, of course, a radical project, and Fanny Maingay's rewritings disrupt the flow of a volume in which poems on domestic subjects are frequently reproduced without alteration. By contrast Carey tended to reproduce Byron's verse in the same form as it appeared in print, but his reproduction of part of chapter 27 of Scott's *Waverley* (1814) reveals a similar personalising of the text.

> 'The woman whom you marry, ought to have affections and opinions moulded upon yours. Her studies ought to be yours; . . . Her wishes, her feelings, her hopes, her fears, should all mingle with yours. <u>She should enhance your pleasures, share your sorrows, and cheer your melancholy</u>.' But no-
> Such were the thoughts of Flora Mac-Ivor. But why should <u>I</u> expect to meet with <u>such</u>. Waverley.
> Friday Novr 5 1835. E.C.

This quotation is written in response to a passage in French by Maingay on the same page, which refers to a man's attempt to efface the evidence of his love, but this choice of a passage on an ideal wife is typical of Carey's use of Scott as a source for images of an idealised domesticity. This kind of rewriting is unusual, but the book created by the Carey-Maingay group confirms that texts could be rewritten to serve new and personal ends. Reading Byron in the Carey anthology is very different to reading the same author in a miscellany that simply reproduces the printed page, or which emphasises his importance as author. The Carey collection thus provides a unique context of interpretation for the individual items that it contains, but it also suggests that the reading communities that produced such manuscript books were not necessarily harmonious groups. Each surviving volume provides detailed information about the ways in which groups used texts, from the playful reworkings of M. A. B. and her friends through to the contested domestic disputes of the Carey-Maingay group. Despite these differences, however, the rules governing the construction of these books seem to have been held in common and were rarely transgressed. Edward Carey's rule breaking – he makes the text *too* personal – exposes the fact that the majority of manuscript books helped to forge and maintain important bonds of friendship or community. Their mode of construction encouraged readers to transcribe passages from texts for purposes quite different to those encouraged by the revived tradition of the commonplace book that also flourished in this period, but the very process of reading with the album in mind, like reading as a member of a particular club or society, may well have restricted the kinds of text read. The vast majority of albums and other manuscript books that have survived from the early nineteenth century suggest that family reading within polite society was not restricted to those authors recommended as suitable for women in the conduct book tradition. But the frequent reproduction of poems such as Mrs Hemans's 'Graves of a Household', with its admittedly very troubled image of domesticity, and of short prose aphorisms from contemporary moralists, suggests something of the role played by these books in the reproduction of the bourgeois ideology of the home.[40]

Reading 'by stealth' – Anne Lister (1791–1840) and the woman reader

During the late Romantic period the discourse of reading played an important role in reinforcing normative ideas about gender and sexuality. Idealised images of the family often focus on reading as a sign of domestic harmony. For example, many of the conduct books published by the London firm of Taylor and Hessey during the 1810s and 1820s included a frontispiece in which a scene depicting reading reinforces the text's message that a woman's ideal role is that of wife and mother. The new edition of Lady Pennington's *A Mother's Advice To Her Absent Daughters* (1761) that they produced in 1811, for example, contains an image of a young married couple illuminated by the glow of the domestic hearth. He is reading aloud from a large folio, probably a Bible, while she nurses a baby and another child plays at her feet. The epigraph reproduced under this image suggests that it represents the ideal of 'uninterrupted domestic harmony' to which all women aspire. Pennington, like most conduct book writers, actually encouraged women to read for themselves, as well as to listen to others reading aloud, and her work is, in part, a guide to those books that she thought it was acceptable for a woman to read. She warns against 'novels and romances' whilst praising sermons, history and some poetry as 'both useful and entertaining' to the woman reader.[41] Other images from this period also tend to use reading as a way of (re)inscribing domestic ideology. For example, the frontispiece to Mrs Taylor's *Practical Hints to Young Females, On the Duties of a Wife, a Mother, and a Mistress of a Family* (1815), reproduced as Figure 5.1, shows a young mother, her sewing put aside for a moment, helping her infant daughter to puzzle out a difficult word in the text she is reading. Although the scene takes place in a room lined with books, with the mother's sewing box propped open on a writing desk, this is not an image of a woman tainted by what Thomas De Quincey was later to call 'the contagion of bookishness'.[42] She is passing on the skills of literacy to her daughter, but women's reading in this image is seen very much as the servant of domesticity, much as it is in Taylor's writing.[43] The reader depicted in both these images is the opposite of the self-absorbed female novel reader so often figured in eighteenth-century representations of reading.

Conduct books were amongst the most frequently reproduced texts of the Romantic period. That a large audience saw the images that they contained is suggested by the fact that *Practical Hints* was in its tenth

Figure 5.1 Frontispiece from Mrs Taylor's *Practical Hints to Young Females, On the Duties of a Wife, a Mother, and a Mistress of a Family*, 10th edition (London: Taylor and Hessey, 1822)

edition by 1822. The lists of approved texts and reading practices that they contained must have been welcomed by many in a world that was frequently anxious about what women were reading. The frontispiece image of the literate, but not bookish woman provided a place for reading within the ideology of the home. Of course, as Jacqueline Pearson has argued many 'real women blithely refused' to fit the categories created for the woman reader by conduct book writers and moralists. The 'respectable' Maria Josepha Holroyd (later Lady Stanley) read conduct books, and the kinds of books that they recommended, but she also had time for Mary Wollstonecraft, Rousseau and the French and German novels that the conduct books invariably condemned.[44] Anne Lister (1791–1840) was a similarly transgressive reader, enjoying Rousseau 'for the style's sake' whilst upholding traditional Tory views that were the opposite of his enlightenment politics. The heiress to the Shibden estate near Halifax, Yorkshire, Lister often deliberately set out to challenge gender norms.[45] In 1817, when she was 26, she began a 'plan of always wearing black' that made her stand out from the majority of young women who, like those depicted in conduct books, tended to wear white.[46] She also cultivated an image of bookishness and literary ambition, which many of her friends noted made her appear 'odd'.[47] Lister was not the only rebel in the neighbourhood, however. She was compared positively by her friends to 'Miss Pickford … a *bas bleu*' (p. 106) who dressed in a similar, masculine fashion and I want to suggest that she used her reading to forge a series of relationships with other women that challenged the normative patterns of gender and 'uninterrupted domestic harmony' that the contemporary discourse of reading tended to enforce.

Lister's journals are well known, of course, because they represent her sexual activity with other women. She had a long running relationship with Marianne Belcombe that continued for the best part of ten years after M (as she is known in the journal) married Charles Lawton in 1815, as well as significant affairs with Isabella Norcliffe ('Tib') and Maria Barlow. In 1834 she entered into a clandestine 'marriage' with Anne Walker, a wealthy heiress. The sexual nature of these relationships, which is recorded in explicit detail, has played a polemical role in recent work on lesbian identity. For example, they are central to the argument of Terry Castle's *The Apparitional Lesbian* (1993) where they are used to discredit the 'no-lesbians-before-1900' myth.[48] This argument is important, of course, but by concentrating exclusively upon the sexual, Castle neglects Lister's search for an emotional partnership with a woman of the kind to which Emma Donoghue pays attention in her re-investigation of the notion of female 'romantic friendship'.[49] Lister considered both

Tib and Mrs Barlow as potential life partners, but found them wanting, and although she sometimes appears disappointed by her relationship with Anne Walker she did succeed in finding a female partner to share her life and help her manage the Shibden Estate, which she inherited on her uncle's death in 1826.[50]

Like her sex life, Lister's reading life is also unusually well documented. The journal that she kept between 1806 and 1840 includes references to books purchased, borrowed and read, as do her letters. The many volumes of 'extracts' that she made provide evidence of the way in which she made sense of these texts. It was Castle who first drew attention to the way in which Lister used the Classics and Byron to communicate with other women in whom she was sexually interested and Anna Clark's discussion of what she terms Lister's 'construction of a lesbian identity' also concentrates on the way in which she made notes on homosexual activity from a wide range of texts including Juvenal and Byron. Similarly, although Clara Tuite's reading of Lister's journals questions the notion of a fixed 'lesbian identity' put forward by Clark, she also concentrates on Lister's 'habitual identification with and mimicry of the suspect models of social, sexual and literary style' associated with two key Romantic writers, Byron and Rousseau.[51] Byron, Rousseau and the Classics were clearly important to Lister's self fashioning, but she also used texts widely available to women during this period, such as Edward Young's *Night Thoughts* and Thomas Campbell's *The Pleasures of Hope*, to signal affection, friendship or sexual interest in other women.

The majority of new books that Lister acquired during the 1810s and 1820s came from the Halifax Subscription Library. Indeed, her desire for new books was so great that she circumvented the rules governing access to this Library by surreptitiously paying the Librarian an additional 10s per year in order to 'have as many books at a time' as she wanted (p. 113). In a culture in which this kind of library going was much more common than library owning, the gift of a book would have been regarded as a token of special friendship. During the period 1819–1824 Lister bought books as presents for four women, Isabella Norcliffe, Miss Browne, Isabella Maclean and Maria Barlow. On 9 September 1819, for example, she arranged to acquire the octavo edition of Thomas Moore's *Lallah Rookh* 'with the illustrations to be bound in crimson morocco, richly guilt [sic] & the inside of the binding lined with green satin' from a local bookseller as a gift for Tib (p. 99). First published in 1817, Moore's poem was in its ninth edition by 1819, but Lister chose to give one of the most expensive versions of the text. *The London Catalogue of Books* records that the illustrated octavo edition would have sold for £1 1s or £2 2s with India Proofs.[52] Even if we assume that Lister chose the cheaper of these two options (and her chosen binding would also have increased the price) this was a major purchase for someone who tended to borrow rather than buy books. Tib had come to stay with Anne at Shibden on 24 June 1819, and they shared a room for a number of months. The diary entries from this period suggest that Lister was testing out her suitability as a long-term partner and companion. Just five days before she ordered the book she noted that: 'She does not suit me. I cannot feel that she is, or ever can be, all to me I want & wish' (p. 98). Throughout the following weeks, however, Lister was uncertain about rejecting Tib altogether, and the gift of the book was probably an attempt to delay the inevitable breakdown of their relationship. Tib didn't share Lister's passion for reading and the latter records that she tried to limit the amount of time that they spent together at the Library because it made Norcliffe 'fidgety & a little impatient' (p. 91). Lister obviously wanted a partner with whom she could discuss her studies and the book may have been an attempt to mould Tib as reader.

The luxurious binding that Lister ordered suggests that the appearance of this book was more important than its contents, but Moore's poetry was a provocative choice. After a conversation with her friends, the Saltmarshes, 'about what books were improper & what not', which took place in March 1821, Lister noted that she thought *Lalla Rookh* 'as much so as Little's poems, or even the first two cantos of *Don Juan*' (p. 151). Clark offers instances of a 'transgressive sexuality' from both Moore and Byron to explain her interest in these poems. Don Juan's cross-dressing may well have interested Lister, as Clark suggests, but I don't think that her reading of these texts can be reduced to a search for such moments.[53] However, Lister quite clearly enjoyed making her friends 'discover' improper moments in texts. That both the Saltmarshe's denied that they could 'find' anything in *Lalla Rookh* (Clark suggests a scene in which slave girls chase each other) indicates that what Lister interpreted as 'improper' about this text is not easy to recover. Taken together, this evidence suggests that Lister gave the book both as a sign of affection and as a symbol of the transgressive nature of her affair with Tib.

The other women to whom Lister gave books shared her passion for reading. For example, she frequently arranged to meet Miss Browne at the Halifax Subscription Library. However, as Lister noted on 18 September 1818, Browne's reading was strictly controlled.

Found she had promised her mother to be back at 5; that her time was seldom her own; 'mama' always inquires where she has been; that she did not like to see her poring over books in the daytime, but that she was kept stitching and attending to domestic concerns. ... She is not brilliant. In fact, she has other things to do & reads by stealth. (p. 59)[54]

References to reading in the journals are often associated with Lister's own freedom from the restraints of domestic ideology, but they also bear witness to the fact that many women shared Browne's ability to read 'by stealth'. Emma Saltmarshe, for example, told Lister that she had read all of *Don Juan*, but must have done so in secret because she would not admit the fact to her husband (p. 125). Despite Mama's control, Browne was particularly well read in Byron's works. In April 1818, she replied 'Yes, perhaps too well' to Lister's question about whether she liked him (p. 42). Tuite argues that her reply, 'ringing with innuendo – doubles for Lister as the hint of reciprocated sexual interest'.[55] When, in March 1819 Lister went to visit Browne and discovered her 'sitting on the sopha [sic] reading the last canto of *Childe Harold*', she refused to 'send for her mother' until they had spent '40 minutes tête-à-tête' together (p. 81). As Castle argues, Lister used the Classics (especially 'the Sixth Satyr of Juvenal' which describes two women who take turns to 'ride each other') to discover whether other women were of the same 'sexual orientation', but Byron's poetry clearly had a similar function.[56] Indeed, the often-quoted conversation with Miss Pickford about Juvenal is presaged by a discussion about Byron, and Maria Barlow chose a French edition of Byron's works as a gift from Lister in the early stages of their affair.[57] That Lister interpreted Browne's reading of *Childe Harold* as a sign that she wanted to spend time alone with her, suggests that his poetry func-tioned as a shared sign of rebellion against the rules of domestic ideol-ogy that included a questioning of the 'compulsory heterosexuality' that was at the heart of this way of thinking about the world.[58] Lister and Miss Browne never slept together, although they kissed, but as Castle notes, their relationship transgressed the rules of female homoso-ciality and became something of a local scandal.[59]

As a result of their first conversation about Byron, Lister considered sending Miss Browne 'a Cornelian heart with a copy of his lines on the subject' and fantasised about giving her 'the 5th canto of Childe Harold' which was not yet available from the Library (p. 42). When she did eventually give a book to Browne, however, it was a text much more suitable for a young woman to receive than anything by Byron. First published in 1799, Thomas Campbell's *The Pleasures of Hope* appears much less open to 'improper' reading than either Byron or Moore, but the diaries make clear that Lister saw the gift as part of a flirtation with a woman who understood her complex sexuality. That Lister also considered giving this volume to M appears to confirm its totemic status: 'I told M – I had just got *The Pleasures of Hope* beautifully bound for Miss Browne, but she should have her choice between the book and the necklace'. Lister's matter-of-fact recording of M's reply, 'She said she had *The Pleasures of Hope* and would take the necklace', is indicative of a moment of crisis in their relationship (p. 106). It is probable that Lister bought the latest 8s edition of Campbell's poem, published in May 1819.[60] As with the book given to Isabella Norcliffe, Lister took great care over the way in which it was bound, but it certainly wasn't as extravagant a gift as that bestowed upon Tib. By giving a book as a gift Lister was clearly reinforcing her reputation for 'bookishness' as well as celebrating the role that reading and the Library played in their relationship. The book may even have been a challenge to mama's diktat against 'poring over books' during the day, but we do not know how it was interpreted or whether they read the book together.

A later gift to another young woman in whom she was sexually interested reveals more about Lister's shared reading practices. Shortly before embarking on a trip to Paris in June 1824, Lister gave Sibella Maclean a copy of Edward Young's *Night Thoughts on Life, Death and Immortality*.[61] Lister doesn't specify which edition it was, but that she regretted 'having given' it 'in such small print' suggests that it was a cheap edition.[62] Young had been part of the core old canon since the mid-1770s, so the book probably came from a series, such as Walker's Classics, which usually cost less than 3s.[63] In this instance, Lister chose the book from amongst her own collection, rather than making a special purchase, but its cheapness meant that she could buy another copy so that she and Maclean could read it together even though they were separated. Lister's letters provide important evidence of how this shared reading worked.

> I long to see all the marks you have made – there is no fear that I should 'quiz' them. How could you think of such a thing? I must quote the following from your letter, or you cannot understand the remarks I mean to make in answer – 'The little volume is at this moment open before me; and the pencil-mark points to these lines, "Heaven gives us friends to bless the present scene, resumes them to prepare us for the next". How true! of every other thing bereft, a friend would still make the present scene blessed. Would you have marked these lines? Not <u>intricate</u> enough for you, Sib says to herself. Are you angry?'. ('Letters', p. 215)

Unfortunately, we are reliant upon Lister for Maclean's side of the correspondence, but the passages that she excerpts in this letter suggest that 'Sib' often deferred to Lister's greater learning, figured here as the love of all things 'intricate'. Both women were particularly fond of using quotation in their letters, and in this exchange the *Night Thoughts* took on a special significance as the source of a series of quotations about friendship that Lister used to encourage a discussion about the nature of their relationship:

I should have marked, and doubtless have done so in my little edition at home, (got another directly), the very lines you mention. I have also marked the following.

> Celestial Happiness! where e'er she stoops
> To visit earth, one shrine the goddess finds
> And one alone, to make her sweet amends
> For absent Heaven – the bosom of a friend;
> When heart meets heart, reciprocally soft,
> Each other's pillow to repose divine

Perhaps the very quoting these lines will almost prove to you how much I agree with you, that, 'of every other thing bereft, a friend might still make the present scene blessed'. 'Tis true, but only true to those few hearts that, constant as the magnet to the pole, 'turn at the touch of joy or woe, but turning tremble too'. It is not everyone to whom you could make a sentiment like this, really intelligible – it would be a stumbling block to many – the foolishness of romance to most. ('Letters', p. 215)

By taking these lines of poetry out of context, where they refer to the superiority of virtuous over sexual friendship, Lister playfully imbued Young's text with a subtle erotic charge. In the rest of the letter she encouraged Maclean to think of their relationship as something more than ordinary friendship:

Friendship is tame in general – it is too much a name – too much the bauble of an hour. Your ideas upon the subject and mine may sometimes play upon the lip, when they have never settled in the heart of those who claim them. [...] You have never met with sentiments more suited to your own? Perhaps you almost doubted that there could be such. ('Letters', p. 215)

Both women refer to annotating the text, to marking out quotations, and it is the process of combining quotations from both Young's text and Maclean's own letters that allowed Lister to turn the discussion away from 'friendship' towards 'romance'.

Lister often described her own love for women as an exaggerated form of friendship.[64] For example, before she started the affair with Mrs Barlow just a few months after writing to Maclean, Lister reacted to the older woman's questions about the rumour that Marie Antoinette 'was too fond of women', by arguing that she 'could go as far in friendship, love as warmly, as most but could not go beyond a certain degree & did not believe that anyone could do it'.[65] In this instance Lister used the concept of 'friendship' in order to suggest to Barlow that she thought of herself as different from the majority of heterosexual women, while at the same time denying any knowledge of lesbian sexual activity. In both these instances Lister is playing with what Lisa Moore has described as a fault-line within the concept of female friendship that allowed some women to engage in sexual relationships under the guise of the kind of close friendship between women that was often idealised in conduct books and other texts concerned with ideas of femininity.[66] That Lister and Maclean were judged to have transgressed the line between friendship and sexual relationship too openly, however, is suggested by the fact that Mariana Lawton informed her that 'much had been said in York' about her 'friendship with Miss Maclean', with one man even going so far as to suggest that 'he would as soon turn a man loose in his house' as allow her to visit.[67] As Tuite has noted, Lister often seems to have enjoyed causing this kind of scandal (it is part of her adoption of a Byronic persona), but I am more concerned here with the way in which the transition from 'friendship' to 'romance' is enacted through the *shared* act of reading, the shared intimacy of the page.[68]

The correspondence with Maclean makes it clear that Lister did not rely solely upon her knowledge of the Classics or Byron to communicate her sexual interest in other women, but it also attests to the liberty of the woman reader to make new and radical meanings from texts that were available as part of the dominant culture. *The Night Thoughts* was widely approved of as suitable reading for young women in this period and is frequently cited in conduct books and other didactic texts aimed at women, including contemporary editions of Pennington's *Advice*.[69] Lister's reading of the poem thus helps to undermine the authority of a text that was recommended as part of a discourse that aimed to limit the freedom of female readers. Indeed, the rest of Lister's flirtatious correspondence with Maclean relies heavily upon texts that were widely reproduced and firmly entrenched within the lists of texts approved for the woman reader, such as William Cowper's poems and John Gregory's conduct book, *A Father's Legacy to His Daughters* (1774).[70] Lister refers to Gregory's advice that 'a woman should never shew the full extent of her regard, even to her husband' in order to subvert it by encouraging Maclean to be open about her feelings ('Letters', p. 193). To use these texts to establish a relationship that undermined the idea of 'uninterrupted domestic harmony' and 'compulsory heterosexuality' that the discourse of reading was used to reproduce in the post-Waterloo period is a truly subversive reading strategy.

Reading as study: Anne Lister's volumes of 'Extracts'

As already noted, Lister followed Benjamin Franklin's advise 'to read with your pen in hand'. Between 1814 and 1838 she completed 11 volumes of 'extracts', using Locke's distinctive method of referencing.[71] This methodology was particularly useful because she tended to make notes from books borrowed from the Halifax Subscription Library, and she sometimes even noted down a text's catalogue numbers so that she could quickly find if again if she needed to.[72] These volumes include notes on homosexual activity from a wide range of texts including the classics in Latin and translation, as both Castle and Clark have noted, but they are often just a by-product of a reading practice that included making notes on a wide range of subjects. Lister often made these extracts just before the book had to be returned. On 9 December 1819, for example, she recorded spending several hours 'making minutes & extracts from Hall's *Travels in France* (it must go back to the library today)' (p. 108).[73]

'Extracts Vol. D', into which notes from Hall's book were written is 223 pages long and contains quotations from books borrowed between 1819 and 1824.[74] The system used to construct this volume reveals a great deal about Lister's reading practices, including her ability to read against the grain. The three extracts from the *Travels in France* (1819) are grouped together under the date 'Thursday Morning 9 December 1819'. Each has a separate subject heading, which has also been entered into the book's index, and is followed by a reference in the style recommended by Locke.[75] Hall's *Travels* appeared in only one edition so it is easy to trace the actual text with which she engaged. The preface was deliberately provocative, drawing attention to Hall's Republican 'sentiments and opinions', and its date ('September 1819') reveals that it was possible for a Library reader in provincial Halifax to engage with a book still hot from the press. As the journal entry on Hall makes clear, transcription provided a particularly useful mode of resistance that allowed Lister to rewrite texts through selective quotation:

> He is an arrant republican in politics & would, perhaps, style himself a philosopher in religion. Consequently his sentiments & mine on these subjects, who [as] a limited monarchist & Protestant Christian according to the established Church of England, are opposite almost to the poles. However, there is some information useful to a tourist. (pp. 108–109)

Lister was reading this volume at a moment after Peterloo in which she was particularly alive to (what she saw as) the dangers of political 'reform'. Her display of political certitude, a kind of right thinking political self, was often brought into play in the face of radical or disturbing texts. By rewriting this text as a series of 'extracts' 'useful to a tourist', Lister should have been able to control the content of Hall's text by stripping it of it's ideological baggage, but only two of the 'extracts' actually work in this way. The third is taken from Hall's chapter on 'the Present Government of France' and is an accurate reproduction of his account of 'The Chamber of Deputies' (including footnotes). Lister counteracted Hall's politics by surrounding the extract with quotations from a number of texts that opposed 'Jacobin' radicalism, including the *British Critic* (on the French electoral process) and *The Anti-Jacobin Review* (on the Jacobin 'atheist cabal'). I have treated this example of resistance to Hall's politics at some length because it is important to locate Lister's queer reading strategies within the context of her other reading projects. Many other forms of resistance to the dominant ideologies of texts are revealed in her autobiographical writings, and it is only by looking at the full range of Lister's reading that we can get any sense of the complex ways in which she used texts to open up new social and sexual possibilities.

The carefully dated and indexed notes on reading contained in the 'extracts' demonstrate the important role that 'study' played in her everyday life and they suggest that the ability to control texts was central to the way in which she thought about herself. Lister frequently constructs herself in the diaries as an eloquent woman with literary ambitions, and as is clearly the case in the correspondence with Maclean, her relationships with other women were often negotiated through a shared reading practice, a mutual understanding of texts. Lister resisted Hall's intended radicalisation of the reader by deploying a counter argument rather than entirely erasing his politics, but she also read this text as research for an extended description of a recent trip to France with her aunt that she was writing at the request of friends in York. After successfully completing this project, she noted that 'I gained a valuable turn towards a habit of patient reference & correction which, should I ever publish, may be of use to me' (p. 111). This is one of several references to becoming a professional author that Lister made during 1819. Although her wish to read texts 'only to improve myself in the hope of a possibility of making something by writing' was probably a rhetorical flourish, and her plans to become an author never came to fruition (p. 102). Lister did intend her studies to provide her with the means to support herself without a husband, as many authors did. Some of the notes that she made were designed to help learn the skills that she knew she would need to manage the Shibden estate. Lister had to teach herself these management skills because she was denied the education that would have been afforded to the son of a minor gentry family as a matter of course. It was the success of the estate, and the financial security that it brought with it, that allowed Lister to live successfully in a lesbian relationship. In this sense, Lister was a particularly effective reader.[76]

Pearson has argued that 'being an effective woman reader acquired the ability of a tightrope walker'. Throughout the period 1750–1835 'literate' or 'learned' women were often depicted negatively in novels, as were those women who read little, or badly.[77] Lister's conspicuous consumption of print and her use of Latin and Greek were amongst the things that signalled her out as an unusual figure in her community. She noted, with some amusement, that 'the Miss Hudsons of Hipperholme ... were frightened of me – my Latin & Greek etc.' (p. 98).[78] She took on the stereotype of the 'literate' or 'learned' woman in order to subvert it. This 'bookish' persona proved an important way for her to demonstrate her rejection of normative gender roles.

This chapter has demonstrated that throughout the late Romantic period, readers continued to engage in collective reading practices. They sometimes bought books in groups and often exchanged texts with friends in manuscript. The popularity of the album suggests that many Romantic readers were transcribers, making copies of texts available from a range of sources that were then represented for public consumption. As Lister's reading notes make clear, however, this shared transcription practice could be used to produce a very individualistic way of reading.

6
Towards a Mass Audience, or, John Clare and the Problem of the Unknown Public

Most work on working-class readers has, of necessity, concentrated on the evidence recorded in the autobiographies of an elite group within that class. From Robert Altick's *The English Common Reader* (1957), through David Vincent's *Bread, Knowledge and Freedom* (1982), to Jonathan Rose's *The Intellectual Life of the British Working Classes* (2001), John Clare's autobiographical writings have played an important role in recovering the history of working-class reading. This chapter looks at the various ways in which Clare and a number of contemporary working-class writers represented reading in order to suggest something of the overdetermined nature of these scenes in working-class autobiography. Despite the derogatory comments that he often makes about other working-class readers, Clare cannot help but acknowledge that he was surrounded by a number of different reading communities as he was growing up in the early years of the nineteenth century. This chapter uses his autobiographical writings to call attention to the complex interpenetration of literate and illiterate communities during the early nineteenth century in order to complicate the picture of dominant reading practices presented in the previous chapter. It then goes on to look at Wilkie Collins's essay on 'The Unknown Public' (1858) in order to suggest that the 'mass' audience who read the new 'penny' press in the 1840s and 1850s still remains largely unexplored by historians of reading. As Collins argues, it is possible to discover something about how this audience responded to these texts via the 'answers to correspondents' columns but these columns suggest many of the difficulties that we face in trying to account for the practices of a mass audience. This leads on to a discussion of two new spaces for reading that were developing at this time, the railway bookstall and the advertising hoarding, which complicate the relationship between reader and text on which this study is predicated.

'Sketches' in the 'Reading Existance' of John Clare (1793–1864)

On 8 August 1825, the working-class poet John Clare recorded the following damning critique of Gillead's *Allworth Abbey, Or, Christianity Triumphant Over Tyranny and Despotism* (1825) in his journal: 'I never saw such a heap of unnatural absurditys and ridiculous attempts at wit and satire strung together in my reading existance'.[1] Clare's 'reading existance', his reading life, has played a significant role in recovering the history of working-class reading practices during the nineteenth century. Richard Altick used evidence taken from Clare's autobiographical 'Sketches in the Life of John Clare' to describe the emergence of the 'self-made reader' in his classic account of the democratisation of print culture, *The English Common Reader* (1957), alongside the autobiographical writings of two other 'peasant' poets, James Hogg (1770–1835) and Ann Yearsley (1752–1806). However, Altick only refers to one working-class poet in any detail, Charles Kingsley's fictional Alton Locke.[2] Subsequent work by David Vincent and Jonathan Rose has helped restore the authentic voice of the 'self-made reader' or autodidact to the history of reading by drawing on a wealth of material that was unavailable to Altick, including the unexpurgated versions of Clare's autobiographical writings published in the 1980s.[3] Even William St Clair, who is largely distrustful of personal reminiscences as a source for recovering the history of reading, has used Eric Robinson's edition of the 'Sketches' to provide evidence of the limited number of texts available to working-class readers at the beginning of the nineteenth century, noting that Clare had to walk six miles in order to get hold of anything other than the 'ballads and chapbooks' that came to his village via the national network of hawkers and chapmen.[4]

The first major study of working-class autobiography, Vincent's *Bread, Knowledge and Freedom* (1982) used 142 documents written between 1790 and 1850 to cautiously generalise about working-class experience (including reading) during a period of rapid social change.[5] Vincent is cautious because writing an autobiography was 'an uncommon activity' amongst working men and women. Indeed, he argues that as 'a mode of expression it was more accessible to those who had prior experience as writers, particularly as journalists or poets, or as activists in the spectrum of working-class organization in the period'.[6] Over a quarter of the texts assembled by Vincent for this study were written by those who held a position of authority within the working-class community, such as Samuel Bamford (1788–1872), Thomas Cooper (1805–1892) and

William Lovett (1800–1877), and several others, including Clare, were well known as professional writers.[7] As a source, working-class autobiography clearly represents a group of unusually articulate *men*. As Jonathan Rose has noted, 'only about 5 percent of the memoirists born before 1870' were women, although by the early twentieth century this figure is closer to 30 percent.[8] There are, of course, some famous autobiographical poems by female writers, such as Ann Yearsley, but other working-class women seem not to have written autobiographies during the early nineteenth century, perhaps because they were excluded from positions of power within the working-class organisations that were emerging at this time.[9]

Vincent's work also suggests that historians of reading need to pay attention to the manner in which these autobiographies were first published as this may well have influenced their contents.[10] Commercial London firms, which served a predominantly middle-class audience, published about a third of the texts in his sample, and each would have gone through a process of editing before publication. Many, including Clare's 'Sketches', were written with a specific section of the mainstream bourgeois audience in mind. Others, such as John Bezer's 'Autobiography of One of the Chartist Rebels of 1848', in which he recounts the importance of Bunyan's *Pilgrim's Progress* to his intellectual development, were published in radical newspapers such as the *Christian Socialist*. Bezer clearly had this audience in mind when he wrote, 'Glorious Bunyan you too were a "Rebel", and I love you *doubly* for *that*'.[11] Even those that remained in manuscript had an intended reader. Vincent argues that the family or local audience that the unpublished memoirist was addressing guarantees a degree of accuracy in the way in which they presented working-class life.[12] As these various determining contexts suggest, any conclusions about individual or collective reading practices derived from these autobiographies needs to take account of the determining factors of both writing *and* publication.

Jonathan Rose's *The Intellectual Life of the British Working Classes* (2001) extends Vincent's work into the twentieth century using many of the 'nearly two thousand documents' listed by Vincent, John Burnett and David Mayall in their *The Autobiography of the Working Class* (1984–1989).[13] Rose argues that these autobiographies allow us into 'the minds of ordinary readers' in order 'to discover what they read and how they read'. Like Vincent, however, he also admits that this source has limitations. It can only tell us about the 'vital minority of self-improving workers' and he uses a range of other sources, including 'library records, sociological surveys, and opinion polls', to offer 'a more representative portrait of the working class as a whole'.[14] However, in the majority of cases, Rose tends to suggest that these other sources simply 'confirm what the memoirists tell us', and his study often risks making the history of a 'vital minority' into that of the many.[15]

If working-class autobiography is a problematic source for recovering anything other than the history of reading amongst those at the forefront of the culture of self-improvement it can also be somewhat limited in what it tells us about the reading practices of this group. As Rose says in defence of using this source, 'in his day the sensational novelist G. W. M. Reynolds outsold Charles Dickens, but in their memoirs Victorian working people repeatedly call on Dickens to represent them, not Reynolds'. Working-class writers have surprisingly little to say about the everyday consumption of 'popular' texts, like Reynolds's novels and newspapers. For Rose, this confirms that some texts 'are consumed like literary chewing gum' whereas others 'transform the lives of their readers'.[16] An autobiography that recreates a reading of Dickens in a style clearly influenced by the great novelist is a sure sign of his 'very great and deep' influence upon the reader, as Rose contends, but I want to argue that the history of reading needs to pay at least some attention to the everyday, non-transformative, kind of reading that is only sometimes described by the 'vital minority' of memoirists.[17] Teresa Gerrard has suggested that if we are ever to get beyond the 'highlighted reading experiences of an exceptional minority' we need to look at alternative sources, such as the 'Answers to Correspondents' columns that appeared in the penny press, but before moving on to consider this source I want to re-examine Clare's 'Sketches' in the light of recent work on the generic constraints of autobiography.[18] For the early part of the nineteenth century a certain amount of evidence about those 'ordinary readers' who did not create autobiographies can be gleaned from the descriptions of reading found within the autobiographies of the 'self-improving' minority. This section reads Clare's 'Sketches' with these figures very much in mind.

Kate Flint has argued that it is important to 'exercise a certain amount of caution when using autobiographical material' because all autobiography is a form of self-fashioning and involves the selection and arrangement of events. This is, of course, also true of other sources used in this study, such as letters and diaries, which involve the framing of events, but it is widely acknowledged that autobiography shares many of the literary techniques associated with fiction.[19] Each author has different reasons for wishing to foreground the importance of reading to their intellectual or emotional development, but they often use established tropes to write about this experience. For example, female memoirists frequently create a scene in which they transgress the rules of reading laid down by a parent or described in a conduct book. As Flint indicates, this way of framing experience provides a substantial body of evidence about the control exercised over young female readers, as well as an important insight into the ways in which such readers nevertheless acquired and enjoyed forbidden texts.[20] Both Vincent and Rose recognise that working-class memoirists often adopted existing fictional tropes to describe their own lives. To compare the school they attended to the one 'out of *Nicholas Nickleby*' is, of course, not to falsify that experience, but such instances underline that these texts need careful reading.[21] Working-class autobiography draws on established modes of life writing, such as spiritual autobiography, and by the middle of the nineteenth century had many of its own distinctive generic rules. Indeed, Alan Richardson has divided published working-class autobiography from this period into two distinct genres. The 'life and struggles' autobiography gives an account of how an individual overcame his (sometimes her) humble origins in order to rise to a position of power, whereas the recollections of the 'uneducated poet' usually record the flowering of an 'untutored genius' lucky enough to be taken under the wing of a patron in order to produce a volume of poems.[22]

The opening of Clare's 'Sketches' indicates that he is indebted to both these genres. There are clear echoes of both the 'uneducated poet' James Hogg's 'Memoir' (1807), with its emphasis upon the enjoyment of writing about the past, and William Cobbett's *The Life and Adventures of Peter Porcupine* (1796).[23] Richardson has argued that Cobbett's widely distributed 'life and struggles' autobiography gave many working-class writers the confidence to celebrate their 'poor but honest' background in a way that subverted the concern with 'ancestry' that characterised middle-class and aristocratic life writing.[24] In the 'Sketches' Clare even goes as far as to admit that his father was 'one of fates chance-lings who drop into the world without the honour of matrimony'.[25] Other recurrent tropes in working-class autobiography include an epiphanic moment in which 'a book's loan or chance discovery or rare purchase … marks an epoch in the self-taught writer's life, particularly in adolescence'.[26] In Hogg's 'Memoir' it is hearing Burns's 'Tam O' Shanter' that begins the 'new epoch' of his life as poet.[27] Clare uses his acquisition of James Thomson's *The Seasons* to mark his transition from reader to writer: 'with reading the book and beholding the beautys of artful nature in the park I got into the strain of descriptive writing on my journey home this was "the morning walk" the first thing I commited to paper' (p. 11). I am not trying to suggest that Thomson was not important to Clare's intellectual development – he clearly was – but we need to recognise that his autobiographical writings are artful. Clare was aware of other autobiographies, including Hogg's 'Memoir', and even his use of the phrase 'written by himself' deliberately echoes the tradition of working-class writing about the self.[28]

Because much of Clare's work remained in manuscript it is tempting to think of it as not having been written for an audience – that it is 'by himself' and for himself. However, as the full title, 'Sketches in the Life of John Clare Written by Himself and Addressed to his Friend John Taylor' reveals, it was written with a specific audience in mind. On 8 February 1821 Clare informed Taylor, who was both his editor and publisher, that he had been 'getting on with my "Memoirs"' and that they would soon be ready for his 'inspection'. Clare sent the manuscript on 3 April 1821, promising Taylor 'sole ownership', a sure sign that he intended the work for publication. However, Taylor chose not to publish and instead used parts of the 'Sketches' in his introduction to Clare's second volume of poetry, *The Village Minstrel*, published in September 1821.[29] Clare and Taylor had carefully constructed an image of the way in which the poet's natural 'genius' had overcome his limited education in the introduction to *Poems Descriptive of Rural Life and Scenery* (in its fourth edition in 1821) and parts of the 'Sketches' are clearly intended to flesh out the account of Clare's life that appeared in that volume. For example, they include a much longer version of an episode that refers to Clare's father reading aloud from a poem by Pomfret.[30] However, the 'Sketches' was also clearly an attempt to forestall criticism about Clare's political beliefs. The reference to reading a 'small pamphlet on the Murder of the French king' that is said to have 'cured' him of 'thinking favourably of radicalism' disassociates him from the 'Radical and ungrateful sentiments' that Lord Radstock (an early reader turned patron) had accused him of holding in the previous year (p. 30).[31] Despite Taylor's unwillingness to publish the 'Sketches', Clare continued to write (and rewrite) his 'life' in the following years. These later autobiographical writings sometimes contradict what is found in the earlier work. A note on a 'Tract ... containing the dreadful end of an atheist who shot his own daughter for going to a Methodist chapple', for example, is described as one of the 'white lies that are hawked about the country to meet the superstitions of the unwary' rather than a 'cure' for radicalism.[32] The writing of the 'Sketches' was clearly overdetermined by these various contexts. As a text intended for publication it needed to play into an already established tradition of writing about the rise of the 'uneducated poet', to flesh out a by now well-known narrative of the poet's early life, and provide evidence of his political quietude in order to please newly acquired patrons, such as Radstock.

Despite these limitations, which call attention to the way in which Clare constructs his own reading life, the 'Sketches' provide an important account of the different reading communities (and different levels of literacy) that surrounded him as he was growing up. Many of the scenes in the 'Sketches' are used rhetorically to signal his difference from his parents or the other members of his community, whom he often associates with illiteracy.

> Both my parents was illiterate to the last degree my mother knew not a single letter and superstition went as far with her that she beleved [sic] the higher parts of learing [learning] was the blackest arts of witchcraft and that no other means could attain them my father could read a little in a bible or testament and was very fond of the supersti[ti]ous tales that are hawked about a sheet for a penny. (p. 2)

Even in this section, which at first appears to suggest that neither of Clare's parents could read, the contrast is in fact between canonical poetry and popular culture ('superstitious tales') rather than literacy and illiteracy. Clare uses the term 'illiterate' here to suggest that his father could not write rather than that he could not read. If we ignore his prejudice against illiteracy we can see that both 'literate' and 'illiterate' lived harmoniously together as part of the same community. Clare's father, Parker Clare, frequently read aloud to his family so that even his 'illiterate' wife was in contact with contemporary print culture. Clare makes this distinction between those who could read 'a little', but not write, and those who could read and write with skill, several times during the 'Sketches'. Although this scene was designed to suggest something of the difficulty of Clare's struggle towards full literacy in an 'illiterate' world, elsewhere in the 'Sketches' he acknowledge that his father's reading aloud stimulated his interest in poetry.

> What first induced me to rhyme I cannot hardly say the first thing that I heard of poetry that can be called poetry was a romantic story which I have since found to be Pomfret's 'Love Triumphant Over Reason' [...] but I could benefit little by this as I used to hear it before I could read and my father was but a sorry reader of poetry to improve his readers by reciting it. (p. 14)

Other sources confirm that many working-class households contained a range of different reading competencies in this way. Clare's description of his father's reading is a useful antidote to over-sentimentalised accounts of reading aloud amongst groups of working-class readers, which tend to imagine solitary reading as a bourgeois practice.[33] It also draws attention to those 'invisible' readers *and* listeners who historians of literacy have tended to condemn as illiterate because they could not write and who figure only briefly in recent accounts of the intellectual life of the working class.[34] Clare appears to share this prejudice, and he may well have exaggerated his father's inability to read aloud in order to emphasise the difference between himself and his parents, but Parker Clare's reading of the Bible, ballads and the poetry of Pomfret is a useful reminder that not all working-class readers were like his son. Working-class memoir often provides glimpses of these other readers who were not able (or did not have the opportunity) to achieve the same levels of literacy as the 'vital minority' who recorded their own lives in such detail.

Most 'life and struggles' autobiographies give some account of the limitations of the contemporary school system that produced readers like Parker Clare. Christopher Thomson (b. 1799), writing in the 1840s with the hope of helping his 'Fellow workers in the holy cause of Self Elevation', described the 'mere apology for learning doled out' to most working-class children at school, which gave them just enough skill to '"get the catechism" and to write their own name'.[35] In one of his many 'digressions' from his own narrative, Clare describes the system of making schoolchildren read only from the Bible and Testament as 'very erroneous' because it encouraged working-class readers to abandon a text that they associated with boredom or punishment: 'a dull boy never turns with pleasure to his school days when he has often been beat 4 times for bad readings in 5 verses of scripture' (p. 6). Clare also describes how his own education was frequently interrupted because anything that he earned as a thresher was valuable to the family economy. By acknowledging their own 'struggles' to gain education writers like Thomson, Cooper and Clare were part of a working-class movement that demanded better education for their children.

Clare's dismissal of a school system that had left him 'nearly as wise as I went, save reading and writing' leads into a section in which he describes his attempts at self-tuition, as 'Sixpenny Romances' (chapbooks) are abandoned and replaced by books on mathematics and other 'puzzling systems' (pp. 6–7). This section is clearly a rejoinder to Taylor's introduction to *Poems Descriptive* which describes this part of Clare's educational programme as learning 'Writing and Arithmetic' with the assistance of a neighbour.[36] In some 'life and struggles' narratives this programme of self-tuition cannot help but expose the tensions within the working class community over the meaning and use of reading. Even writers such as Thomas Cooper, who benefited from much greater access to mutual improvement groups than Clare, found that other members of this community could be dismissive of his learning. He notes that he was often asked, 'Who was I, that I should sit on the cobbler's stall, and "talk fine!"'.[37] Clare also refers to similar tensions. His parents supported his reading programme when they thought that it might lead to a better job, but discouraged him from buying books when it was clear that he intended to remain a labourer. He records that some of his neighbours thought his reading was 'for no other improvement then [sic] quallyfiing [sic] an idiot for a workhouse' (p. 5). Scenes in which he was forced to hide his reading from his neighbours occur several times in the course of the narrative of his intellectual development. He explains that a common association of books with 'laziness' often led to his hiding in the fields in order to read chapbooks on Sundays (p. 6). Even in the famous episode in which he looked into his own copy of Thomson's *Seasons* for the first time, he claims that he climbed over the wall into Burghley Park because he 'did not like to let anybody see me reading on the road of a working day' (p. 11). In another passage he notes that he was afraid to show anyone his poetry because in 'our unletterd villages ... the labouring classes remain as blind in such matters as the slaves in Africa', whilst their betters read little more than weekly papers, almanacs and prayer books (p. 18). This is clearly a useful rhetorical strategy as it underlines the difference between the 'lettered' poet and his 'unlettered' community that is necessary to maintain his claim to the 'natural genius' of the poet. It is repeated often enough, however, to suggest that there was a genuine tension over the meaning of reading for self-improvement within Clare's community.

Despite Clare's references to 'unletterd villages' and the ignorance of the 'labouring classes', the 'Sketches' cannot help but reveal that he was neither the only reader in his village, nor solitary in his reading habits. His 'confidential friend' Thomas Porter was a 'lover of books' who pored 'over old book stalls at a fair' (p. 19). Clare describes how the two men met regularly over a number of years to talk about their reading and that a neighbour, John Turnhill, helped him to learn mathematics. He recounts that he borrowed books from the uncle of a boy at school and 'a companion'. Even his decision to buy a *Universal Spelling Book* in order to learn grammar was taken on 'the advice of a friend' (p. 17). This friend may well have been Porter, of course, but he also writes about discussing texts with his better-educated 'companions' (p. 16). As David Vincent has noted, most of the autobiographies include references to a meeting with, or the companionship of, another 'lover of books'. These men were often brought together by the mutual recognition of shared 'intellectual hardship'.[38] Clare seems to have found a number of companions with whom to share books in this way, but he was not completely isolated from those who did not share his aim of self-improvement. In all of these instances, Clare maintains his difference from these other readers by insisting that they did not understand poetry or his urge to write. Thomas Porter's tastes are described as the same 'excepting poetry' and Clare's friends are said to dismiss his observations on the beauty found 'in a wild flower or object in the surrounding scenery' as 'droll fancies' (pp. 16–17). Rather than an 'unletterd village' full of ignorant labourers, Clare's 'Sketches' reveal a diversity of different reading communities and the overlapping of different competencies, or types of literacy.

This overlapping of different reading communities is made particularly clear in the episode in which Clare first gets a glimpse of Thomson's *Seasons*. In Taylor's introduction to *Poems Descriptive* it is said that this book was shown to him by 'another boy', but in the 'Sketches' it is a damaged copy that belonged to a Methodist 'weaver, much older then [sic] myself, then in the village' who also shows him a copy of Wesley's *Hymns* 'as a rival of exellence'. Once again this scene works rhetorically to suggest that Clare appreciates poetry more than anyone else that he meets – the poem makes his 'heart twitter with joy' but is 'reckoned nothing of' by the weaver and his friends – whilst at the same time underlining his religious orthodoxy in a way that suited his new patrons. The Methodists are dismissed as 'fanatics' some of whom will only read books containing the words 'Lord and God' (p. 10). As already suggested, this episode was clearly intended as an emblematic moment – it leads eventually to the writing of his first poem – but as with so many other episodes in the 'Sketches' it cannot help but reveal that Clare was a part of a community in which a range of different interpretive modes were possible.

David Vincent has argued that 'eclecticism was at once a necessity and a virtue for the reader of limited means'.[39] The intellectual life of many of the elite of working-class readers who produced autobiographies consisted of gathering together a library that often contained obsolete texts and cheap editions, a patchwork of what was available. In an autobiographical fragment written after the completion of the 'Sketches', Clare lists more than 40 'old books of motley merits' that he had 'gotten together by savings' by the 1810s. This list includes books on botany, mathematics, surveying and history, as well as poetry by canonical writers such as Thomson, Milton and Waller, and famous prose works by Bunyan and Defoe. He notes that he 'happened to meet' with some of these texts 'second hand', but that most were acquired relatively cheaply from a bookseller in nearby Stamford. The later self of Clare's autobiography is quite dismissive of this list, which he says made him imagine 'that I was book learnd' (p. 61).

William St Clair's work on the publishing industry during the Romantic period suggests that later Clare was right to be dismissive of this 'motley' collection. He saw little or nothing of any of the new writers of this period before he became famous because most new books were very expensive and produced in only limited print runs. Working-class readers could only afford 'old canon' writers (such as Thomson) whose work could be bought for as little as 1s by the 1810s.[40] In the episode in which he describes seeing the weaver's copy of Thomson's *Seasons*, for example, it is clearly an old canon edition for he notes that it was worth 1s 6d. Clare was particularly pleased when he eventually managed to buy his own copy for just one shilling. As St Clair makes clear, the old canon was important because it allowed readers who had never before been able to afford substantial texts to join the reading nation, but the relatively small libraries gathered together by Clare and other working-class readers suggests that they were still very much luxury items.[41] There was no such thing as an average working-class wage during the early nineteenth century. Clare earned just 8s per week in 1814, but even in the 1830s agricultural labourers were often paid less than 2s per day.[42] In this context, it is not surprising to find Clare celebrating his 6d saving. When Edward Drury took over as proprietor of the New Public Library in Stamford, Clare owed the previous tenant the considerable sum of 15s.[43] The old canon may well have been the 'first truly national literature' read from 'Lord to cottager', as St Clair argues, but the evidence from working-class autobiographies suggests that the 'cottager' often struggled to afford even these cheap books in any number.[44]

Titles from the old canon appear in the lists of books read by most autodidacts along with the other most frequently reproduced texts of the age, such as the Bible, religious tracts and chapbooks. 'Self-censorship' by the publishers patrolling 'the textual limits' of what was available in the lower price ranges meant that much that was widely available during this period was ideologically conservative.[45] Even conduct books and volumes of literary theory, such as Blair's *Lectures*, which helped to police reading practices, were to be found in working-class collections. Clare, for example, lists owning a copy of Gregory's *A Father's Legacy* (the same title was owned by Anne Lister), although his copy of Blair's *Sermons*, a text that St Clair describes as particularly common, was a later gift, acquired when he was already famous.[46] Widely available in abridged versions and anthologised in school textbooks, to be a reader during this period was to experience these texts. As noted in Chapter 1, St Clair argues that they formed a conservative 'horizon of expectations' from which it took an act of will on the reader's part to deviate.[47] Of course, many of the working-class memoirists were able to find texts that helped form, or support, radical ideas. Christopher Thomson read both the old canon and radical newspapers, such as Cobbett's *Register* and Wooler's *Black Dwarf*, but conservative pamphlets and religious tracts, often issued in opposition to the radical's cause, had the advantage of being given away for free.[48] During the 1840s the Religious Tract Society distributed more than 23 million items.[49]

As already noted, Clare records both an orthodox, politically conservative, response to a pamphlet against radicalism ('on the Murder of the French king'), and a resisting reading of a 'Tract ... containing the dreadful end of an atheist', which was handed to him by one of his neighbours. The context of the 'Sketches' perhaps suggests a certain amount of political expediency in producing an image of himself as an obedient reader, but it is possible that he engaged in both sorts of reading during his long and complex 'reading existance'. Individual reading practices do not have to be consistent. However, Clare was not the only working-class reader of his generation to feel that the rhetorical strategies used in the texts disseminated by the Religious Tract Society and others were too obvious to be taken seriously. Joseph Mayett (1783–1839), writing in the 1830s, recalled that 'those kind of books were often put into my hands in a dictatorial way in order to convince me of my errors'. He lists a number of texts that he argues were 'designed' to 'perswade poor people to be satisfied in their situation and not to murmur at the dispensations of providence'. Like Clare, Mayett describes a childhood in which a few books, such as the Bible, Bunyan's *Pilgrim's Progress* and the *Reading Made Easy*, were all that were available.[50] Mayett was taught to read by his mother and he uses his autobiography to recount how his gradual acquisition of a set of sophisticated reading strategies led him to reject both the state religion, espoused in tracts, and the radical politics of Cobbett, Wooler and Carlile that he was at one time attracted to. It was Mayett's reading of Bunyan that convinced him to become a Baptist, and although he continued to read widely in his later life, he told his own readers that they should 'always prefer the bible before any other book'.[51]

Jonathan Rose has argued that historians of reading need to take account of this sort of 'working-class cultural conservatism'. As an example he notes that the 'only books John Clare repeatedly read were

Paradise Lost, Thomson's *Seasons*, *Robinson Crusoe*, *Tom Jones*, and the *Vicar of Wakefield*: he had no desire to read Scott or any other contemporary novelist'.[52] Although it is true that Clare was not very interested in contemporary fiction, it seems a little unfair to make him into a culturally conservative figure because of this. Indeed, the first paragraph of the autobiographical passage referred to by Rose in fact details his 'irregular' reading habits: 'I cannot and never coud plod thro every book in a regular mechanical way – as I meet with [it] I dip into it here and there and if it does not suit I lay it down and seldom take it up again but in the same manner[.]'

The only volumes of poetry that he had 'regularly read thro' (i.e. read from beginning to end) at the time this passage was written were, he claims, the *Seasons* and *Paradise Lost*. Rather than a culturally conservative rereading of texts, Clare is describing a radical lack of respect for old canon texts that are discarded if they do 'not suit' (p. 56). This is a very different kind of reading practice to that engaged in by some of his contemporaries, such as Thomas Cooper, who spent many hours memorising passages from Shakespeare and other canonical writers.[53] Many of the autobiographies written by the working-class elite of Clare's generation describe reading the same texts – the Bible, religious tracts, chapbooks, *Robinson Crusoe*, *Pilgrim's Progress*, and the pre-Romantic poets, not because of any deep seated conservatism, but because they were the books that were most widely available to this generation. Mayett, Clare and Cooper found these texts radically 'acculturating' – to use Chartier's phrase – but what about those other working-class readers, like Parker Clare, who did not have the skill to record how they reacted to texts? Like Rose, I want to supplement this picture of autodidact reading strategies by looking at a survey from the 1830s that provides 'a more representative portrait of the working class as a whole'.

Surveying the working-class reader

During the 1830s the Central Society of Education (CSE) began to investigate the reading habits of the working class by sending out investigators to survey a mixture of urban and rural parishes. In 1838 the barrister Frederick Liardet produced perhaps the best known of these surveys.[54] He was asked to investigate Boughton-Under-Blean, Hernhill and Dunkirk, located on the London road between Faversham and Canterbury in Kent, because the CSE wanted to explain why 'Sir William Courtenay' (actually John Thom, a maltster from Cornwall) had been able to persuade about 40 of the villagers from this area to join in a millenarian revolt that ended in the deaths of eight men after they attacked a party of militia.

The CSE was particularly worried because, as Liardet notes, 'the greater part of Courtenay's followers believed him to be Jesus Christ, and considered that they were not only justified in obeying him as their lord, but that disobedience would entail upon them eternal damnation'.[55] Barry Reay has used this survey along with a range of other sources detailing literacy in these villages to argue that for many agricultural labourers during the first half of the nineteenth century, 'reading *was* literacy'. It is perhaps not surprising to find that Parker Clare was more typical than his son John, but Reay insists that in order to understand how these rural communities functioned we need to recognise the interaction between different levels of literacy within the rural community. He gives the example of a newspaper reporter who discovered one of Thom's followers carrying a Bible even though he couldn't 'read nor write' who explained that 'his wife read the book to him every night, and said that some such person as Sir William Courtenay was spoken of in it'.[56]

Many of the labourers interviewed by Liardet replied to the question 'Can you read?' with the 'usual answer ..."Yes, a little in the Testament"'.[57] It is interesting to note that Clare used this same phrase to describe his father's reading ability. Liardet's research supports those autobiographies that describe the poor standard of schooling provided for working-class children. For example, in Hernhill he discovered that 35 of the 51 children aged over 14 who lived in the village could read, but only 11 could both read *and* write. He argues that this was because only one of the three schools in the village taught writing, and even there, those pupils who wanted 'reading, writing and arithmetic' were charged a higher fee than those who wanted (or could afford) 'reading only'. The other schools taught 'nothing but sewing and reading' usually from a limited number of religious texts, such as 'the Bible, the Testament, Catechism and some religious tracts' (p. 111). In a brilliant example of how material forms affect meaning, he demonstrates that children taught to read in these schools could in fact *only* read from the texts that they were familiar with: 'they have read and heard read, the same thing so often, that the sound of one word suggests the following one. They even remember some words from their length or form, and the position they occupy in the page which they would not know in another book' (p. 112).

The books used in school as teaching aids were also those most frequently found in the villagers' cottages. In Hernhill, 34 of the village's 51 families owned the Bible or another religious book, with 'in some instances a few religious tracts'. Only four houses contained any secular reading whatsoever and Liardet makes no reference to old canon writers or imaginative literature of any sort other than to note that the walls of some of the cottages were adorned with images cut from old ballads. He is shocked to find that none of the publications distributed by the Society for the Publication of Useful Knowledge, such as *The Penny Magazine*, were available in the village (p. 108). As Reay notes, 40 per cent of those interviewed by Liardet 'possessed absolutely no reading material whatsoever'. Given the limited range of material available, it is perhaps not surprising that only 13 of the families interviewed claimed to read in the evening.[58]

Of course, as with all surveys, Liardet had a point to prove: the late revolt had been caused by the participants' lack of education rather than any political belief or desire for change. He argues throughout that 'exclusive religious reading' has 'a tendency to narrow the mind, and instil fallacious ideas' and emphasises that out of those who took part 'very few could write their own names; and those who could read, rarely ventured upon any other book than the Testament or Bible' (p. 96). His praise of *The Penny Magazine* is part of a rhetorical strategy that aims to suggest that the villagers would have been less vulnerable to Courtenay's machinations if this diet of religious books had been leavened by works of 'useful knowledge'. And Liardet's interests go beyond the immediate context. Although he was keen to emphasise that the lack of new texts in the village was a sign of the inhabitants 'indifference to mental recreation of any sort', the report is designed to act as a warning against 'the folly and danger of leaving the agricultural population in the debasing ignorance that now exists among them' (p. 97). In many ways he speaks with the same voice of protest found in many of the working-class autobiographies. Like Thomson, Cooper, Clare and William Lovett, Liardet had faith in the power of print to transform the minds and lives of those who read regularly.

If we put aside Liardet's dismissive attitude towards those who could not read or write fluently we can reconstruct a detailed picture of what reading meant in these rural communities. Some of Courtenay's followers were clearly regular readers of the Bible. Liardet claims to have discovered one of the women who had persuaded many to support Courtenay reading from the Bible when he made the survey, and he recalls that she told him that after the riot in which Courtenay was killed she and a friend spent the night reading passages from the Bible together in the hope of his resurrection.[59] He boasts that by questioning her about her beliefs he was able to prove 'that her boasted knowledge of the Scriptures was of the most superficial kind', but if his evidence is accurate, she clearly had an unwavering faith in the Bible even after Courtenay had been proved false (p. 93). Her brother, William Wills, who was amongst those imprisoned after the riot, converted others to the cause by 'showing' them a passage in Revelations which described the Saviour's return on a white horse like that ridden by Courtenay (p. 91). His success suggests something both of the authoritative status of the Bible in these villages, and of the presence of a literate hierarchy whose interpretive strategies were taken seriously by other members of the community. Liardet notes that Wills was considered 'quite a learned man' by almost everyone that he met and that he and his sister were considered 'prodigies of learning' by some of their neighbours (pp. 90, 96).

Other sources reveal a somewhat different picture. For example, *The Times* looked at the graffiti created by the rioters. The text left by William Wills on the door of the tithe barn in Hernhill, 'o that great day of gudgement is close at hand ... our rites and liberties We Will have', combines the Bible with the language of contemporary radicalism.[60] This language may well have come from conversation rather than reading, of course, and it is significant that Liardet makes no mention of finding any text associated with the contemporary radical canon in the cottages that he surveyed. Indeed, Liardet has little to say about the political beliefs of the rioters because this suits his argument that the 'late disturbance was undoubtedly of a religious character' (p. 133). In the last few pages of his report, however, he is forced to acknowledge that Courtenay 'often hinted at a more equable distribution of property' and that several of the labourers that he interviewed entertained 'very erroneous notions ... respecting the rights of property' (p. 133). This was usually put down to 'ignorance', as when a man who admitted that he had never seen the *Penny Magazine* or read a newspaper but could 'read a little in the testament', informed him that 'everybody ought to have land' because God had given the land 'to *all*' (p. 134). Barry Reay has argued that those villagers who used the Bible to dispute with Liardet demonstrate that people do not need to be widely read, or indeed be able to write, in order to 'think in a non-passive way'.[61] Given William St Clair's description of the conservative 'horizon of expectations' created by school textbooks, anthologies, sermons and other religious materials with which working-class readers were supplied by the Religious Tract Society, these labourers were engaged in a particularly radical appropriation of one of the key texts of the dominant ideology. Liardet records that he needed to intervene so that the 'rights of property' were no longer threatened by what he regarded as a misreading of the Bible.

It is not my intention to argue that all working-class readers performed such radical acts of appropriation during the early nineteenth century, or indeed that all working-class readers thought in 'a non-passive way'. Some of those interviewed by Liardet appear to have had little interest in reading or in Courtenay's cause. However, as Reay argues, the fact that not all of Courtenay's supporters could read suggests that we should think of rural society as 'a range of cultures, of *literacies* rather than literate and non-literate (or illiterate)'.[62] How those who couldn't write reacted to texts is always going to be in a sense unknowable, but as Clare's autobiography and Liardet's survey suggest, it is possible to reconstruct something of the shared practices that pertained in communities that contained a vast range of different reading (and listening) skills.

The problem of 'The Unknown Public': mass literacy and new print spaces

Wilkie Collins's essay 'The Unknown Public', which first appeared in *Household Words* in August 1858, has proved an inspiration for many historians of Victorian reading practices. I want to use it here as a departure point in order to think about some of the new print spaces that emerged during this period, including the 'Answers to Correspondents' columns of the penny weekly press that he is so concerned with in this essay. According to Collins 'the unknown public' consisted of the millions of readers who regularly saw copies of the 'penny-novel Journals', as he calls them.[63] Patrick Brantlinger has argued that Collins's essay reads like one of his 'sensation novels': 'it is a mystery story, with Collins as literary detective, trying … to fathom the nature and composition of the "*monster* audience of at least three millions" he purports to have detected'.[64] This anxiety about who was reading these new periodicals, and how, was shared by many of his contemporaries. Texts such as *The London Journal*, *Reynolds's Miscellany*, *Cassell's Illustrated Family Paper* and *The Family Herald* were amongst the most discussed texts of the 1850s because they offered cheap fiction for a new mass audience that Victorian writers tended to describe as 'the million'. The circulation figures for such newspapers are not always reliable, but Altick suggests that many sold more than 250,000 copies of each issue in the mid 1850s, with both *The Family Herald* and *London Journal* sometimes selling over 300,000 copies per week.[65]

If Liardet was worried about how literate members of the working class were interpreting sacred texts, Collins and his contemporaries were anxious about mass literacy and the mass readership of the secular periodical press that 'arose with capitalism, urbanization, industrialization, and the progress of education'.[66] For example, Margaret Oliphant's

'The Byways of Literature', which appeared in *Blackwood's Magazine* in the same month as Collins's essay, suggests that the optimistic view of earlier commentators, who believed that 'reading was of itself ... a virtuous and improving exercise', should be made to examine the new market driven publications that had replaced 'the Penny Magazines and Cyclopaedias' offered by the now forgotten 'Societies for the Diffusion of Knowledge'.[67] However, Collins's investigation of this new audience begins by defining the 'known' public. These readers he declares 'are easily discovered and classified' and he goes on to describe 'the religious public', the public that 'patronizes' circulating libraries and railway bookstalls in search of 'amusement' and the public which 'reads nothing but newspapers'. The language of classification used in this essay echoes that found in the great social documentaries of the period, such as *London Labour and the London Poor* (1849–1854), but this audience doesn't need to be sought out, or interviewed as Mayhew's did: 'We all know where to lay our hands on the people who represent these various classes. We see the books they like on their tables. We meet them out at dinner, and hear them talk of their favourite authors' (p. 252).[68] Collins it seems is overly familiar with the 'known public', and as such, he doesn't need to describe them in any detail. This inclusive use of 'we' in this essay has the effect of heightening the difference between the 'known', the reader with whom 'we' are familiar enough to dine, and the 'unknown public' with whom 'we' never will. Lorna Huett has argued that the 'superior identity' that Collins constructs here is in fact part of an attempt to *create* a middle-class audience for a journal that was ambiguously positioned in the market. *Household Words* was a tuppenny weekly that prominently featured fiction, and as Deborah Wynne has noted, even its title was 'redolent of its even cheaper counterparts' such as *The Family Herald*.[69] The way in which Collins writes about working-class readers clearly embodies some anxieties about the status of his own audience.

Both Collins and Oliphant tend to write about the readers of the penny press as though they were a uniform 'multitude'. As Patricia Anderson has argued, however, the market for periodicals in the 1850s is best thought of as part of a new and developing 'mass culture' that was characterised by its 'social diversity': 'such a culture was never exclusively the experience of any one group or class, and for this reason "mass" must be understood to designate multiple social layers'.[70] Writing in 1854, Charles Knight argued that the audience for periodicals such as *The London Journal* and *The Family Herald* included 'the schoolboy, the apprentice, the milliner, the factory girl, the clerk and the small shopkeeper'.[71] The experience of this diverse 'mass' public is, of course, difficult to recover. Indeed, Jonathan Rose has noted that while the working-class autobiographers are 'forthcoming about some forms of popular literature (such as school stories) they tell us almost nothing about others (notably women's magazines)'.[72] Faced with the same problem of a lack of direct evidence (no one would 'answer the inquiry, "Do you subscribe to a penny journal?" plainly in the affirmative'), Collins tried several different strategies to find out more about these readers (p. 252). First he adopted 'the character of a member of the unknown public' in order to buy copies and question various shopkeepers about their stock. Although he was met with a friendly reception, he claims to have learnt little from these men other than the fact that each title consisted of a 'good pennorth' (pp. 253, 255). Despite being informed by one shopkeeper that all of the penny journals that he stocked would be sold out by the evening, Collins chose not to interview any of these customers, but took his purchases home with him in order to reconstruct the 'real reader' from the answers to correspondents' pages.

The 'Notices to Correspondents' column that appeared in *The London Journal* on 15 November 1851 is fairly typical of the genre. In this instance the column begins with a letter to the editor, but in most penny journals this section was made up entirely of the editor's answers, preceded by the signature or pseudonym of the correspondent.[73] These columns fascinated Collins and other middle-class commentators and in 'The Unknown Public' he argues that a close examination of their contents will reveal 'the average intelligence of the unknown public' (p. 256). Collins makes a little too much of his 'impartiality' in selecting from these pages and it is worth dwelling for a moment on the paragraph that precedes the long sequence of extracts from the 'answers' that he reproduces.

> I have not waited for bad specimens, or anxiously watched for good: I have impartially taken my chance. And now just as impartially, I dip into one journal after another, on the Correspondents' page, exactly as the five happen to lie on my desk. The result is that I have the pleasure of presenting to those ladies and gentlemen who may honour me with their attention, the following members of the Unknown Public, who are in a condition to speak quite unreservedly for themselves. (p. 256)

This paragraph re-inscribes the class position that Collins desired for his own audience – 'ladies and gentlemen' – before making the claim that he will let the unknown, working-class audience speak for itself. Recent work on this sort of column in the women's magazines of the 1890s suggests that they were constructed from real readers' letters, rather than created by the editor, but they were nevertheless highly mediated. As Lynne Warren has argued, even if the readers are real we tend to hear only the editorial voice and she reads such columns as constructing something between an ideal reader and a corporate identity for a product that needed to encourage readers to return, to purchase the next issue. 'Controlling the opportunities for correspondence – by fragmentation and by "silencing" the readers' voice', she notes, allowed the magazine 'to present these columns as having a nominally independent status while preserving its own dominant position'.[74] These columns, you might say, keep readers in their place. The editor of the *London Journal* even used this column as a marketing tool by encouraging readers to buy back issues in his answers. Collins's extracts are, of course, doubly distanced from the original correspondents and he uses the various quotations that he assembled in tandem with extracts from fiction in order to argue that 'the unknown public is, in a literary sense, hardly beginning, as yet, to learn to read'. He gives examples of readers 'not certain what the word Poems means; not certain that Mazeppa was written by Lord Byron; not certain whether there are such things in the world as printed and published lives of Napoleon Bonaparte' (p. 257). The analysis of the stories contained in these magazines that he then goes on to make is based upon the state of ignorance that he discerns from the editor's answers.

Teresa Gerrard has argued that the 'Answers to Correspondents Column' has been neglected by historians of working-class reading practices because of the mocking tone used to describe them by Collins and other middle-class commentators in the late 1850s.[75] Oliphant's 'The Byways of Literature' certainly suggests that they contain little of value. Indeed, she argues that these columns are like a printed form of graffiti with some readers writing in purely for 'the pleasure of seeing their self-chosen names in print'. She notes that answers to questions about handwriting, pronunciation and etiquette were particularly common and that the 'Oracle' of the back pages also gave out much advice on medical and legal matters. There is a gentle mockery throughout of working-class ambitions to learn '"manners" and be fine like their heroes and heroines'. Oliphant uses these columns to make working-class readers appear strange by asking her own audience to imagine how ridiculous it would be for them to write into a monthly magazine, such as her own 'Maga', for advice. Like Collins, Oliphant moves swiftly on to the fiction contained in these texts in order to reassure her readers that even the 'rather villainous' looking *Reynolds's Miscellany* contained nothing offensive.[76] By contrast, Gerrard's research into the contents of the 'Answers to Correspondents' columns of *The Family Herald* uncovers an audience struggling to acquire cultural capital and eager to learn about canonical texts. In 1860, for example 'roughly one in eight' of the answers refer to texts other than the *Family Herald* itself. Readers of this newspaper, like Collins's reader 'not certain that Mazeppa was written by Lord Byron', were clearly looking to improve their reading.[77] Gerrard is right to suggest that these columns put us in touch with a rarely documented aspect of working-class reading, but her conclusion that many working-class readers wanted to know more about the canon seems to support Rose's idea that 'the classics were an unambiguously emancipating force for working-class readers'.[78] However, I'm not sure that those who wrote in and had their letters processed by an editor can represent all of the readers of these journals, the entire 'unknown public', or that we can gauge the 'average intelligence' of the audience by assessing their contents, as Collins suggests, or as Gerrard seems to imply.

Even in Collins's construction of the 'real reader' there are moments of slippage in which he suggests that those who wrote in represented only a 'portion' of the 'unknown public' (p. 259). Indeed, Collins's own arch, facetious and mocking tone suggests another reading practice that could be brought to bear on these columns. He may claim that 'nothing is exaggerated for the sake of a joke', but his account is designed to engage his own audience who he imagines as reading for both information and amusement. For example, he mocks the way in which an answer, given 'it is to be hoped, by a straight-legged editor', recommends that two knock-kneed readers peruse an earlier issue in which a similar enquiry had already been answered (p. 257). Collins is clearly laughing at working-class ignorance here, but I think it is also possible that some sections of the 'mass' readership of the penny press read these columns in exactly this way. For example, the editor of the *London Journal's* reply to a reader known as W. T. B, 'You quarrel with your sweetheart; and instead of going to her, you came to us to make up!' was clearly designed as much to amuse as to advise. Such instances may, as Warren argues, create an editorial voice that appears 'naturally superior' to that of the correspondent, but the reader of the column shares in the editor's power over his or her fellow reader at these moments.[79] As Andrew King has argued, despite the dismissive comments of Oliphant and others, the serialised fiction that appeared in the penny press demanded quite sophisticated reading strategies. Many of the readers who made sense of these texts may well have been adept at searching out these nuggets of amusement amongst the 'Answers'.[80] Even Oliphant's account of these columns gives room to those who 'enjoy' the 'answers' as 'a peep into somebody's secrets'.[81]

Recent work on the Victorian periodical press as a series of structured reading communities tends to suggest that the 'answers' columns reveal the implied, or ideal reader constructed by the editorial practices of a given title rather than the real reader.[82] In the case of *The London Journal* the 'notices to correspondents' suggests something of the broad audience to which it was intended to appeal. In November 1851, for example, answers to men, women and children were printed side by side with extracts from letters that show-off the correspondent's education by challenging the contents of articles from earlier issues. Notes from autodidacts asking about French lessons, or the standard of their handwriting rub shoulders with appeals from women, such as 'Agnes and Bessie' who were 'anxious to change their present legal appellations for the more honoured ones of wives'.[83] And even if the editor's comments do tend to produce a hierarchical relationship between reader and text – the editor always knows best – there is at least room for some readers to share in the jokes aimed at correspondents, such as W. T. B, who were prepared to discuss their love lives in public. Like *Household Words*, the penny press had a dual purpose – to instruct and amuse, and we mustn't lose sight of the 'conscripted' reader who turned to these columns, like Collins, for the pleasure of reading the editor's terse replies. As Warren has argued, 'answers' columns and letters pages (the latter a rarity before the 1890s) show that some readers wanted to take an active part in the construction of the magazine or newspaper. They use it as a space to try out a textual identity that is in part shaped by the discursive limits of the space allowed to the reader.[84] By examining these spaces in the penny press, as Gerrard has done, it is possible to recover something of the experience of those readers uncertain about Byron, or confident enough to challenge the editor. Such evidence tends to confirm the picture of the culture of 'self-improvement' revealed by working-class autobiographies – even the reader ignorant of what a poem is wants to improve – but those readers for pleasure whose presence is implied by the editor's sarcastic or witty comments left little trace either on the pages of the magazines that they read (by writing in) or by writing their own accounts of reading. Such real readers, if they existed at all, remain stubbornly 'unknown' and unknowable. The majority of readers never wrote in at all, and the responses that we do have don't suggest how readers made sense of any part of the journal, other than the correspondents' page itself.

In a recent overview of work on the Victorian reader, Leah Price argued that historians of reading are now beginning to pay attention to those forms of reading that left little trace. The 'sheer bulk of many Victorian genres', she argues, required 'their consumers to skip and to skim, to tune in and zone out'. Although these practices are more diffi-cult to theorise than 'readerly engagement', in part because they leave none of the traces (marginalia, underlining etc.) with which historians usually deal, Price notes that some recent investigations of the reader have been able to spot these moments of *disengagement*, and to look at forms of reading that don't leave any mark on the page.[85] Garret Stewart's reading of George Dunlop Leslie's painting *Alice in Wonderland*, for example, deals with the way in which the intoxication of a reader lis-tening to a text leaves little trace even on the body. He describes the lis-tening girl's 'blank, unseeing' stare as 'scarcely disengaged' and he goes on to argue that painting, by its very nature, cannot represent the 'somatic rhythms of reading'.[86] Given this concern with the untrace-able, I now want to examine two new print spaces that began to flourish in the 1840s and 1850s, the railway bookstall and the advertising hoard-ing, which might be thought to exemplify disengaged forms of reading that left no trace either on the body or the page.

Reading at the railway bookstall

The image of readers at a railway bookstall reproduced as Figure 6.1 appeared under the title 'Street Sketches' in *The Leisure Hour* in March 1870. Founded in 1852, *The Leisure Hour* was a penny magazine published by the Religious Tract Society as a respectable alternative to *Reynolds's Miscellany* and the other penny weeklies founded during the 1840s. Hilary Fraser, Stephanie Green and Judith Johnston have noted that this image 'reveals something of the anxieties that surrounded the idea of the female reader, as well as suggesting the role assumed by the periodical press in protecting, directing, circumscribing and policing women's reading'.[87] The quotation under the heading 'reading of the period' is taken from a review in *The Times* of the novel *Annals of An Eventful Life*, which was praised because it did not contain 'that crew of demireps, forgers, bigamists, pretty murderesses, and the ladies of equivocal reputation whom the British Paterfamilias admits into his drawing-room, provided they are wrapped up in the pages of fiction'. The full review praised the novel as the excellent production of a 'male pen' whilst castigating women writers for producing novels that were either too 'sanctimonious' or too 'sensa-tional'.[88] The sketch builds on this review to construct an image of read-ing that is rigidly gendered. The two young women in the foreground are looking at an advertisement that displays the illustrated covers of 'novels of the period', with titles such as 'Suicide', 'Bigamy', 'Incest' and 'Murder',

STREET SKETCHES.

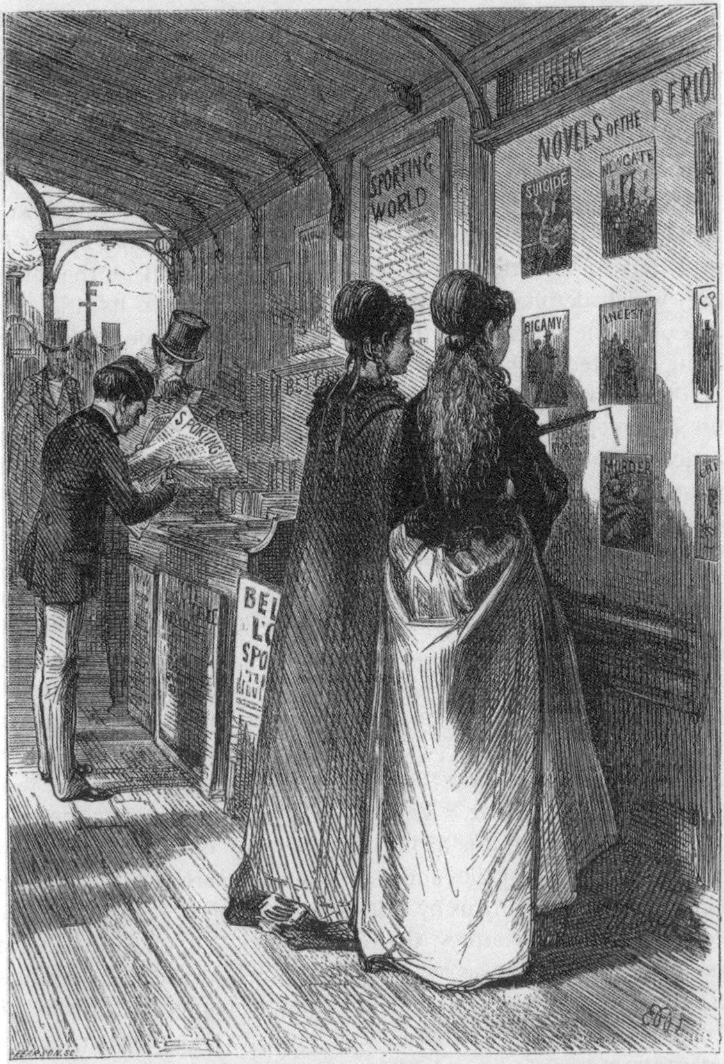

READING OF THE PERIOD.

"That crew of demireps, forgers, bigamists, pretty murderesses, and the ladies of equivocal reputation whom the British Paterfamilias admits so complacently into his drawing-room, provided they are wrapped up in the pages of fiction."—*Times*.

Figure 6.1 'Street Sketches' from *The Leisure Hour*, 19 (1870), p. 201

while in the background two men (the elder of which is presumably the father of the two young women) read through the *Sporting World*. To the left of the women is an advertisement for the newspaper *Bell's Life in London*, which as Richard Altick has noted was the favourite reading of 'male and female devotees of the fast life', such as the heroine of Elizabeth Braddon's *Aurora Floyd* (1863).[89]

This image is about the irresponsibility of the 'British Paterfamilias' who allows his children to be enticed by the vivid advertising next to the stall while he checks the latest racing results. It was followed in *The Leisure Hour* by an article 'On the Education of the Girls of the Middle Class', which despite the focus on women's reading in its title, is an attack upon the education system that allowed the gendered pattern of reading depicted in the sketch to emerge.[90] Image and article reinforce each other. Both foreground women's reading in order to suggest that there is something fundamentally wrong with contemporary reading practices. The article doesn't target yellowback fiction or the railway bookstall, but their presence in the image belies a particular anxiety about the stall as a site of undisciplined reading that can be traced back to the moment when the stalls first became particularly visible as a cultural phenomenon in the late 1840s. By 1848 there were already at least 21 stalls on the London and North Western Railway (LNWR) between London and Manchester and by the early 1860s W. H. Smith and Son owned nearly 200 in England and Wales.[91] As early as 1849 *The Dublin University Magazine* was drawing its readers' attention to the 'itinerant vendors' of the LNWR who pushed 'certain curious little volumes with embellished covers' into the 'face of the traveller' as he or she sat waiting for the train to depart.[92] By 1851 *The Times* was decrying the influence of the stalls upon the 'mental development' of the nation. Having witnessed 'two young ladies and a boy' in a first-class carriage 'amusing themselves and alarming us by a devotion to a trashy French novel' for an entire three-hour journey, the reporter took it upon himself to see whether similar 'trash' was available at all the bookstalls. An extended version of this report published in sixpenny pamphlet form as *The Literature of the Rail* noted that Eugene Sue's novels and other items of 'literary trash' were to be found at every station in London except that run by Smith and Son at Euston Square.[93] 'Cheap' literature was associated with obscenity throughout the 1850s (the decade in which the Obscene Publications Act became law) and despite Smith's reputation for ridding trash from the rails the association of railway bookstalls with immorality continued into the 1860s and 1870s.[94] In 1863 the *Quarterly Review* thought that 'keepers of bookstalls as well as of refreshment-rooms, find an advantage in offering their customers something hot and strong, something that may catch the eye of the hurried passenger, and promise temporary excitement to relieve the dullness of a journey'. This essay blames 'periodicals, circulating libraries and railway bookstalls' for the rise of the 'Sensation Novel'.[95] In the same year the *Christian Remembrancer* advised 'husbands and fathers' to protect their 'young ladies' against Sensation fiction in the guise of 'the popular romance' by scrutinising 'the parcel that arrives from Mudies'.[96] The independent-minded and passionate heroine of these novels is often figured as a threat to domestic harmony in such essays. The image from *The Leisure Hour* plays on these fears of the bookstall and circulating library as a source of 'sensation' by emphasising the dangers of unsupervised female reading. From 1860 Smith's stalls included a circulating library and sold cheap copies of 'books of the season' that had been withdrawn from its stock, but it is significant that this image focuses on the power of advertising to lead women into temptation rather than the book itself.

Of course, books were publicly displayed in the street long before the introduction of stalls to the railways in the 1840s. Cruikshank's famous illustration for *Oliver Twist* (1838) of a customer so absorbed in his reading that he doesn't notice his pocket being picked shows a bookshop that opens onto the street, but there was something fundamentally different about the railway bookstall; it was there to be browsed, to occupy the time spent waiting for a connection or a late running train, to sell texts that were designed to be ephemeral, that were to last the journey.[97] Its advertisements and the cries of the newsboys patrolling the platform were intended to encourage impulse buying. By the 1850s the novels that it stocked were excitingly packaged, cheap and small and complete in one volume. Surviving inventories of stock show that the bookstall was a cornucopia of printed artefacts, including books, newspapers, magazines, pamphlets, engravings, 'chromotypes and coloured photographs'. Respectably expensive newspapers, like *The Times*, were sold alongside 'penny-novel journals' such as *The London Journal* and *The Family Herald*.[98] Later photographs celebrate the stall, the staff and the stock, but ignore the customer. The image from *The Leisure Hour* is valuable because it gives at least some sense of the way in which readers acted at the stall – of reading standing up, awkwardly hunched, of browsing the headlines, perhaps without any intention to purchase. I want to suggest that although such readers did engage with individual texts at the stall – as the man reading the newspaper in this image is doing – each potential customer had first to read the stall in its entirety, to make sense of the range of texts on offer, to encourage or avoid the attentions of the bookstall clerk. Despite the discursive power of such sites, reading at the railway bookstall has left little trace in the sources (such as diaries and autobiographies) usually used to construct the history of reading.

The two young women in this image are, of course, not actually reading sensation novels but looking at an advertisement for 'novels of the period' made up of lurid looking covers. Reading advertisements was an important part of the bookstall experience. W. H. Smith and Son entered into advertising contracts with the LNWR and the Midland railway companies in 1851. Photographs taken in the 1860s and 1870s suggest that advertising was the most visible aspect of contemporary print culture on the platform. And, unlike the bookstall itself, it could not be avoided.[99]

The 'Language of the Walls'

Spectacular advertising of the sort depicted in the frontispiece to Henry Sampson's *A History of Advertising* (1875) was probably only found at the major London railway stations, but from the early 1850s onwards the railway platform provided advertisers with a unique opportunity to engage with a captive audience.[100] Smith's contracts give some sense of the kinds of material that surrounded railway travellers as they waited for the train or browsed the bookstall. The agreement with the Midland drawn up in July 1851 is typical. It allowed Smith's to exhibit 'advertisements, announcements, handbills and placards' upon 'the fences or partitions adjoining the stations', the walls of the station itself, and in the waiting rooms and booking offices. Each advert had to be mounted in a proper frame so that it was clearly displayed and the stationmaster could remove anything 'immoral, libellous, seditious or offensive'. Those for competing railway companies, 'workmen in combination against their employers' and 'relating to medicines for complaints or ailments of an indecent or indelicate nature' were banned.[101] This was a disciplined space for advertising to a bourgeois, consumer audience who did not want to be reminded about indelicate subjects or striking workmen. The careful display of each advert in its own frame made this a quite different place to read than the street, which as many contemporaries noticed showed the fiercely competitive nature of capitalism, with one poster quickly replaced or pasted over with another.

In a brilliant examination of the 'ubiquitous nature' of street advertising that appeared in *Household Words* in March 1851, Dickens describes how if he had an enemy he would take revenge on him by posting bills around London that would 'darkly refer' to something that 'sat heavy on his conscience'.

> Thus, if my enemy passed an uninhabited house, he would see his conscience glaring down on him from the parapets, and peeping up at him from the cellars. If he took a dead wall in his walk, it would be alive with reproaches. If he sought refuge in an omnibus, the panels thereof would become Belshazzar's palace to him. If he took a boat, in a wild endeavour to escape, he would see the fatal words lurking under the arches of the bridges over the Thames.

As this essay makes clear there was no escape from advertising in the modern urban landscape. To look down was to see the pavement 'made eloquent by lamp-black lithograph' and even the streets were filled with advertising vans, 'each proclaiming the same words over and over again'.[102] London was, of course, a particularly modern place, but photographic records suggest that most Victorian towns and cities included uninhabited buildings wrapped in layer-upon-layer of posters.[103] Advertising was everywhere. Dickens describes his 'intimate' knowledge of the decaying posters covering an old warehouse in some detail and notes how the names of companies and slogans, such as 'Better to be bald as a Dutch-cheese than come to this', had become part of his internal mental universe through repeated exposure.[104]

The anonymous author of *The Language of the Walls*, published some four years later, describes a similar inability to zone out and ignore these signs of the modern capitalist world. She/he is fascinated by the kinds of material excluded from the railway station, including posters for pills which help 'the unfortunate victims of self-debasement' and appeals to help men striking for the protection of 'what they conceive their rights'. And, as in 'Bill-sticking', she/he notes that the undisciplined nature of street advertising often leads to strange and amusing conjunctions, as when a poster for a performance of the 'Ups and Downs of the Life of a Showman' partially covers an announcement that a 'Noble Lord' is to 'preside at a Grand Protection Meeting'. The narrator explains how other posters conjure up narratives. Advertisements for auctions disposing of a family's furniture create a haunting image of domestic bliss rent asunder by tragic events.[105] As with Dickens's re-imagining of the poster as a form of 'terrible revenge', this is an artful and amusing account of a particularly modern experience: the repeated, involuntary consumption of a text. As the unexpected conversion of an auction poster into a narrative of wrecked domestic peace suggests, however, the relationship between reader and text in the case of the advertising hoarding is not as transparent as one might imagine. It is difficult to theorise this relationship because the known and the unknown public, the literate and the illiterate shared many of these new print spaces, including the railway bookstall. Dickens noted that even some billstickers could not read.[106] Both 'Bill-Sticking' and *The Language of the Walls* suggest that at least some members of the literate audience treated street advertising as a text to be manipulated playfully, but these essays also prefigure Modernism's distaste for the ubiquitous advertising jingle, the all pervasive text that lodges itself in the brain.[107] Dickens's reader haunted by advertising slogans suggests that some found it difficult to disengage from reading adverts, but he was also intrigued by how the illiterate reacted to such texts. In *Bleak House* (1852–1853), for example, he wants to know what it must be like to be Jo the illiterate crossing sweeper surrounded by 'those mysterious symbols, so abundant over the shops, and at the corners of streets, and on the doors, and in the windows!'.[108] Dickens suggests that watching others read these signs increases Jo's sense of isolation, but reconstructing the actual responses of the illiterate to the 'ubiquitous nature' of advertising is a difficult task.

The author of *The Language of the Walls* sees advertising as a reflection of all that is most negative in the modern world, but those few working-class memoirists who mention advertising tend to do so in a positive manner. Charles Manby Smith, also writing in the 1850s, argued that 'it is an awful blunder to suppose that those only profit by the display in shop-windows who are in a position to purchase. … To the moneyless million, the shops of London are what the university is to the collegian: they teach them all knowledge'.[109] John Clare recalled that he 'greedily lookd over' the advertisements for books that wrapped his purchases of pencils and paper in the days when he could not afford the books themselves.[110] Jonathan Rose uses several other positive accounts of reading adverts, including that by 'one of the most priggish proletarian evangelists of "useful knowledge"', Thomas Carter, in order to argue that working-class readers were particularly adept at appropriating texts that were designed for a completely different audience. Manby Smith's description of 'the mechanic and artisan, out of work and out of money' reading the shop-windows of London in order 'to dissipate the weary hours of enforced idleness' is certainly a form of appropriation, but as with Clare's celebration of reading what was available to him, we need to be cautious about celebrating a reading practice that was developed to cope with cultural deprivation. Carter may well have been able to 'develop his defences against all kinds of propaganda' by learning to decode the language of advertising, as Rose argues, but he is right to be cautious about suggesting that others read in this fashion.[111]

This book has been predicated on the idea that individual readers are free to make meaning within certain parameters. The various literary and autobiographical accounts of advertising that I have been dealing with in this section show that even those texts designed to sell products or publicise events could be read in a variety of different ways, from Clare's straightforward delight in finding out about a world of print, through to the troubled construction of a narrative of threatened domesticity produced by the author of *The Language of the Walls*. Most of these accounts work by converting these products of a consumer society into the form of a traditional text that could be read as a narrative, but Dickens's consideration of the illiterate crossing sweeper's experience of advertising and the way in which slogans from posters seeped into his own subconscious, suggest other, less artful, reading practices. In order to understand what reading meant in the mid-nineteenth century, therefore, we will need to reconstruct those print spaces that were traversed by members of the public with a vast range of different reading competencies. Historians of reading who want to know how the Victorians interpreted the new cities that they were building will need to reconstruct the print spaces that were such an important part of their everyday lives.

Conclusion: Texts Consumed

This study has examined a range of sources, from manuscript books to autobiographies, which describe the complex responses of individual readers. The journals of Gertrude Savile (1697–1758) capture both her confident recitation of some of the most popular dramatic works of the 1720s and her uncertain reaction to the new 'amatory' fiction of the same period. They show that she engaged in various modes of reading, from listening to her servants through to the silent perusal of texts in her own closet. Her commonplace book is equally revealing, however, suggesting that she must often have read with its 27 categories very much in mind. This suggests that in order to understand how readers made sense of texts we need to discover as much evidence about them as possible by gathering together a variety of sources. The diaries of John Dawson (1692–1765), for example, reveal little about his reading, but the chance survival of his library shows someone who customised his books in order to put them to work. If anything unites the readers of the period 1695–1770 looked at in this study, it is that they often read with the pen in hand.

Savile's contemporary, Dudley Ryder (1691–1756) also seems to have been uncertain about what strategies to apply to the interpretation of fiction, but this is a rare moment of coincidence. This study suggests that more often different readers put the *same* texts to quite different uses. For example John Clare (1793–1864) used old canon reprints in a way quite different to Anne Lister (1791–1840). For the working-class Clare, being able to get hold of the work of out of copyright authors such as James Thomson and Oliver Goldsmith was a radically accultur-ating experience that eventually led to his becoming a published author. Lister had access to a far greater range of books, including contemporary work by Byron, but she sometimes engaged in playful and subversive readings of the old canon as part of her questioning of heterosexual norms. Diaries from the Romantic period also show that different readers could use the same institutions of reading in quite different ways. Those who 'did not want to read' attended the new commercial libraries that were springing up in the late eighteenth century because they were fashionable places to be seen, whereas other readers used them as a vital source of books for study.

Much of the evidence examined in this study is intensely personal, but the sense of self constructed in reading diaries and autobiographies is often produced by describing the perceived difference between the creator and the other members of his or her reading community. Clare, for example, often contrasts his well-developed reading and writing skills with those of his 'illiterate' parents and neighbours. Despite his frequent references to the 'unlettrd', his autobiographical writings provide a convincing picture of a rural community that included a range of different literacies. Complex accounts of reading, such as those constructed by Ryder and Clare, allow the reconstruction of what Radway calls the 'event' of reading.[1] Amongst Ryder's friends, conversation frequently 'turned' on books and his reading was often the prelude to a social event. He read *for* the coffee house as well as *in* the coffee house. Members of his social circle had to be readers in order to join, but he and his friends also frequently talked about texts that only some of them had actually read. The diaries of Joseph Hunter (1783–1861) also give a sense of what reading meant to a small group of readers at a particular moment. It was only when the subscription library to which he belonged began to remove the texts associated with political radicalism from its shelves that he began to conceive of himself as a 'jacobinical' reader. His description of the development of a new book club that continued to take radical texts despite the widespread attack on Jacobinism led by the *Anti-Jacobin Review*, suggests that it is possible to discover how communities of readers reacted to, and were formed by, specific circumstances.

The records of book clubs and reading societies from throughout the period 1770–1840 demonstrate that although the text itself was often consumed privately, reading maintained a public dimension. Texts borrowed from these sorts of institutions were often discussed (using the monthly Reviews) before they were ordered, or at a formal meeting once they had been in circulation. If anything unites the readers of the period 1770–1840, it is that they were more often library-goers than library owners, but the difference between the resort libraries visited by Charlotte Francis (1786–1870) and the radical book club used by Hunter, demonstrates something of the range of different reading communities that existed in the late 1790s.

Much of the evidence that we have for these communities comes from those readers who transcribed sections of the books that they borrowed into commonplace books and albums. While this study has insisted upon the freedom of individual readers to make meaning, it has also suggested that it is possible to discern something of the general culture of reading in which they operated. As Heather Jackson insists Romantic readers often engaged in the same sorts of annotation practices, which included the making of extracts.[2] This study shows that the middle-class readers of the 1820s and 1830s often created albums and other manuscript books into which favourite poems and other short texts were copied. Such books show that reading was used to cement bonds of friendship and strengthen familial ties in much the same way as reading aloud. Taken together these practices suggest something of the sociable nature of reading in the early part of the nineteenth century. Of course, not everyone read in this way, but the survival of so many albums suggests that this *type* of reader was a familiar figure in the bourgeois world of this period. There were many M. A. B's with their grey goose quills and their albums.

The manuscript book constructed by the Carey-Maingay group in the 1830s is quite different to that compiled by Charles Caesar some 125 years earlier. That transcription practices should have changed in the intervening period is, of course, not surprising, although the movement from the book constructed by an individual to the collective compilation goes against the traditional narrative of progression from communal to solitary reading over the course of the long eighteenth century. As the evidence presented in this study suggests the experience of reading before and after 1750 was not monolithic, and I have not attempted to replace the traditional notion of a transition from intensive to extensive practices with a new grand narrative. My concern throughout has been with the way in which individuals made meaning as part of small reading communities rather than national readerships, but readers such as Gertrude Savile in her purchase of duodecimos often reflect the national trends detected by book historians. I hope that these case studies have demonstrated that it is possible to recover and explore 'the often conflicting, contradictory ways in which general social changes and individual experience interact'.[3] There is, however, still a need to multiply these case studies. I am conscious of the many different communities of reading ignored by this study. I have made no mention, for example, of immigrant reading communities, or those readers who spoke little, or no, English.

Working-class readers of Welsh and Gaelic were often surveyed in much the same way as the English peasantry.[4] There is I am sure a wealth of material still to be unearthed in local record offices and research libraries that will deepen our understanding of what reading meant to these and other communities.

Notes

Introduction: Consuming Texts

1. Voltaire, *Candide and Other Stories*, trans. by Roger Pearson (Oxford: Oxford University Press, 1990), p. 80.
2. Lucien Dallenbach, *The Mirror in the Text*, trans. by Jeremy Whitley and Emma Hughes (Cambridge: Cambridge University Press, 1989).
3. Jacqueline Pearson, *Women's Reading in Britain 1750–1835: A Dangerous Recreation* (Cambridge: Cambridge University Press, 1999), pp. 1–21 (p. 10).
4. Leah Price, 'Reading Matter', *PMLA*, 121, 1 (January 2006), 9–16 (11).
5. William Coe, 'The Diary of William Coe, 1693–1729', in *Two East-Anglian Diaries 1641–1729*, ed. by Matthew Storey (Woodbridge: Boydell Press, 1994), p. 250.
6. Jonathan Rose, 'Rereading the English Common Reader: A Preface to a History of Audiences', *Journal of the History of Ideas*, 53 (1992), 47–70, reprinted in *The Book History Reader*, ed. by David Finkelstein and Alistair McCleery (London: Routledge, 2002), pp. 324–339 (p. 325); Margaret Beetham, 'In Search of the Historical Reader', *Siegener Periodicum zur Internationalen Empirischen Literaturwissenschaft* [*SPIEL*], 19 (2000), 89–104 (92–95).

1 Reading Has a History

1. Robert Darnton, 'First Steps Toward a History of Reading', *Australian Journal of French Studies*, 23 (1986), 5–30, reprinted in *The Kiss of Lamourette: Reflections in Cultural History* (London: Faber & Faber, 1990), pp. 154–187 (p. 155).
2. Richard D. Altick, *The English Common Reader: A Social History of the Mass Reading Public 1800–1900* (Chicago: University of Chicago Press, 1957), pp. 379–380.
3. William St Clair, *The Reading Nation in the Romantic Period* (Cambridge: Cambridge University Press, 2004), p. 9.
4. Altick, *Common Reader*, p. 347.
5. Altick, *Common Reader*, p. 259; Jonathan Rose, 'How Historians Study Reader Response: Or, What Did Jo Think of *Bleak House*?', in *Literature in the Marketplace*, ed. by John O. Jordan and Robert Patten (Cambridge: Cambridge University Press, 1995), pp. 195–212 (p. 195); Altick's findings are confirmed by Jonathan Rose, *The Intellectual Life of the British Working Classes* (New Haven: Yale University Press, 2001) and St Clair, *Reading Nation*.
6. R. K. Webb, *The British Working Class Reader 1790–1848* (London: Allen & Unwin, 1955); Richard Hoggart, *The Uses of Literacy* (London: Chatto & Windus, 1957).
7. Q. D. Leavis, *Fiction and the Reading Public* (London: Chatto & Windus, 1932); Raymond Williams, *Culture and Society, 1780–1950* (London: Chatto & Windus, 1958), p. 310.

8. Richard Hoggart, *A Sort of Clowning* (London: Oxford University Press, 1991), quoted in Rose, *Intellectual Life*, p. 366.

9. Roger Chartier, 'Texts, Printing, Readings', in *The New Cultural History*, ed. by Lynn Hunt (Berkeley: University of California Press, 1989), pp. 154–175 (p. 172).

10. James Raven, Helen Small and Naomi Tadmor, 'Introduction: The Practice and Representation of Reading in England', in *The Practice and Representation of Reading in England*, ed. by J. Raven et al. (Cambridge: Cambridge University Press, 1996), p. 4.

11. David McKitterick, 'Book Catalogues: Their Varieties and Uses', in *The Book Encompassed: Studies in Twentieth-Century Bibliography* ed. by Peter Davison (Cambridge: Cambridge University Press, 1992), pp. 161–175 (p. 162).

12. *Under the Hammer: Book Auctions since the Seventeenth Century*, ed. by Robin Myers et al. (New Castle: Oak Knoll, 2001).

13. Jason Scott-Warren, 'News, Sociability, and Bookbuying in Early Modern England: The Letters of Sir Thomas Cornwallis', *The Library*, n.s. 1, 4 (2000), 381–402; David McKitterick, 'Women and Their Books in Seventeenth-Century England: The Case of Elizabeth Puckering', *The Library*, n.s. 1, 4 (2000), 359–380; *A Radical's Books: The Library Catalogue of Samuel Jeake of Rye, 1623–1690*, ed. by Michael Hunter et al. (Woodbridge: D. S. Brewer, 1999).

14. St Clair, *Reading Nation*, pp. 103–210 (p. 196).

15. St Clair, *Reading Nation*, p. 118.

16. St Clair, *Reading Nation*, p. 133, p. 138.

17. Simon Eliot, 'The Reading Experience Database; or, What Are We to Do About the History of Reading', *The Reading Experience Database* <http://www.open.ac.uk/Arts/RED/redback.htm>

18. William Sherman, *John Dee and the Politics of Reading and Writing in the English Renaissance* (Amsherst: University of Massachusetts Press, 1995), p. 55.

19. Elizabeth Freund, *The Return of the Reader: Reader Response Criticism* (London: Methuen, 1987), p. 7.

20. Sherman, *John Dee*, p. 59.

21. Robert Darnton, 'First Steps Toward a History of Reading', *Australian Journal of French Studies*, 23 (1986), 5–30. Reprinted in *The Kiss of Lamourette: Reflections in Cultural History* (London: Faber & Faber, 1990), pp. 179–182 (181).

22. Roger Chartier, *The Order of Books: Readers, Authors and Libraries in Europe Between the Fourteenth and the Eighteenth Centuries*, trans. by Lydia Cochrane (Cambridge: Polity Press, 1994); Kevin Sharpe, *Reading Revolutions: The Politics of Reading In Early Modern England* (London: Yale University Press, 2000); Sherman, *John Dee*, p. 59; St Clair, *Reading Nation*, pp. 4–5.

23. Roland Barthes, 'The Death of the Author', in *Image, Music, Text*, trans. by Stephen Heath (London: Fontana, 1977), pp. 142–148, reprinted in *The Norton Anthology of Theory and Criticism*, ed. by William E. Cain et al. (New York: W. W. Norton, 2001), pp. 1466–1470 (p. 1470).

24. Roland Barthes, 'From Work to Text', in *Image, Music, Text*, pp. 155–164, reprinted in *Norton Anthology*, pp. 1470–1475.

25. Andrew Bennett, 'Introduction', in *Readers and Reading*, ed. by Andrew Bennett (London: Longman, 1995), pp. 1–19 (p. 4).

26. Wolfgang Iser, *The Act of Reading: A Theory of Aesthetic Response* (Baltimore: Johns Hopkins University Press, 1978).
27. Terry Eagleton, *Literary Theory* (London: Blackwell, 1983), p. 79.
28. *The Book History Reader*, ed. by David Finkelstein and Alistair McCleery (London: Routledge, 2002), p. 289; Vincent B. Leitch, 'Reader Response Criticism', in *Readers and Reading*, pp. 32–65 (p. 53).
29. H. R. Jauss, 'Literary History as a Challenge to Literary Theory', in *Toward An Aesthetic of Reception*, trans. by Timothy Bahti (Minneapolis: University of Minnesota Press, 1982), reprinted in *Norton Anthology*, pp. 1550–1564 (p. 1551, p. 1555, p. 1556, p. 1562).
30. Kate Flint, *The Woman Reader, 1837–1914* (Oxford: Clarendon Press, 1993), p. 42.
31. Heidi Brayman Hackel, *Reading Material in Early Modern England: Print, Gender, and Literacy* (Cambridge: Cambridge University Press, 2005), p. 7.
32. Bennett 'Introduction', pp. 2–4 (p. 4).
33. Bennett 'Introduction', p. 9. Work by all of these theorists is included in Bennett, *Readers and Reading*.
34. Sherman singles out Blanchot's insistence on the 'essential solitude' of reading for particular criticism, *John Dee*, p. 56.
35. Derek Alsop and Chris Walsh, *The Practice of Reading: Interpreting the Novel* (Houndmills: Macmillan Press, 1999), p. 23.
36. Michel de Certeau, *The Practice of Everyday Life*, trans. by Steven Randall (Berkeley: University of California Press, 1984), pp. 165–176, reprinted as 'Reading as Poaching' in *Readers and Reading*, pp. 150–163 (p. 156, p. 157).
37. Alsop and Walsh, *The Practice of Reading*, p. 94.
38. Certeau, 'Reading as Poaching', p. 159.
39. Certeau, 'Reading as Poaching', pp. 157–158.
40. David Vincent, *The Rise of Mass Literacy: Reading and Writing in Modern Europe* (Cambridge: Polity Press, 2000), p. 144, pp. 146–147.
41. Chartier, *Order of Books*, p. 23, p. 5.
42. Stanley Fish, 'Interpreting the *Variorum*', *Critical Inquiry*, 2 (1976), 465–485, reprinted in *Norton Anthology of Theory*, pp. 2071–2089 (p. 2085).
43. Fish, 'Interpreting the *Variorum*', p. 2084, p. 2085, p. 2088.
44. Fish, 'Interpreting the *Variorum*', p. 2088.
45. Fish, 'Interpreting the *Variorum*', p. 2089, p. 2078.
46. Chartier, *Order of Books*, p. 3.
47. Jerome McGann, 'The Text, the Poem and the Problem of Historical Method', *New Literary History*, 12, 2 (1981), 269–288, reprinted in *Modern Literary Theory: A Reader*, ed. by Philip Rise and Patricia Waugh, 2nd edition (London: Edward Arnold, 1989), pp. 289–306 (p. 294, p. 293).
48. Jerome McGann, *The Textual Condition* (Princeton: Princeton University Press, 1991).
49. Janine Barchas, *Graphic Design: Print Culture and the Eighteenth-Century Novel* (Cambridge: Cambridge University Press, 2003), pp. 1–18 (p. 8, p. 18).
50. Barbara Benedict, *Making the Modern Reader: Cultural Mediation in Early Modern Literary Anthologies* (Princeton: Princeton University Press, 1996).
51. D. F. McKenzie, 'Typography and Meaning: The Case of William Congreve', in *Buch und Buchhandel in Europa im achtzehnten Jahrundert*, ed. by Giles Barber and Bernhard Fabian (Hamburg: Hauswedell, 1981), pp. 81–126,

reprinted in D. F. Mckenzie, *Making Meaning: 'Printers of the Mind' and Other Essays*, ed. by P. D. McDonald and M. F. Suarez (Amherst: University of Massachusetts Press, 2002), pp. 198–237 (p. 212, p. 233).

52. D. F. McKenzie, *Bibliography and the Sociology of Texts*, 2nd edition (Cambridge: Cambridge University Press, 1999), p. 25.

53. William Wimsatt and Monroe Beardsley, 'The Intentional Fallacy', reprinted in *Norton Anthology*, pp. 1374–1387.

54. McKenzie, *Bibliography*, pp. 18–25 (p. 25).

55. McKenzie, *Bibliography*, p. 20, p. 19.

56. Chartier, *Order of Books*, p. 11, p. 13.

57. Chartier, *Order of Books*, p. 21; Roger Chartier, *The Cultural Uses of Print in Early Modern France* (Princeton: Princeton University Press, 1987), p. 7.

58. Rose, *The Intellectual Life*, p. 92; Chartier, *Cultural Uses of Print*, pp. 334–335.

59. Janice Radway, *Reading the Romance: Women, Patriarchy, and Popular Literature* (London: Verso, 1987), p. 7, p. 86.

60. Radway, *Reading the Romance*, p. 8.

61. Harold Love, *Scribal Publication in Seventeenth-Century England* (Oxford: Clarendon Press, 1993).

62. Sharpe, *Reading Revolutions*, p. 60, p. 307.

63. Sharpe, *Reading Revolutions*, p. 44, p. 61.

64. Sharpe, *Reading Revolutions*, p. 61; Carlo Ginzburg, *The Cheese and the Worms: The Cosmos of a Sixteenth-Century Miller* (Baltimore: Johns Hopkins University Press, 1992).

65. Darnton 'First Steps', p. 155; Robert Darnton, *The Great Cat Massacre* (London: Allen Lane, 1984), p. 216.

66. Lisa Jardine and Anthony Grafton, '"Studied for Action": How Gabriel Harvey Read his Livy', *Past and Present*, 129 (1990), 30–78 (48).

67. Jardine and Grafton, 'Studied', p. 31, p.51.

68. Sharpe, *Reading Revolutions*, p. 295.

69. Anthony Grafton, 'Is the History of Reading a Marginal Enterprise?: Guillaume Bude and His Books', *Papers of the Bibliographical Society of America*, 91 (1997), 139–157 (156).

70. Earle Havens, *Commonplace Books: A History of Manuscripts and Printed Books from Antiquity to the Twentieth Century* (Yale: University Press of New England, 2001), p. 40.

71. Kevin Sharpe, 'Uncommonplaces? Sir William Drake's Reading Notes', in *The Reader Revealed*, ed. by Sabrina Alcorn Baron et al. (Washington: Folger Library, 2001), pp. 58–65 (p. 60); Sharpe, *Reading Revolutions*, p. 282.

72. Steven N. Zwicker, 'The Constitution of Opinion and the Pacification of Reading', in *Reading, Society and Politics in Early Modern England*, ed. by Kevin Sharpe and Steven Zwicker (Cambridge: Cambridge University Press, 2003), pp. 295–316 (p. 299, p. 297).

73. Hackel, *Reading Material*, p. 3.

74. Darnton, *Cat Massacre*, p. 217.

75. Darnton, *Cat Massacre*, p. 219, p. 222, p. 223.

76. Darnton, *Cat Massacre*, p. 249.

77. Darnton, *Cat Massacre*, p. 251, p. 252.

78. Robert Darnton, 'Extraordinary Commonplaces', *New York Review of Books*, 21 December 2000, 82–87 (87).

79. Rolf Engelsing, *Der Burger als Leser: Lesergeschichte in Deutschland 1500–1800* (Stuttgart: Metzler, 1974); David Hall, 'The Uses of literacy in New England, 1600–1850', in *Cultures of Print: Essays in the History of the Book*, ed. by David D. Hall (Amherst: University of Massachusetts Press, 1996), pp. 36–76.
80. Darnton 'First Steps', p. 156.
81. John Brewer, 'Reconstructing the Reader: Prescriptions, Texts and Strategies in Anna Larpent's Reading', in *The Practice and Representation of Reading in England*, ed. by James Raven et al. (Cambridge: Cambridge University Press, 1996), pp. 226–245 (p. 244).
82. Arianne Baggerman, 'The Cultural Universe of a Dutch Child: Otto Van Eck and His Literature', in *Eighteenth Century Studies*, 31, 1 (1997), 129–134.
83. Robert DeMaria, *Samuel Johnson and the Life of Reading* (London and Baltimore: Johns Hopkins University Press, 1997).
84. Grafton, 'Is the History of Reading a Marginal Enterprise?', p. 141, p. 143.
85. James Raven, 'New Reading Histories, Print Culture and the Identification of Change: the Case of Eighteenth-Century England', *Social History*, 23, 3 (1998), 268–287 (271, 279); Margaret Spufford, 'First Steps in Literacy: The Reading and Writing Experience of the Humblest Seventeenth-Century Spiritual Autobiographers', *Social History*, IV (1979), 407–435; David Vincent, *Literacy and Popular Culture: England 1750–1914* (Cambridge: Cambridge University Press, 1989); Rose, *Intellectual Life*. The Reading Experience Database (RED) is designed to bring such case studies together. The RED input page is available on the Internet: www.open.ac.uk/Arts/RED/
86. Jacqueline Pearson *Women's Reading in Britain 1750–1835: A Dangerous Recreation* (Cambridge: Cambridge University Press, 1999), pp. 122–151, pp. 10–11.
87. Pearson, *Women's Reading*, p. 10; Garrett Stewart, *Dear Reader: The Conscripted Audience in Nineteenth-Century British Fiction* (Baltimore: Johns Hopkins, 1996), pp. 133–172.
88. Patrick Brantlinger, *The Reading Lesson: The Threat of Mass Literacy in Nineteenth-Century British Fiction* (Bloomington and Indianapolis: Indiana University Press, 1998), p. 19.
89. Flint, *Woman Reader*, p. 4, p. 13, p. 10.
90. Elizabeth Long, *Book Clubs: Women and the Uses of Reading in Everyday Life* (Chicago: University of Chicago Press, 2003), pp. 2–16; William Beatty Warner, 'Staging Readers Reading', *Eighteenth-Century Fiction*, 12, 2–3 (January–April 2000), 391–416.
91. Long, *Book Clubs*, pp. 31–58 (p. 31); Jenny Hartley, *Reading Groups* (Oxford: Oxford University Press, 2001), pp. 1–23.
92. Elizabeth McHenry, *Forgotten Readers: Recovering the Lost History of African American Literary Societies* (Durham: Duke University Press, 2002).
93. Bill Bell, 'Bound for Australia: Shipboard Reading in the Nineteenth Century', in *Journeys through the Market: Travel, Travellers and the Book Trade*, ed. by R. Myers and M. Harris (New Castle: Oak Knoll Press, 1999), pp. 119–140; 'The Scottish Emigrant Reader in the Nineteenth Century', in *Across Boundaries: The Book in Culture and Commerce*, ed. by Bill Bell, Philip Bennett and Jonquil Bevan (New Castle: Oak Knoll, 2000), pp. 116–129.

94. D. R. Woolf, *Reading History in Early Modern England* (Cambridge: Cambridge University Press, 2000); Adam Smyth, *'Profit & Delight': Printed Miscellanies In England, 1640–1682* (Detroit: Wayne State University Press, 2004).

95. Heather Jackson, *Romantic Readers: The Evidence of Marginalia* (New Haven: Yale University Press, 2005), p. 303, p. 300.

96. St Clair, *Reading Nation*, p. 5, pp. 374–375. Further references are given in the text.

97. St Clair, *Reading Nation*, pp. 307–338.

98. Jonathan Rose, 'Rereading the English Common Reader: A Preface to a History of Audiences', *Journal of the History of Ideas*, 53 (1992), 47–70, reprinted in *The Book History Reader*, ed. by David Finkelstein and Alistair McCleery (London: Routledge, 2002), pp. 324–339 (p. 332).

99. Pearson, *Women's Reading*, pp. 137–142, p. 13.

100. Flint, *Woman Reader*, p. 187.

101. Scott-Warren 'News, Sociability, and Bookbuying in Early Modern England', 402; Grafton, 'Is the History of Reading a Marginal Enterprise?', p. 141.

102. Hackel, *Reading Material*, p. 7.

103. Adrian Johns, *The Nature of the Book: Print and Knowledge in the Making* (Chicago: University of Chicago Press, 1998), p. 47.

104. *The Cambridge History of the Book in Britain, Volume Four, 1557–1695*, ed. by John Barnard, D. F. McKenzie and Maureen Bell (Cambridge: Cambridge University Press, 2001).

105. St Clair, *Reading Nation*, pp. 84–121.

106. On print production in the later nineteenth century, see Simon Eliot, *Some Patterns and Trends in British Publishing, 1800–1919*, Occasional Papers of the Bibliographical Society 8 (London: Bibliographical Society, 1994). The continued importance of case studies of individual readers is suggested by Rose, *Intellectual Life*.

2 Reworking the Word: Readers and their Manuscript Books, 1695–1730

1. Rolf Engelsing, 'Die Perioden der Lesergeschicte in der Neuzeit', *Archiv fur Geschichte des Buchwesens*, 10 (1969), 946–1002; Engelsing, *Der Burger als Leser: Lesergeschichte in Deutschland 1500–1800* (Stuttgart: Metzler, 1974); Robert DeMaria, *Samuel Johnson and the Life of Reading* (Baltimore: the Johns Hopkins University Press, 1997), pp. 1–19 (p. 4), p. 139.

2. John Brewer, *The Pleasures of the Imagination: English Culture in the Eighteenth Century* (London: Harper Collins, 1997), pp. 167–197.

3. William Coe, 'The Diary of William Coe, 1693–1729', in *Two East-Anglian Diaries 1641–1729*, ed. by Matthew Storey (Woodbridge: Boydell Press, 1994), pp. 203–260 (p. 240).

4. Harold Love, *Scribal Publication in Seventeenth Century England* (Oxford: Clarendon Press, 1993).

5. Peter Beal, 'Notions in Garrison: The Seventeenth-Century Commonplace Book', in *New Ways of Looking at Old Texts*, ed. by W. Speed Hill (New York: Renaisance English Texts Society, 1993), pp. 131–147 (p. 134).

6. Desiderius Erasmus, *On Copia of Words and Ideas*, trans. by Donald B. King (Milwaukee: Marquette University Press, 1963).

7. Robert Darnton, 'Extraordinary Commonplaces', *New York Review of Books*, 21 December 2000, pp. 82–87 (p. 82).

8. Roger Chartier, *Publishing Drama in Early Modern Europe: The Panizzi Lectures 1998* (London: British Library, 1999), p. 57. The classic account is, G. K. Hunter, 'The Marking of *Sententiae* in Elizabethan Printed Plays, Poems and Romances', *The Library*, 5th Series, 6, 3–4 (1951), 171–188.

9. William H. Sherman, 'Toward a History of the Manicule', in *Owners, Annotators and the Signs of Reading*, ed. by Robin Myers et al. (London: British Library, 2005), pp. 19–48 (pp. 41–42).

10. Beal 'Notions in Garrison', p. 137; Ann Moss, *Printed Commonplace Books and the Structuring of Renaissance Thought* (Oxford: Clarendon Press, 1996), pp. 275–276.

11. Kevin Sharpe, 'Uncommonplaces? Sir William Drake's Reading Notes', in *The Reader Revealed*, ed. by Sabrina Alcorn Baron et al. (Washington: Folger Library, 2001), pp. 58–65 (p. 60); Heidi Brayman Hackel, *Reading Material in Early Modern England: Print, Gender, and Literacy* (Cambridge: Cambridge University Press, 2005), pp. 176–187. See especially Hackel's discussion of Folger Library MS Add. 774, which dates from the early to middle seventeenth century, p. 177.

12. Moss, *Printed Commonplace Books*, pp. 279–280.

13. Earle Havens, *Commonplace Books: A History of Manuscripts and Printed Books from Antiquity to the Twentieth Century* (Yale: The Beinecke Rare Book and Manuscript Library, Yale University, and University Press of New England, 2001), p. 73. An extract from this 'anonymous commonplace book written about 1660–90' is reproduced on p. 76.

14. G. K. Hunter, 'The Marking of *Sententiae*' (1951), suggests that the appearance of these marks in printed texts began to decline from the 1660s onwards, p. 171.

15. Moss, *Printed Commonplace Books*, p. 280.

16. John Locke, 'A New Method of a Commonplace Book' in *The Posthumous Works of Mr John Locke* (London: John Churchill, 1706), pp. 311–336.

17. Joseph Hunter in Chapter 4 and Anne Lister in Chapter 5.

18. On Locke, see Beal, 'Notions in Garrison', pp. 140–142; Moss, *Printed Commonplace Books*, pp. 278–280; Havens, *Commonplace Books*, pp. 55–58.

19. Harold Love, 'How Personal is a Personal Miscellany? Sarah Cowper, Martin Clifford and the "Buckingham Commonplace Book"', in *Order and Connexion: Studies in Bibliography and Book History*, ed. by R. C. Alston (Woodbridge: Boydell and Brewer, 1997), pp. 111–126 (p. 111, p. 112).

20. Harold Love, *English Clandestine Satire 1660–1702* (Oxford: Oxford University Press, 2004), p. 286.

21. Cedric Brown, 'The Black Poet of Ashover: Leonard Wheatcroft', *English Manuscript Studies*, 11 (2002), 181–202.

22. Love, 'How Personal', p. 126.

23. 'Commonplace Book of Charles Caesar, 1705', British Library, Add. MSS 43410. I have been unable to trace the other volumes that the British Library Catalogue suggests remained in private hands after this volume was deposited.

24. Edmund Lodge, *Life of Sir Julius Caesar* (London: Hatchard, 1827), p. 40.
25. British Library, Add. MSS 43410, ff.31–34, ff.167–168, f.187r, f.2r, f.10r. Further references are given in the text.
26. The page references that Caesar gives for these extracts correspond with the nearest contemporary edition, George Herbert, *The Temple: Sacred Poems and Private Ejaculations* (London: Jeffrey Wale, 1703). Caesar also copied Herbert's 'Anagram on the virgin Mary' in full.
27. John James Caesar, *The Glorious Memory of a Faithful Prince ... Upon the Most Lamented Death of King William Third* (London: Henry Mortlock, 1702).
28. Samuel Wallas, *The Good Angel of Stamford* (London: S. N., 1659); Francois Perrault, *The Divill of Mascon* (Oxford: R. Davis, 1659); *A Brief Character of the Protector Oliver Cromwell with an Account of the Slavery He Left the Nation Under at his Death Comprehended in a Seasonable Speech, Made by a Worthy Member of Parliament, in the House of Commons ... March 1659* (London: R. Taylor, 1692). This was a new version of Silius Titus's, *A Seasonable Speech, Made by a Worthy Member of Parliament ... March 1659* (London: n. p. 1659).
29. Francis Quarles, *Divine Fancies Digested into Epigrams, Meditations and Observations* (London: J. Williams and C. Skegness, 1687); Martin Lister, *A Journey to Paris in the Year 1698* (London: Jacob Tonson, 1699); [Thomas Flatman], *Heraclitus Ridens; or, A Discourse Between Jest and Earnest, Where Many a True Word is Spoken in Opposition to all Libellers Against the Government*, Aug. 1682, no. 8.
30. Edward Ward, *All Men Mad: Or, England a Great Bedlam* (London: n. p., 1704), British Library, 164.1.67.
31. On the relationship between the book trade and scribal publication, see Peter Beal, *In Praise of Scribes: Manuscripts and Their Makers in Seventeenth-Century England* (Oxford: Clarendon Press, 1998).
32. Moss, *Printed Commonplace Books*, pp. 255–281.
33. Adam Smyth, *'Profit and Delight': Printed Miscellanies in England, 1640–1682* (Detroit: Wayne State University Press, 2004), pp. 118–26 (p. 126).
34. Even personal miscellanies of clandestine satire often include notes on authorship or the source of the original.
35. *Poems on the Affairs of State* (London: n. p., 1703), p. 101.
36. *Poems on the Affairs of State*, p. 241.
37. Peter Beal, *Index of English Literary Manuscripts Volume II: 1625–1700* (London: Mansell, 1993). Beal notes that John Dunton added the text to a manuscript miscellany originally constructed in 1704, c.1724, Bod., MS Rawl. Poet. 173, f.1.
38. *The Literary Works of Matthew Prior*, ed. by H. B. Wright and M. K. Spears, 2 Vols (Oxford: Clarendon Press, 1959), II, pp. 878–879.
39. *Poems on the Affairs of State*, p. iii. Further references are given in the text.
40. Francis Quarles, *The Shepherd's Oracles: Delivered in Certain Eclogues* (London: John Marriot & Richard Marriot, [1645]). The sentence, 'A prince, that (briefly to characterise him) wants nothing, but a people, how to prize him' is part of a passage on a 'Pious Prince', spoken by 'Orthodoxus' in Eclogue X.
41. Adam Smyth, '"Read in One Age and Understood i' th' Next": Recycling Satire in the Mid-Seventeenth Century', *Huntington Library Quarterly*, 69, 1 (2006), 1–16 (9).

42. On the post-Revolution political consensus that began to emerge during the reign of Queen Anne, see W. A. Speck, *Literature and Society in Eighteenth-Century England: Ideology, Politics and Culture, 1680–1820* (London: Longman, 1998), pp. 31–46.

43. Love, *English Clandestine Satire*, pp. 266–73.

44. Elizabeth Freke, *The Remembrances of Elizabeth Freke 1671–1714*, edited by Raymond Anselment, Camden Fifth Series, Volume 18 (Cambridge: Cambridge University Press, 2001), p. 3.

45. Raymond A. Anselment, 'Elizabeth Freke's Remembrances: Reconstructing a Self', *Tulsa Studies in Women's Literature*, 16 (1997), 57–75 (67, 57).

46. Freke, *Remembrances*, p. 139, p. 133.

47. Freke, *Remembrances*, p. 156. Further references are given in the text.

48. D. R. Woolf, *Reading History in Early Modern England* (Cambridge: Cambridge University Press, 2000), pp. 104–108 (p. 106, p. 105).

49. Elizabeth Freke, 'Commonplace Book of Elizabeth Freke', British Library, Add. MSS 45718, f.254v. This volume may well be made up of two separate manuscripts that were later bound together. ff.1–104 includes much of the 'remembrances', the emblems and accounts. The transcripts begin at the reverse of this volume and run from ff.245–108. Further references are given in the text.

50. John Philips, *Sportive Wit: The Muses Merriment – A New Spring of Witty Drollery, Joviall Fancies and a la Mode Lampoones* (London: Nath. Brook, 1656). For a discussion of this volume, see Smyth, *'Profit and Delight'*, pp. 132–137.

51. Thomas Percy, *Reliques of Ancient English Poetry* (London: Dodsley, 1765), pp. 327–329.

52. Harold Love's 'First-Line Index to Selected Anthologies of Clandestine Satire' contains three references to manuscript collections that include 'The French King's Cordiall'. See his *English Clandestine Satire*, pp. 303–414.

53. *Poems on the Affairs of State*, p. 267. Further references are given in the text. Love's 'First-Line Index' does not give any references to scribal versions of this text.

54. Freke, *Remembrances*, pp. 173–177 (p. 174, p. 175).

55. G. W. Story, *A True and Impartial History of … Ireland During the Last Two Years* (London: Chiswell, 1691); Freke, *Remembrances*, pp. 139–152 (p. 139). Further references are given in the text.

56. *Poems on Affairs*, p. 266, p. 401, p. 320.

57. DeMaria, *Samuel Johnson*, p. 4.

58. Gertrude Savile, *Secret Comment: The Diaries of Gertrude Savile 1721–1757*, ed. by Alan Saville (Nottingham: The Thoroton Society, 1997). This is an edited transcript of the surviving journals, which cover the years 1721–1722, 1727–1731 and 1737–1757. Not all of the references to reading are reproduced in this edition, however, and I have also consulted the original manuscripts where necessary. 'Gertrude Savile's Journal, 1721–31', Nottinghamshire Archives, Nottingham, DD.SR 212/10–11.

59. Lorna Weatherill, *Consumer Behaviour and Material Culture in Britain* (New York: Routledge, 1988).

60. James Raven, 'Publishing and Bookselling 1660–1780', in *The Cambridge History of English Literature, 1660–1780*, ed. by John Richetti (Cambridge: Cambridge University Press, 2005), pp. 11–36 (p. 16).

61. Ros Ballaster, *Seductive Forms: Women's Amatory Fiction from 1684 to 1740* (Oxford: Clarendon Press, 1992), p. 36; William St Clair argues that 'most plays' were produced in editions of between 750–1,000 copies, *The Reading Nation in the Romantic Period* (Cambridge: Cambridge University Press, 2004), pp. 467–468.

62. For an alternative assessment of the audience for the novel, see J. Paul Hunter, *Before Novels: The Cultural Contexts of Eighteenth-Century English Fictions* (New York: Norton, 1990), pp. 61–88.

63. Savile, *Secret Comment*, p. 41, p. 46. Further references are given in the text.

64. Marjorie Penn, 'The Account Books of Gertrude Savile, 1736–58', *Thoroton Society Record Series*, 24 (1967), 99–152 (115).

65. Savile, 'Journal, 1728', MS DD.SR 212/10/4, f.14v.

66. George Stanhope, *A Paraphrase and Comment on the Epistles* (London: Parker, Williamson and Motte, 1726); Savile, *Secret Comment*, p. 144.

67. Samuel Clarke, *A Demonstration of the Being and Attributes of God* (London: James and John Knapton, 1728).

68. Savile, *Secret Comment*, p. 86, p. 116.

69. DeMaria, *Samuel Johnson*, p. 12.

70. St Clair, *Reading Nation*, p. 3.

71. Nicholas Rowe, *The Ambitious Stepmother* (London: J. Darby, A. Bettesworth, F. Clay, 1727).

72. Brewer, *The Pleasures of the Imagination*, p. 354.

73. John Gay, *The Beggar's Opera* (London: John Watts, 1728).

74. Frances Harris, 'The Englishwoman's Private Library in the 17th and 18th Centuries', in *Libraries in Literature*, ed. by Peter Vodosek and Graham Jefcoate (Wiesbaden: Harrasowitz Verlag, 1999), pp. 189–203 (p. 198).

75. Savile 'Journal 1728', DD.SR 212/10/4, ff.10v–11r.

76. Richard Steele, *The Conscious Lovers: A Comedy. As it is Acted at the Theatre Royal in Drury-Lane* (London: Jacob Tonson, 1723), p. iii.

77. Harold Love, 'Restoration and Early Eighteenth-Century Drama', in *The Cambridge History of English Literature, 1660–1780*, pp. 109–131 (p. 110).

78. [James Shirley], *Double Falshood: Or, the Distrest Lovers ... Written Originally by W. Shakespeare* (London: J. Watts, 1728); John Sturmy, *Sesostris: Or, Royalty in Disguise* (London: J. Crokatt, 1728).

79. Savile 'Journal, 1728', DD.SR 212/10/3, f.7v.

80. Savile 'Journal, 1727', DD.SR 212/10/2, f.13v.

81. 'The Commonplace Book of Gertrude Savile', DD SR 212/12.

82. Elijah Fenton, *Mariamne: A Tragedy* (London: J. Tonson, 1723). There was also a 1728 edition published by Thomas Astley. Savile included extracts in her journal during October 1728 and January 1729, Savile, *Secret Comment*, p. 143, p. 159.

83. Savile, 'Commonplace Book', DD.SR 212/12, f.6r.

84. Love, 'Restoration', p. 119.

85. Sturmy, *Sesostris*, p. vi.

86. Love, 'Restoration', p. 113.

87. Discussed in David W. Lindsay, *The Beggar's Opera and Other Eighteenth-Century Plays* (London: J. M. Dent, 1993), p. xxiii.

88. Joseph Addison, *Cato: A Tragedy* (London: J. Tonson, 1728); Nicholas Rowe, *Ulysses* (London: Jacob Tonson, 1726); Charles Sedley, *The Mulberry*

Garden: A Comedy (London: H. Herringman, 1675); Thomas Rymer, *Edgar: Or, the English Monarch* (London: J. Knapton, 1693); Samuel Daniel, *Hymens Triumph* (London: Francis Constable, 1615).

89. Madeleine de Scudery, *Clelia: An Excellent Romance* (London: Herringman [and eight others], 1678).

90. *The Spectator*, 37, Thursday, 12 April 1711, 140–144 (141).

91. Ros Ballaster, *Seductive Forms: Women's Amatory Fiction from 1684 to 1740* (Oxford: Clarendon Press, 1992), p. 49.

92. *The Spectator*, 37, p. 143.

93. On the representation of the 'learned woman', see Jacqueline Pearson, *The Prostituted Muse: Images of Women and Women Dramatists 1642–1737* (London: Harvester, 1998), pp. 83–85.

94. For an overview, see *Popular Fiction by Women 1660–1730: An Anthology*, ed. by Paula Backscheider and John Richetti (Oxford: Clarendon Press, 1996).

95. Aphra Behn, *All the Histories and Novels of the Late Ingenious Mrs Behn* (London: A. Bettesworth and F. Clay, 1722).

96. Savile, *Secret Comment*, pp. 55–57.

97. Savile, *Secret Comment*, p. 55. Further references are given in the text.

98. Balaster, *Seductive Forms*, p. 82; Eliza Haywood, *The Perplex'd Dutchess* (London: J. Roberts, 1727); [Haywood, trans.], *Memoirs of the Baron de Brosse*, 2 vols (London: D.Browne Junr and S. Chapman, 1725–1726); Haywood, *The British Recluse* (London: D. Browne Junr, W. Chetwood, J. Woodman and S. Chapman, 1722); Madame de Gomez [trans. Haywood], *La Belle Assemblee, or, The Adventures of Six Days* (London: D. Browne Junr and S. Chapman, 1724); *The Prude: A Novel Compleat in Three Parts*, 3 vols (London: J. Roberts, 1724–1726); Jean Regnaauld de Segrais, *Three Novels* (London: D. Browne Junr, 1725); Haywood, *The Arragonian Queen* (London: J. Roberts, 1724); Penelope Aubin, *The Noble Slaves* (London: E. Bell [and nine others], 1722); Aubin, *The Strange Adventures of the Count de Vinevil* (London: E Bell [and nine others], 1721); *Nunnery Tales Written by a Young Man* (London: the Booksellers of London and Westminster, 1727); E. le Noble, *Zulima, Or, Pure Love* (London: J. Hooke and J. Roberts, 1719); Pierre Villiers, *Female Falsehood, or, The Life and Adventures of a Late French Nobleman … Digested by Monsieur St. Evremont* (London: John Walthoe, 1722).

99. William B. Warner, 'Novels on the Market', in *The Cambridge History of English Literature 1660–1780*, ed. by John Richetti, pp. 87–105 (pp. 90–91).

100. Backscheider and Richetti, *Popular Fiction by Women*, p. xx.

101. Eliza Haywood, *The City Widow: Or, Love in a Butt. A Novel* (London: J. Roberts, 1729), p. 14.

102. Ballaster, *Seductive Forms*, p. 170.

103. Warner 'Novels on the Market', p. 95

104. [Jean Paul Bignon], *The Adventures of Abdallah Son of Hanif*, 3 vols (London: R. Newton, 1729), p. i.

105. Aubin, *The Noble Slaves*, pp. xi–xii.

106. Penelope Aubin, *The Strange Adventures of the Count de Vinevil and his Family* (London: E. Bell, J. Darby, A. Bettesworth [and seven others], 1721), reproduced in Backscheider and Richetti, *Popular Fiction by Women*, pp. 112–151 (p. 114).

107. Backscheider and Richetti, *Popular Fiction by Women*, p. 114, p. xix.

108. The 'story of Almoraddin', for example, is said to warn against 'the bewitching power of love, which hurries its votaries into Ruin, without sufficient precaution', vol 1, opp. p. 82.

109. [Pierre Villiers], *Female Falsehood, Or, The Life and Adventures of a Late French Nobleman*, 3 vols (London: John Walthoe, 1722), vol 2, p. 2.

110. Alain Rene Le Sage, *The History and Adventures of Gil Blas* (London: Jacob Tonson, 1716), [p. ii].

111. Behn's suggestion that 'Women enjoy'd, are like Romances read' in *The Unfortunate Bride* (1698) is discussed in Ballaster, *Seductive Forms*, p. 31. Haywood's embedding of the 'anti-novel' discourse in her texts is noted by Warner, 'Novels on the Market', p. 94.

3   Diversities of Reading Practice, 1695–1770

1. James Raven, 'New Reading Histories, Print Culture and the Identification of Change: the Case of Eighteenth-Century England', *Social History*, 23, 3 (1998), 268–287 (p. 272).

2. Stuart Sherman, 'Diary and Autobiography', in *The Cambridge History of English Literature 1660–1780*, ed. by John Richetti (Cambridge: Cambridge University Press, 2005), pp. 649–672 (pp. 650–651). See also his *Telling Time: Clocks, Diaries, and English Diurnal Form, 1660–1795* (Chicago: Chicago University Press, 1996).

3. John Beadle, *The Journal or Diary of a Thankful Christian* (London: Thomas Parkhurst, 1656), p. iiv. Quoted in Sherman, 'Diary and Autobiography', p. 651.

4. Elizabeth Freke, *The Remembrances of Elizabeth Freke 1671–1714*, ed. by Raymond Anselment, Camden Fifth Series, Volume 18 (Cambridge: Cambridge University Press, 2001), p. 83.

5. William Coe,'The Diary of William Coe, 1693–1729', in *Two East-Anglian Diaries 1641–1729*, ed. by Matthew Storey (Woodbridge: Boydell Press, 1994), pp. 203–260 (p. 204, p. 207). Further references are given in the text.

6. Samuel Cradock, *Knowledge and Practice, Or, A Plain Discourse on the Chief Things Necessary to be Known, Believ'd and Practised in Order to Gain Salvation. Useful for Private Families*, 3rd edition (London: Grantham, Mortlock and Miller, 1673), pp. 137–138.

7. Thomas Comber, *A Discourse Concerning the Daily Frequenting of Common Prayer* (London: Charles Brome, 1687). Coe also transcribed a prayer 'for any time of the day' from Patrick Simon's *The Devout Christian* (London: R. Royston, 1673); Coe, *The Diary of William Coe*, p. 264.

8. Anne Kugler, *Errant Plagiary: The Life and Writing of Lady Sarah Cowper 1644–1720* (Stanford: Stanford University Press, 2002), pp. 3–7.

9. D. R. Woolf, *Reading History in Early Modern England* (Cambridge: Cambridge University Press, 2000), p. 119.

10. Woolf, *Reading History*, p. 121, p. 123.

11. *The Diary of Dudley Ryder, 1715–1716*, ed. by William Matthews (London: Methuen, 1939).

12. *The Diary of Dudley Ryder*, p. 29. Further references are given in the text.

13. *An Essay Upon Study, More Particularly the Study of Philosophy* (London: Richard Wilkin, 1713). This essay argues against the kind of reading associated with

the compilation of a commonplace book, although it does maintain that it is useful to gather notes that can later be arranged under relevant headings.

14. Woolf has noted that Ryder often read the same text in a number of different locations, taking his copy of Salust with him 'to dinner one day, dipping back into it after practicing his viol another', *Reading History*, p. 124.

15. John Macky, *A Journey through England* (London: J. Roberts and T. Caldecott, 1714), p. 205.

16. *The Diary of Dudley Ryder*, p. 104, p. 122. On bookselling in London, see Giles Mandelbrote, 'From the Warehouse to the Counting-House: Booksellers and Bookshops in late 17th–Century London', in *A Genius for Letters: Booksellers and Bookselling from the 16th to the 20th Century*, ed. by Robin Myers and Michael Harris (Winchester and Delaware: St Paul's Bibliographies and Oak Knoll Press, 1995), pp. 49–84 (p. 53).

17. Mandelbrote 'From the Warehouse', pp. 56–60.

18. *The Persian and the Turkish Tales* (London: W. Mears and J. Browne, 1714). Alternatively, Ryder may have been reading *The Thousand and One Days: Persian Tales* (London: J. Tonson, 1714).

19. On the coffee house as a site for reading scribally produced newsletters and satires, see Harold Love, *Scribal Publication in Seventeenth Century England* (Oxford: Clarendon Press, 1993), p. 206.

20. Jurgen Habermas, *The Structural Transformation of the Public Sphere*, trans. by Thomas Burger and Frederick Lawrence (Cambridge Mass.: MIT Press, 1989), p. 57; Steve Pincus, ' "Coffee Politicians", Does Create: Coffee Houses and Restoration Political Culture', *The Journal of Modern History*, 67 (December 1995), 807–834; Daniel Woolf, 'News, History and the Construction of the Present in Early Modern England', in *The Politics of Information in Early Modern Europe*, ed. by Sabrina Baron and Brendan Dooley (New York: Routledge, 2001), pp. 80–118 (p. 92).

21. Pincus, ' "Coffee Politicians" ', p. 822.

22. Gilbert Burnet, *The History of the Reformation of the Church of England* (London: Richard Chiswell, 1683). An abridged edition was published in 1705.

23. Lisa Jardine and Anthony Grafton, ' "Studied for Action": How Gabriel Harvey Read His Livy', *Past and Present*, 129 (1990), 30–78.

24. George Berkeley, *A Treatise Concerning the Principles of Human Knowledge* (Dublin: Jeremy Pepyat, 1710).

25. 22 July 1715, *The Diary of Dudley Ryder*, p. 59

26. 9 September 1715, *The Diary of Dudley Ryder*, p. 93.

27. Stefanie Lethbridge, 'Anthological Reading Habits in the Eighteenth Century: The Case of Thomson's *Seasons*', in *Anthologies of British Poetry: Critical Perspectives from Literary and Cultural Studies*, edited by Barbara Korte, Ralf Schneider and Stefanie Lethbridge (Amsterdam: Rodopi, 2000), pp. 89–104 (p. 99).

28. *The Spectator*, i, (1711), p. 6.

29. *Diary of Dudley Ryder*, pp. 101–102.

30. Woolf, *Reading History*, p. 124.

31. Lorna Weatherill, *Consumer Behaviour and Material Culture in Britain, 1660–1760*, 2nd edition (London: Routledge, 1996), p. 49.

32. *A Radical's Books: The Library Catalogue of Samuel Jeake of Rye, 1623–1690*, ed. by Michael Hunter et al. (Woodbridge: D. S. Brewer, 1999), p. xxxii. On the spread of coffee houses throughout the nation, see Pincus, Coffee Politicians.

33. For a description of the Dawson Collection at the Hackney Archives Department, London, see, R. C. Bloomfield, *A Directory of Rare Book and Special Collections in the United Kingdom and the Republic of Ireland*, 2nd edition (London: Library Association, 1997), pp. 230–231.

34. 'The Life of John Dawson; Officer of Excise', West Yorkshire Archive Service, Kirklees, Huddersfield, MS: KC688.

35. 'John Dawson's Book; January 8, 1730', Hackney Archives Department, London, D/F/DAW-/2, pp. 167–177.

36. *The True State of England. Containing the Particular Duty, Business and Salary of Every Officer, Civil and Military* (London: King, Stagg, Francklin and Browne, 1729), pp. 124–128; Weatherill, *Consumer Behaviour*, pp. 93–111.

37. 'John Dawson's Book; January 8, 1730', Hackney Archives, London, D/F/DAW-/2, pp. 231–232.

38. 'A Catalogue of the Books of Mr John Dawson of Hoxton Deceased, Left by Will to the Vicars of S. Leonard in Shoreditch, 1765', Hackney Archives, D/F/DAW-/1. For a reconstruction of the library based on this catalogue and the surviving books, see Tony Brown, 'John Dawson: His Life and Library', Library Association Thesis, 1973.

39. Dawson, 'A Catalogue of My Books', Hackney Archives, D/F/DAW-/2, pp. 155–163.

40. For a transcript of this catalogue, see Stephen Colclough, ' "A Catalogue of My Books": The Library of John Dawson (1692–1765), "Exciseman and Staymaker", c.1739', *Publishing History*, 47 (2000), 45–66.

41. *The Term Catalogues 1668–1709 A.D.; With a Number for Easter Term, 1711 A.D.*, 3 vols, ed. by Edward Arber (London: Edward Arber, 1903–1906); *The Gentleman's Magazine 1731–51: The Lists of Books, Collected with Annual Indexes and the Index to the First Twenty Years*, English Bibliographical Sources Series 1, No. 6, (London: Gregg Press, 1966); *The Monthly Catalogue, 1723–30*, English Bibliographical Sources Series 1, No. 2 (London: Gregg Press, 1964).

42. Only three of the surviving volumes date from before 1678, the oldest being Luis de Granada's *Of Prayer and Meditation* (London: W. Wood, 1599).

43. Richard Allestree, *The Whole Duty of Man* (London: M.Garthwait, 1670); Antonio Gavin, *A Short History of Monastical Orders* (London: W. Bentley, 1693); Thomas Salmon, *The Chronological Historian* (London: W. Mears, 1733); Abel Boyer, *The History of King William the Third*, 3 vols (London: A. Roper and F. Coggan, 1702–1703).

44. John Barnard, 'Introduction', in *The Cambridge History of the Book in Britain, Volume Four, 1557–1695*, ed. by John Barnard, D.F. McKenzie and Maureen Bell (Cambridge: Cambridge University Press, 2001), pp. 1–28 (p. 8); E. S. Leedham-Green, *Books in Cambridge Inventories*, vol. I (Cambridge: Cambridge University Press, 1986), pp. 588–592; The library of Thomas Baker (1656–1740) of Cambridge University contained 4290 items, including 90 incunabula. See Frans Korsten, *A Catalogue of the Library of Thomas Baker* (Cambridge: Cambridge University Press, 1990).

45. David McKitterick, 'Book Catalogues: Their Varieties and Uses', in *The Book Encompassed: Studies in Twentieth-Century Bibliography*, ed. by Peter Davison (Cambridge: Cambridge University Press, 1992), pp. 161–175.

46. The passage, 'none of our newspapers comes to us now; but gives us some dismall Relation of Damages done by floods', appears in both the diary and

the life, where it is dated July 1725, 'The Life of John Dawson', f.45v. The miscellany is bound with the second volume of the diary, 'John Dawson's Diary, II', Hackney Archives, D/F/DAW-/3/2, ff.1–80.

47. William Sherman, *John Dee: the Politics of Reading and Writing in the English Renaissance* (Amherst: University of Massachusetts Press, 1995); Jardine and Grafton, 'Studied', 30–78.

48. Kevin Sharpe, *Reading Revolutions: The Politics of Reading in Early Modern England* (London: Yale University Press, 2000); Steven N. Zwicker, 'The Reader Revealed', in *The Reader Revealed*, ed. by Sabrina Alcorn Baron et al. (Washington: Folger Shakespeare Library, 2001), pp. 11–17 (p. 15).

49. H. J. Jackson, *Marginalia: Readers Writing in Books* (London: Yale University Press, 2001); H. J. Jackson, *Romantic Readers* (New Haven: Yale University Press, 2005).

50. Anthony Grafton, 'Is the History of Reading a Marginal Enterprise?: Guillaume Bude and His Books', *Papers of the Bibliographical Society of America*, 91 (1997), 139–157.

51. Jackson, *Marginalia*, p. 255. Further references are given in the text.

52. Adam Smyth, 'Profit and Delight': *Printed Miscellanies in England, 1640–1682* (Detroit: Wayne State Press, 2004), pp. 40–59; Heidi Brayman Hackel, *Reading Material in Early Modern England* (Cambridge: Cambridge University Press, 2005), pp. 156–175.

53. On the marginalia of Johnson, Swift and Locke, see Robert DeMaria, *Samuel Johnson and the Life of Reading* (London and Baltimore: Johns Hopkins University Press, 1997), pp. 20–57.

54. This survey looked at 100 books located using Robin Alston's, *Books With Manuscript: A Short Title Catalogue of Books with Manuscript Notes in the British Library* (London: British Library, 1994) and the British Library Catalogue.

55. David McKitterick, *A History of Cambridge University Press: Printing and the Book Trade in Cambridge, 1534–1698* (Cambridge: Cambridge University Press, 1992), p. xiii.

56. John Flavell, *Sacramental Meditations* (London: N. Crouch, 1700), British Library [hereafter BL], 875.a.10.

57. Thomas Salmon, *A Review of the History of England*, 2 vols (London: C. Rivington, 1724), BL, 598.e.16. This text was later owned by Francis Hargrave (1741–1821).

58. Robert Samber, *On the Passion of Our Blessed Saviour* (London: S. Battersbury, 1708), BL, 1608/5623.

59. Edward Laurence, *The Duty and Office of a Land-Steward* (Dublin: Samuel Fuller, 1731), BL, 1508/1236.

60. [J. Arbuthnot], *Law is a Bottom-less Pit* (London: John Morphew, 1712), BL, 12314.aa.16.

61. John Feather, 'British Publishing in the Eighteenth Century: A Preliminary Subject Analysis', in *The Library*, 6: 8, I (1986), 32–46 (37).

62. [J. Peirce], *An Essay in Favour of the Ancient Practice of Giving the Eucharist to Children* (London: J. Noon and J. Gray, 1728), BL, 117.g.56, p. 57.

63. DeMaria, *Samuel Johnson*, p. 52.

64. David McKitterick, 'Women and Their Books in Seventeenth-Century England: The Case of Elizabeth Puckering', *The Library* n. s. 1, 4 (2000), 359–380 (380).

65. John Holwell, *A Sure Guide to the Practical Surveyor, in Two Parts* (London: Christopher Hussey, 1678). Hackney Archives. Annotated by John Dawson.

66. This is the shelf mark for his copy of [Arthur Collins], *The Peerage of England Or a Genealogical and Historical Account of All the Flourishing Families of this Kingdom ... From Saxon Times to this Present Year, 1711*, 2 vols (London: Sanger and Collins, 1711). Hackney Archives. Annotated by John Dawson.

67. Laurence Echard, *The Gazetter's; or, Newsman's Interpreter* (London: John Nicholson, 1704) Hackney Archives. Annotated by John Dawson.; *The Merchant and Tradesman's Daily Companion* (London: Midwinter, 1729). Hackney Archives. Annotated by John Dawson.

68. Woolf, *Reading History*, p. 156.

69. Henry Isaacson, *Saturni Ephemerides Sive Tabula Historica – Chronologica* (London: Henry Siele & Humphry Robinson, 1633) valued at 12s; Laurence Echard, *The History of England* (London: Jacob Tonson, 1707) valued at £2 2s; William Camden, *Britannia or a Chronological Description of Great Britain and Ireland* (London: J. & J. Knapton, 1722), valued at £3.

70. 'Even in 1700 when the titles available had expanded enormously, most catalogs [sic] would contain no more than a fifth-part historical matter, and generally somewhere in the range of 10–15 percent', Woolf, *Reading History*, p. 157.

71. [Arthur Collins], *The Peerage of England ... Volume II. Part I* (London: Sangar and Collins, 1711). Hackney Archives. Annotated by John Dawson.

72. This annotation system is continued in *The Peerage of England: or, an Historical Account of the Present Nobility*, 4th edition, 2 vols (London: W. Taylor, 1717), which contains ten pages of "tables" listing dukes, earls, viscounts and barons.

73. Samuel Von Puffendorf, *An Introduction to the History of the Principal Kingdoms and States of Europe* (London: J. Knapton, D. Midwinter [and 3 others], 1728).

74. *Atlas Geographus: Or a Compleat System of Geography Ancient and Modern*, 2 vols (London: John Nutt, 1711). The passage on 'women in men's apparel' is on p. 1054 of volume II, Dawson's notes appear after p. 1336.

75. Woolf, *Reading History*, p. 90.

76. Salmon, *The Chronological Historian*. Only a few pages from the list of parliaments has survived bound into the front pages of this volume, but a further 32 manuscript pages (including the list of kings) have been bound into the back of this volume.

77. For an example of the symbols used by Harvey, see Sherman, *John Dee*, p. 109. Bodin is discussed in, Anthony Grafton, 'Discitur ut Agatur: How Gabriel Harvey Read his Livy', in *Annotation and Its Texts*, ed. by Stephen A. Barney (Oxford: Oxford University Press, 1991), pp. 108–129 (pp. 117–118).

78. Salmon, *Chronological Historian*, p. 113.

79. Dawson, 'The Life of John Dawson', MS: KC688.

80. Abel Boyer, *The History of the Reign of Queen Anne, Digested into Annals*, 11 vols (London: A Roper & F. Coggan, 1703–1713). Hackney Archives. Annotated by John Dawson.

81. For example, a passage in the 'Life' for 21 September 1710 records that parliament was 'dissolv'd by proclamation', a fact that is noted in the table of 'Parliaments in Queen Ann's Reign' in his copy of Salmon, 'The Life of John Dawson', f.13r.

82. Salmon, *Chronological Historian*, p. 366.

83. Dawson, 'The Life of John Dawson', f.15v.
84. *English Advice to the Freeholders of England* (London, n. p., 1714). The *Remarks on a Late Libel Privately Dispers'd by the Tories Entituled English Advice to the Freeholders of England* (London: J. Roberts, 1715) which accuses the author of the *English Advice* of being 'against the Protestant succession' gives some sense of the debate surrounding this pamphlet.
85. Woolf, *Reading History*, p. 121, p. 123.

4 The Circulating Library, Book Club and Subscription Library: Readers and Reading Communities, 1770–1800

1. 'New Reading Histories, Print Culture and the Identification of Change: the Case of Eighteenth-Century England', *Social History*, 23, 3 (1998), 268–287. For the figures from the *ESTC*, see 275, note 37.
2. William St Clair, *The Reading Nation in the Romantic Period* (Cambridge: Cambridge University Press, 2004), pp. 186–209, p. 256.
3. Raven 'New Reading Histories', 279.
4. William Beatty Warner, 'Staging Readers Reading', *Eighteenth-Century Fiction*, 12, 2–3 (January–April 2000), 391–416 (408, 404). Both paintings are reproduced in this article, 403, 409.
5. Elizabeth Long, *Book Clubs: Women and the Uses of Reading in Everyday Life* (Chicago: University of Chicago Press, 2003), pp. 2–31 (p. 31).
6. Jacqueline Pearson, *Women's Reading in Britain 1750–1835: A Dangerous Recreation* (Cambridge: Cambridge University Press, 1999), p. 172.
7. For a discussion of the representation of the circulating library in the fiction of the period see, Christopher Skelton-Foord, 'Surveying the Circulating Library Scene: Popular British Fiction, 1770–1830', in *Bibliotheken in der Literarischen Darstellung: Libraries in Literature*, ed. by Peter Vodosek and Graham Jefcoate (Wiesbaden: Harrassowitz Verlag, 1999), pp. 89–113.
8. Pearson, *Women's Reading*, pp. 162–69 (p. 164).
9. Reproduced in John Brewer, *The Pleasures of the Imagination: English Culture in the Eighteenth Century* (London: HarperCollins, 1997), p. 178.
10. Pearson, *Women's Reading*, p. 163.
11. Jane Austen, *Mansfield Park*, 3 vols (London: Egerton, 1814), III, Ch. 9, p. 101.
12. Keith Manley, 'Booksellers, Peruke-Makers and Rabbit Merchants: The Growth of Circulating Libraries in the Eighteenth Century', in *Libraries and the Book Trade*, ed. by Robyn Myers, Michael Harris and Giles Mandelbrote (Delaware: Oak Knoll Press, 2000), pp. 29–50.
13. Jan Fergus, 'Eighteenth-Century Readers in Provincial England: The Customers of Samuel Clay's Circulating Library and Bookshop in Warwick, 1770–72', in *Papers of the Bibliographical Society of America*, 78, 2 (1984), 155–213.
14. Manley 'Booksellers, Peruke-Makers', p. 30. See also his 'Lounging Places and Frivolous Literature: Subscription and Circulating Libraries in the West Country', in *Printing Places: Locations of Book Production and Distribution Since 1500*, ed. by John Hinks and Catherine Armstrong (London: The British Library, 2005), pp. 107–120.

15. Paul Kaufman's groundbreaking essays on the various libraries available in Britain are gathered in his *Libraries and Their Users* (London: Library Association, 1969). See also, St Clair, *Reading Nation*, pp. 235–267.

16. John Button, *The Lewes Literary Society* (1804), quoted in St Clair, *Reading Nation*, p. 249.

17. St Clair, *ReadingNation*, p. 259.

18. *A Catalogue of the Library Belonging to the Book Society Held at the House of Esther Caterer in Surry Street, Sheffield* (Sheffield: Pierson, 1798).

19. Kaufman, *Libraries and Their Users*, pp. 28–35.

20. James Raven, 'From Promotion to Prescription: Arrangements for Reading and Eighteenth-Century Libraries', in *The Practice and Representation of Reading in England*, ed. by James Raven et al. (Cambridge: Cambridge University Press, 1996), pp. 175–201 (p. 182, p. 196).

21. *Hall's New Margate and Ramsgate Guide* (Margate: Joseph Hall, [1790?]), pp. 10–11.

22. This image is reproduced and discussed in Lee Erickson, *The Economy of Literary Form: English Literature and the Industrialization of Publishing, 1800–1850* (London: Johns Hopkins University Press), p. 124, p. 129.

23. *The New Margate and Ramsgate Guide* (London: H. Turpin and T. Wilkins, n. d), pp. 13–15. A contemporary guidebook notes that 'an extensive assortment of stationery, perfumery, [and] jewellery' was 'on constant sale' in resort libraries. *A Guide to All the Watering and Sea-Bathing Places* (London: Richard Philips, 1803), p. 79.

24. Erickson, *The Economy of Literary Form*, p. 129.

25. *Diary and Letters of Madame D'Arblay: Edited by Her Niece*, 7 vols (London: Henry Colburn, 1842–1846); Charlotte Francis, 'Journal of What Passed in an Excursion to Brighton', British Library, Egerton MSS 3706A.

26. Keith Manley's Library History Database, hosted at www.r-alston.co.uk, includes entries for three Circulating Libraries in Brighton during this period, Donaldson & Wilkes' 'Marine Library', Frederick Fisher's Circulating Library and James Gregory's Circulating Library.

27. Charlotte Francis 'Excursion to Brighton', British Library, Egerton MSS 3706A, f.14r. Further references are given in the text.

28. Erickson, *The Economy of Literary Form*, p. 130.

29. *The New Margate and Ramsgate Guide*, pp. 14–15. For gambling in the Brighton libraries, see Robert Bisset, *Modern Literature; A Novel*, 3 vols (London: T. N. Longman & O. Rees, 1804), Vol 2, pp. 20–22.

30. There is some evidence to suggest that Francis borrowed at least one book from Donaldson's (f.40r) but its title is not recorded in the diary.

31. Bisset, *Modern Literature*, Vol 2, pp. 20–22.

32. 'After dinner I wrote a little and read to Mamma' (f.17r).

33. *A Guide to all the Wateringand Sea-Bathing Places* (London: Richard Philips, 1803)., for example, records that 'the daily papers are regularly laid on the reading tables', p. 78.

34. *A Guide to all the Watering Places*, p. 80. The subscription fees of 5s per month and 10s for three months would have been high enough to maintain social boundaries.

35. On a reluctant young reader from the 1790s, see Arianne Baggerman, 'The Cultural Universe of a Dutch Child: Otto Van Eck and His Literature', *Eighteenth Century Studies*, 31, 1 (1997), 129–134.

36. Erickson, *The Economy of Literary Form*, p. 128.
37. [Sylvester Hunter], *A Brief Memoir of the Late Joseph Hunter, F.S.A.* (London: John Edward Taylor, 1861).
38. Joseph Hunter, 'The Journal of Joseph Hunter', British Library, Add. MSS 24, 879.
39. Hunter, 'Journal of Joseph Hunter', f.5r. Further references are given in the text.
40. Ann Radcliffe, *A Journey Made in the Summer of 1794*, (London: G. G. and J. Robinson, 1795); Edmund Lodge, *Illustrations of British History*, 3 vols (London: G. Nicol, 1791).
41. The diary of Otto Van Eck, who was Hunter's senior by just two years, was regularly scrutinised by his parents. Baggerman, 'The Cultural Universe of a Dutch Child', p. 130.
42. John Brewer, 'Reconstructing the Reader: Prescriptions, Texts and Strategies in Anna Larpent's Reading,' in *The Practice and Representation of Reading in England*, ed. by James Raven et al. (Cambridge: Cambridge University Press, 1996), pp. 226–245. Baggerman, 'The Cultural Universe of a Dutch Child', 129–134. For a discussion of audience formation in the 1790s see, Jon P. Klancher, *The Making of English Reading Audiences, 1790–1832* (Madison: University of Wisconsin Press, 1987), pp. 18–47.
43. Kaufman, *Libraries and Their Users*, pp. 28–35. For an examination of a single subscription library, see M. Kay Flavell, 'The Enlightened Reader and the New Industrial Towns: A Study of the Liverpool Library, 1758–1790', *British Journal of Eighteenth Century Studies*, 8 (1985), 17–35.
44. [John Robinson], *A Directory of Sheffield Including the Manufacturers of the Local Villages* (Sheffield: James Montgomery, 1797), p. 12. Robinson compiled the population figures from the parish registers. He estimated that the population of Sheffield had increased by nearly 4,000 between 1788 and 1796.
45. Hunter's normal practice was to record the date on which a text was borrowed or purchased and to then record his response to it on the day it was returned or completed. The figures are a record of the number of volumes that he acquired and read rather than the number of titles, as this provides a more accurate representation of his reading experience. Texts that were read in part have been included in the figures for texts read.
46. The name of this institution does not seem to have been formalised until the nineteenth century when it became the Sheffield Library. In the diary, Hunter refers to this subscription library as the 'book society,' 'the library' and the 'Surry Street Library'. Each of these descriptions is used in the 1798 catalogue, *A Catalogue of the Library Belonging to the Book Society Held at the House of Esther Caterer in Surry Street, Sheffield*.
47. 'Saw in Woollen's (the caricature shop) a neat view of the Cotton Mill' (f.38r). 'Saw at Book Johns ... New Memoirs of Literature for the Year 1725' (f.30v). Hunter transcribed a passage from 'the printed description' which accompanied a medal given to him by Mr Scholfield (f.19v).
48. Gabriel Silvertongue [James Montgomery], *The Whisperer* (Sheffield: Montgomery, 1798), George Smith, *A Sermon Delivered in the Parish Church of Sheffield to the Original United Lodge of Odd Fellows ... July 9 1798* (Sheffield: Montgomery, 1798).
49. Hunter recorded a visit to this shop on 19 May 1798 (f.16r). It acted as the main retailer of texts printed by Montgomery.

50. Klancher, *Making of English Reading Audiences*, pp. 44–45.
51. There are numerous volumes that include the phrase a 'Petition to the House of Commons' in their title.
52. Evans attempted to acquire an Encyclopaedia at an auction on 20 April 1797, without any success (f.8v).
53. Hunter recorded reading only 11 of the 28 texts that he received from friends and family during 1798, but much of this deficit is accounted for because he did not record reading each of the 12 numbers of the *Monthly Magazine* that were lent to him by Miss Haynes.
54. Anthony Robinson, *A View of the Causes and Consequences of English Wars* (London: Johnson, 1798).
55. Kaufman, *Libraries and Their Users*, p. 34.
56. [John Robinson], *A Directory of Sheffield*, p. 34.
57. [Mrs Harley], *The Castle of Mowbray: An English Romance by the Author of St. Bernard's Priory* (London: C. Stalker & H. Setchell, 1788).
58. Brewer, *Pleasures of the Imagination*, p. 182.
59. Brewer, *Pleasures of the Imagination*, p. 180.
60. *A Catalogue of the Library*, i–iv; Sara E. Joynes, 'The Sheffield Library, 1771–1907', *Library History*, 2 (1971), 91–116 (113).
61. Evans was president in 1773, 1776 and 1784. T. A. Ward, *Short Account of the Sheffield Library* (Sheffield: Bacon, 1825), p. 4.
62. Four of the texts that he borrowed were new acquisitions and therefore not included in the 1798 catalogue. These include John Gifford, *A Short Address to the Members of the Loyal Association* (London: T. N. Longman, 1798), and Frederick Morton Eden, *The State of the Poor; Or an History of the Labouring Classes in England, 3 vols* (London: J. Davis, 1797), which may be classified as political texts.
63. Ann Radcliffe, *The Mysteries of Udolpho*, 4 vols (London: G. G. & J. Robinson, 1794).
64. Kaufman, *Libraries and Their Users*, p. 31.
65. Hunter catalogued the 723 volumes contained in Evan's library in April 1797, f.7r.
66. On 17 June 1798 he recorded that 'Mr Evans preached at Sheff[iel]d. We afterwards drank tea with my grandmother & Mr Williams at Miss Haynes's', f.19v.
67. Brewer suggests that in the last quarter of the eighteenth century 'a substantial history or a piece of travel literature or biography was more expensive than an annual subscription', *Pleasures of the Imagination*, p. 178; George Leonard Staunton, *An Authentic Account of an Embassy From the King of Great Britain to the Emperor of China*, 2 vols (London: Nicholson, 1797); Robert Townson, *Travels in Hungary With a Short Account of Vienna, in the Year 1793* (London: Robinson, 1797).
68. Hunter borrowed 123 texts in total. He read at least 88, and recorded 97 separate acts of reading in the 1798 sequence.
69. Fines were imposed at the rate of 'a halfpenny for every day the book is kept after the time limited'. Any books lost had to be paid for in full, *A Catalogue of the Library*, p. iii.
70. Alternatively he could use a different institution to complete the text as occurred in April 1797, when he used Lindley's library to acquire the first volume of a novel (f.9v).

71. Helen Maria Williams, *A Tour in Switzerland; or a View of the Present State of the Government and Manners of Those Cantons, With Comparative Sketches of the Present State of France*, 2 vols (London: G. G. & J. Robinson, 1798).
72. Ann Radcliffe, *The Italian: Or, the Confessional of the Black Penitents* (London: T. Cadell Jun and W. Davies, 1797).
73. *A Catalogue of the Library*, p. iv.
74. Hunter quotes directly from the notice of publication that appeared in the *Monthly Magazine*, 6 (September 1798), 214.
75. 'They voted the works of H. Walpole ... into the Library before they were published but now they are published they have not sent for them, probably on account of the price' (f.30r).
76. On 4 August 1798 Hunter recorded: 'I am much pleased with the account of Mr Lambton in the Monthly Mag. The Walpoliana is also very entertaining' (f.24r). The *Monthly Magazine* began to publish 'Walpoliana; or Bon-mots, Apothegms, Observations on Life and Literature, with Extracts from the Original Letters of the Late Horace Walpole', in March 1798. It was published in book form as *Walpoliana*, 2 vols (London: R. Phillips, 1799).
77. *Biographical Anecdotes of the Founders of the French Republic* (London: R. Philips, 1797). A second volume was published in 1798 as Hunter notes.
78. H. J. Jackson, *Marginalia: Readers Writing in Books* (New Haven: Yale University Press, 2001), p. 78; St Clair, *Reading Nation* p. 259.
79. For a discussion of Gilray's *The New Morality*, see Kenneth R. Johnson, *The Hidden Wordsworth* (London: Pimlico, 2000), pp. 434–437.
80. Hunter records that the 'news of the victory of Horatio Nelson' reached Sheffield on 3 October 1798 and was met with 'bells, cannons & rockets' (f.35).
81. Mary Wollstonecraft, *Historical and Moral View of the Origin and Progress of the French Revolution* (London: J. Johnston, 1794); Wollstonecraft, *Letters Written During a Short Residence in Sweden, Norway, and Denmark* (London: J. Johnston, 1796).
82. *The Spirit of the Public Journals for 1797: Being an Impartial Selection of the Most Exquisite Essays and J'eux D'esprits* (London: R. Philips [and four others], 1798), p. iii.
83. Anne Janowitz, 'Amiable and Radical Sociability: Anna Barbauld's "Free Familiar Conversation"', in *Romantic Sociability*, ed. by Gillian Russell and Clara Tuite (Cambridge: Cambridge University Press, 2002), pp. 62–81.
84. Richard Cronin, *The Politics of Romantic Poetry: In Search of the Pure Commonwealth* (Basingstoke: Macmillan Press, 2000), pp. 61–82 (p. 62); *The Anti-Jacobin or Weekly Examiner*, 1, 3–4, quoted in Cronin, *Politics of Romantic Poetry*, p. 64.
85. St Clair, *Reading Nation*, pp. 257–259 (p. 257).
86. Cronin, *Politics of Romantic Poetry*, p. 82.
87. James L. Machor, 'Historical Hermeneutics and Antebellum Fiction: Gender, Response Theory, and Interpretive Contexts', in *Readers in History: Nineteenth-Century American Literature and the Contexts of Response*, ed. by James L. Machor (Baltimore: John Hopkins University Press, 1993), pp. 54–84 (pp. 64–65, p. 70).
88. S. J. Pratt, *Gleanings Through Wales, Holland and Westphalia, With Views of Peace and War* (London: T. N. Longman and L. B. Seeley, 1795); Staunton's *An*

Authentic Account and Townson's *Travels in Hungary*, were reviewed in *Monthly Review* 24 (1797), 1–9, 67–77, 121–36, 169–76.

89. The 'New Idea of a Novel' is item 51 in the *Walpoliana*. It reads, 'I am firmly convinced that a story might be written, of which all the incidents should appear supernatural, yet turn out natural. (This remark was made in 1784)', *Monthly Magazine*, 5 (May 1798), 358.

90. *A Journey Made in the Summer of 1794, Through Holland and the Western Frontier of Germany* (London: Robinson, 1795). Hunter borrowed the first volume of *The Italian* (1797) on 20 March 1797 (f.3v). The same entry notes that he had already read her *The Castle of Athlin and Dunbayne, A Sicilian Romance* (1790), *The Romance of the Forest* (1791) and *The Mysteries of Udolpho* (1794).

91. [William Coombe], *Fragments; in the Manner of Sterne*, (London: Debrett, Murray & Highley, 1797).

92. 'Some readers may, *in the present temper of the times*, censure the author for giving to it the appearance a *party* production, in which occasion is often taken ... to display the cruelty of war ... In a word the political cast of this performance will appear to different persons in different lights', *Monthly Review*, 24 (October 1797), 271–274 (272).

93. John Ferrier, 'Comments on Sterne', *Memoirs of the Literary and Philosophical Society of Manchester*, iv (1793), 45–86; 'Extracts from the Port Folio of a Man of Letters: Poetical or Prose Imitations and Similarities', *Monthly Magazine*, 5 (May 1798), 365–367.

94. Machor, 'Historical Hermeneutics', pp. 66–79.

95. The *Monthly Review*, 22 (1797), 282–284.

96. Brewer argues that for Larpent, 'reading, even the reading of fiction, ... becomes purposive, disciplined, a means of overcoming rather than encouraging female frivolity,' 'Reconstructing the Reader', p. 235.

97. Thomas Pennant, *Outlines of the Globe Volume One: The View of Hindoostan* (London: Henry Hughes, 1798).

98. 'I took Radcliffe's Tour to the Library. I was not so much entertained with it as I expected, tho her descriptions are very fine' (f.18v).

99. 'Saw ... in the possession of one of our men the Spy, a periodical ... in which were some very keen things against the Ministry' (f.38r).

100. Charles Macklin, *The Man of the World* (London: John Bell, 1785); Donald Campbell, *A Journey Over Land to India*, 4 vols (London: Cullen & Co., 1795).

101. Brewer has argued that 'intensive' and 'extensive' reading acted as alternate, rather than exclusive, reading strategies in the 1790s, 'Reconstructing the Reader', pp. 239–240.

102. A further 35 texts were borrowed and remained unread or their reading remained unrecorded (see Figure 4.1).

103. 'Brought the 2[n]d volume of the Antiquarian Repertory; I have read it before but there was a picture in it I wished to draw' (f.12r).

104. Hunter was inspired to keep a commonplace book after reading John Locke's 'A New Method of a Commonplace Book' in April 1797, f.6r. He recorded that he had started 'another paper of anecdotes for my collection of writings relative to Sheffield' on 28 May 1798, that he had begun 'a book' in which he intended to write 'the plans of some of the best novels,' on

14 August 1798 (f.26r), and that he was transcribing material from *The Gentleman's Magazine* into his 'commonplace' on 5 July 1798 (f.21r).

105. Johann Georg Zimmerman, *Solitude Considered With Respect to Its Influence Upon the Mind and Heart ... Translated From the French of J.B. Mercier* (London: C. Dilly, 1797).

106. Brewer, 'Reconstructing the Reader', pp. 239–244.

107. Brewer, 'Reconstructing the Reader', p. 244.

5 Communal Practice and Individual Response: Reading in the Late Romantic Period

1. Zachary Leader, *Revision and Romantic Authorship* (Oxford: Clarendon Press, 1996); Jeffrey N. Cox, *Poetry and Politics in the Cockney School: Keats, Shelley, Hunt and Their Circle* (Cambridge: Cambridge University Press, 1998). For a summary of work on collaboration, see Gillian Russell and Clara Tuite, 'Introducing Romantic Sociability', in *Romantic Sociability: Social Networks and Literary Culture in Britain*, ed. by Russell and Tuite (Cambridge: Cambridge University Press, 2002), pp. 1–23.

2. 'Correspondents on all Subjects of Literature and Science', *Monthly Magazine* 51 (June 1821), 397–398.

3. William St Clair, *The Reading Nation in the Romantic Period* (Cambridge: Cambridge University Press, 2004), pp. 264–266. St Clair estimates that the national population was about 15 million in the 1820s.

4. The Hackney Reading Society was founded *c.*1815. 'Hackney Reading Society: Minutes, Records of Books Distributed, Accounts and Rules, April 1815–September 1828', Hackney Archives Centre, London, D/S/2/1. The 'Rules' are included on a printed insert.

5. St Clair, *Reading Nation*, pp. 252–255.

6. 'Hackney Reading Society: Minutes, 1828–1846', Hackney Archives, D/S/2/2, f.12.

7. 'Hackney Reading Society: Rules', D/S/2/1.

8. 'Minutes of the Eclectic Book Society, 1812–20', Guildhall Library, London, MS 988A, f.124.

9. 'Walworth Book Society, 1835–1840', Southwark Local Studies Library, MS11220.

10. St Clair, *Reading Nation*, p. 255.

11. [Charles Dickens], *Sketches by Boz*, 2 vols (London: J. Macrone, 1836).

12. 'Hackney Reading Society: Records of Books Distributed, 1828–1844', D/S/2/2, ff.45–46.

13. *The Times*, 16 December 1813, p. 3. col. e. Leonore Davidoff and Catherine Hall, *Family Fortunes: Men and Women of the English Middle Class 1780–1850*, 2nd edition (Routledge, 1992), pp. 419–420; Paul Kaufman, *Libraries and Their Users* (London: The Library Association, 1969), p. 58.

14. *The Times*, 16 December 1813, p. 3. col. e.

15. Of course, some groups came together to share and promulgate political ideas. The radical Corresponding Societies of the 1790s are the best documented because of the way in which the Government tried to repress them, but such organisations also flourished in the 1810s. See, Margaret C. Jacob, 'Sociability and the International Republican Conversation' in *Romantic Sociability* ed. by Russell and Tuite, pp. 24–42.

16. Harold Love, 'Oral and Scribal Texts in Early Modern England', in *The Cambridge History of the Book in Britain: Volume IV, 1557–1695*, ed. by John Barnard, D. F. Mckenzie and Maureen Bell (Cambridge: Cambridge University Press, 2002), pp. 97–121 (110–111).

17. Many of the books consulted for this project are part of William St Clair's private collection. Those contained in research libraries and public archives are described in Stephen Colclough, *Reading Experience 1700–1840: An Annotated Bibliography of Sources for the History of Reading in the British Isles* (Reading: History of the Book On-Demand Series, 2000).

18. *A New Commonplace Book: Being an Improvement on that Recommended by Mr Locke* (London: Walker, 1799), British Library, 8405.cc.21.

19. Anne Lister, 'Extracts 1817–1819', SH: 7/ML/Ex/3-, f.1, Calderdale Archives, Halifax Central Library.

20. [Hannah More], *Hints Towards Forming the Character of a Young Princess* (London: Thomas Cadell, 1805), p. 44.

21. Jane Austen, *Northanger Abbey*, ed. by Marilyn Butler (London: Penguin, 1995), p. 15, 35; *Pride and Prejudice* ed. by R. Irvine (Ormskirk: Broadview, 2002), p. 47.

22. This book is part of the private collection of William St Clair. Unless noted, all of the other manuscript books referred to in this chapter come from this collection.

23. 'Commonplace Book of Emma Knight', British Library, c.152.d.1.

24. James Raven, *Judging New Wealth: Popular Responses to Commerce in England, 1750–1800* (Oxford: Clarendon Press, 1992), p. 54.

25. For a discussion of this manuscript, see Stephen Colclough, 'Recovering the Reader: Commonplace Books and Diaries as Sources of Reading Experience', *Publishing History*, XLIV (1998), pp. 5–37.

26. Robert White, *Autobiographical Notes* (Newcastle: Newcastle University Library, 1966), p. 5.

27. St Clair, *Reading Nation*, p. 196.

28. St Clair, *Reading Nation*, p. 246.

29. *The Literary Souvenir* (London: Longman, Rees, Orme, Browne and Green, 1828), p. 196.

30. On Clare and the annuals, see Stephen Colclough, '"Designated in Print as Mr John Clare": The Annuals and the Field of Reading, 1827–1835', *John Clare Society Journal*, 25 (2005), 52–68.

31. For the complex publication history of this poem, see *The Complete Poetical Works*, ed. by Jerome McGann, 7 vols (Oxford: Oxford University Press, 1980–1993), III, p. 494.

32. Roger Chartier, *The Order of Books: Readers, Authors and Libraries in Europe between the Fourteenth and the Eighteenth Centuries*, trans. by Lydia Cochrane (Cambridge: Polity Press, 1994), pp. 3–6; D. F. McKenzie, *Bibliography and the Sociology of Texts*, 2nd edition (Cambridge: Cambridge University Press, 1999), p. 29.

33. Arthur F. Marotti, *Manuscript, Print and the English Renaissance Lyric* (London: Cornell University Press, 1995), p. 135.

34. Marotti, *Manuscript*, pp. 145–146.

35. Anne Lister, *I Know My Own Heart: The Diaries of Anne Lister (1791–1840)*, ed. by Helena Whitbread (London: Virago Press, 1988), p. 49.

36. St Clair, *Reading Nation*, p. 228.

37. Robert Charles Dallas, 'Stanzas: Introductory to a Friend's Album', from *Adrastus, A Tragedy: Amabel and the Cornish Lovers and Other Poems* (London: James Cawthorn, 1823), p. 134.

38. *The Remembrance*, ed. by Thomas Roscoe (London: Jennings and Chaplin, 1831), p. 100.

39. Carey appears to have married Fanny's sister, Margaret Maingay, in 1836. See William Wilfred Carey, *The History of the Careys of Guernsey* (London: J. M. Dent, 1938).

40. Felicia Hemans, 'The Graves of a Household', in *Records of Woman* (Edinburgh: Blackwood, 1828), pp. 302–304.

41. Sarah Pennington, *An Unfortunate Mother's Advice To Her Absent Daughters* (London: S. Chandler and S. Bristow, 1761), p. 39; Sarah Pennington, *A Mother's Advice To Her Absent Daughters* (London: Taylor and Hessey, 1811).

42. Thomas De Quincey, 'Style' (1840), in *De Quincey as Critic*, ed. by John E. Jordan (London: Routledge, 1973), p. 78.

43. Mrs Taylor, *Practical Hints to Young Females* (London: Taylor and Hessey, 1815).

44. Jacqueline Pearson, *Women's Reading, 1750–1835: A Dangerous Recreation* (Cambridge: Cambridge University Press, 1999), p. 43.

45. Jill Liddington, 'Beating the Inheritance Bounds: Anne Lister (1791–1840) and her Dynastic Identity', *Gender and History*, 7 (1995) 260–274; Extracts from Lister's (often coded) journals have been published as Anne Lister, *I Know My Own Heart: The Diaries of Anne Lister (1791–1840)*, ed. by Helena Whitbread (London: Virago, 1988); Anne Lister, *No Priest But Love: Excerpts from the Diaries of Anne Lister, 1824–1826*, ed. by Helena Whitbread (Otley: Smith Settle, 1992) and in Jill Liddington, *Female Fortune: Land, Gender and Authority – The Anne Lister Diaries and Other Writings 1833–36* (London: Rivers Oram, 1998).

46. Lister, *Own Heart*, p. 14.

47. Lister, *Own Heart*, pp. 89–90. Further references are given in the text.

48. Terry Castle, *The Apparitional Lesbian: Female Homosexuality and Modern Culture* (New York: Columbia University Press, 1993), pp. 92–106 (96).

49. Emma Donoghue, *Passions between Women: British Lesbian Culture* (London: Scarlet Press, 1993).

50. Lister suggested to M that Tib was prepared to 'willingly marry me in disguise at the altar', *Own Heart*, p. 105.

51. Anna Clark, 'Anne Lister's Construction of Lesbian Identity', *Journal of the History of Sexuality*, 7, 1 (1996), 23–50 (31); Clara Tuite, 'The Byronic Woman: Anne Lister's Style, Sociability and Sexuality', in *Romantic Sociability*, pp. 186–210 (187).

52. *London Catalogue of Books Published in Great Britain* (London: Sampson Low, 1851).

53. Anna Clark, 'Lesbian Identity', 38. Lister also read extracts from a review of *Lalla Rookh* to her aunt in 1817, *Own Heart*, p. 12.

54. For other references to their use of the library as a place to meet see Lister, *Own Heart*, p. 77, p. 81.

55. Tuite, 'The Byronic Woman', p. 193.

56. Castle, *Apparitional Lesbian*, pp. 102–103. Castle suggests that Lister used references to the classics as a 'secret language or semaphor' in order to talk to other lesbians, p. 102. Similarly, Clark argues that Lister formed her 'sexual identity by creatively reading two main sources: the classics and romantic writers', 'Lesbian Identity', 31.

57. 'Followed Miss Pickford into the [lecture] room. Talked a few minutes. She thought Lord Byron the best poet of the day', Lister, *Own Heart*, p. 237. Lister, *No Priest*, p. 54. Unlike the English edition, it included *Don Juan*.
58. Tuite uses this phrase, adapted from Adrienne Rich, to denote 'the social enforcement' of 'constructions of gender' in the post-Waterloo period, 'The Byronic Woman', p. 187.
59. Castle, *Apparitional Lesbian*, p. 58; Lister, *Own Heart*, p. 84.
60. Thomas Campbell, *The Pleasures of Hope* (London: Longmans, 1819).
61. Lister, *No Priest*, p. 346.
62. Muriel M. Green, 'A Spirited Yorkshire-Woman: The Letters of Anne Lister of Shibden Hall, Halifax', Library Association Thesis, 1939, p. 215. Further references are given in the text as 'Letters'.
63. On Young's place in the old canon, see St Clair, *Reading Nation*, pp. 525–534.
64. Lisa Moore, '"Something More Tender Still Than Friendship": Romantic Friendship in Early Nineteenth Century England', *Feminist Studies* 18, 3 (Fall 1992), 510–513. The title for this article is taken from Lister's diaries.
65. Lister, *No Priest*, p. 32.
66. Moore, 'Something More', p. 513.
67. Lister, *No Priest*, p. 127.
68. Tuite, 'The Byronic Woman', p. 202.
69. Pearson, *Women's Reading*, p. 25, p. 58.
70. John Gregory, *A Father's Legacy to His Daughters* (Edinburgh. W. Creech, 1774). This text was widely reprinted.
71. Anne Lister, 'Extracts From Books Read, 1814–1838', Calderdale Archives, Halifax Central Library, SH: 7/ML/Ex/1–11.
72. Anne Lister, 'Extracts 1819–1823', SH:7 ML Ex/4, ff.135–137.
73. Francis Hall, *Travels in France* (London: Longman, Hurst, Rees, Orme & Brown, 1819).
74. Lister, 'Extracts 1819–1823', SH:7 ML Ex/4.
75. Lister, 'Extracts 1819–1823', ff.75–77.
76. For Lister's management of the Shibden estate, see Jill Liddington, 'Gender, Authority and Mining in an Industrial Landscape: Anne Lister 1791–1840', *History Workshop Journal* 42 (1996), 68–86.
77. Pearson, *Women's Reading*, p. 15.
78. As Pearson notes, women who wished to attain a familiarity with the classics in the original were often treated satirically in the fiction of the Romantic period because these texts were seen as keys to the 'education and socialization' of boys, *Women's Reading*, p. 69.

6   Towards a Mass Audience, or, John Clare and the Problem of the Unknown Public

1. *John Clare By Himself*, ed. by Eric Robinson and David Powell (Ashington and Manchester: Carcanet, 1996). p. 240.
2. Richard D. Altick, *The English Common Reader: A Social History of the Mass Reading Public, 1800–1900* (Chicago: University of Chicago Press, 1957), pp. 240–259.

3. Altick used *Sketches in The Life of John Clare,* ed. by Edmund Blunden (London: Cobden-Sanderson, 1931). The manuscript version of the 'Sketches' was published as *John Clare's Autobiographical Writings,* ed. by Eric Robinson (Oxford: Oxford University Press, 1986).

4. William St Clair, *The Reading Nation in the Romantic Period* (Cambridge: Cambridge University Press, 2004), p. 339.

5. David Vincent, *Bread, Knowledge and Freedom: A Study of Nineteenth-Century Working Class Autobiography* (London: Methuen, 1982).

6. Vincent, *Bread,* p. 9.

7. Samuel Bamford, *Early Days* (London: Simpkin, Marshall, 1849); *The Life of Thomas Cooper: Written By Himself* (London: Hodder and Stoughton, 1872); William Lovett, *Life and Struggles of William Lovett* (London: Trubner, 1876).

8. Jonathan Rose, *The Intellectual Life of the British Working Classes* (New Haven: Yale University Press, 2001), p. 2.

9. Ann Yearsley, *Poems on Several Occasions* (London: Thomas Caddel, 1785); *Poems on Various Subjects* (London: Robinson, 1787).

10. Vincent, *Bread,* pp. 9–10.

11. John James Bezer, 'The Autobiography of One of the Chartist Rebels of 1848', in *Testaments of Radicalism: Memoirs of Working Class Politicians 1790–1885,* ed. by David Vincent (London: Europa: 1977), p. 167.

12. Vincent, *Bread,* p. 5.

13. Rose, *Intellectual Life,* p. 2; *The Autobiography of the Working Class: An Annotated Critical Bibliography,* ed. by John Burnett, David Vincent and David Mayall, 3 vols (Brighton: Harvester, 1984–1989).

14. Rose, *Intellectual Life,* pp. 1–2.

15. Rose, *Intellectual Life,* p. 2.

16. Jonathan Rose, 'Rereading the English Common Reader: A Preface to a History of Audiences', *Journal of the History of Ideas,* 53 (1992), 47–70, reprinted in *The Book History Reader* ed. by David Finkelstein and Alistair McCleery, (London: Routledge, 2002), pp. 324–339 (pp. 329–330).

17. Rose, *Intellectual Life,* pp. 111–112.

18. Teresa Gerrard, 'New Methods in the History of Reading: "Answers to Correspondents" in the *Family Herald,* 1860–1900', *Publishing History,* 43 (1998), 52–69 (54).

19. Kate Flint, *The Woman Reader 1837–1914* (Oxford: Clarendon Press, 1993), p. 187.

20. Flint, *The Woman Reader,* pp. 209–218.

21. Vincent, *Bread,* pp. 22–23; Rose, *Intellectual Life,* p. 112.

22. Alan Richardson, *Literature, Education and Romanticism: Reading as Social Practice, 1780–1832* (Cambridge: Cambridge University Press, 1994), p. 233.

23. James Hogg, 'Memoir of the Author's Life', in *Altrive Tales: Featuring a 'Memoir of the Author's Life',* ed. by Gillian Hughes (Edinburgh: Edinburgh University Press, 2005), pp. 11–52. The 'Memoir' was first published in *The Mountain Bard* (1807); William Cobbett, *The Life and Adventures of Peter Porcupine* (Philadelphia: William Cobbett, 1796). An English edition was published in 1797.

24. Richardson, *Literature, Education,* p. 235.

25. Clare, *By Himself,* p. 2. Further references are given in the text.

26. Richardson, *Literature, Education,* p. 236.

27. Hogg, 'Memoir', p. 18.
28. Even the most recent biography of Clare fails to acknowledge the artful nature of his autobiography. See Jonathan Bate, *John Clare: A Biography* (London: Picador, 2003), pp. 89–109.
29. Clare, *By Himself*, pp. xvi–xvii. Robinson and Powell's introduction to this volume contains a detailed history of the context of the manuscript's creation.
30. John Clare, *Poems Descriptive of Rural Life and Scenery*, 4th edition (London: Taylor and Hessey, 1821), p. ix.
31. This episode is discussed in Richardson, *Literature, Education*, p. 255.
32. Clare 'Religious Tracts', quoted in George Deacon, *John Clare and the Folk Tradition* (London: Sinclair Browne, 1983), p. 33. Clare's other autobiographical writings are collected in *By Himself*.
33. Roger Chartier, *The Order of Books: Readers, Authors and Libraries in Europe Between the Fourteenth and the Eighteenth Centuries*, trans. by Lydia Cochrane (Cambridge: Polity Press, 1994), p. 22.
34. For a discussion of those readers 'invisible' to traditional studies of literacy, see Barry Reay, 'The Context and Meaning of Popular Literacy: Some Evidence from Nineteenth-Century Rural England', *Past and Present*, 131 (1991), 89–129 (114).
35. Christopher Thomson, *The Autobiography of an Artisan* (London: John Chapman, 1847), pp. vi–vii, p. 19.
36. Clare, *Poems Descriptive*, p. ix.
37. Cooper, *The Life*, p. 56.
38. Vincent, *Bread*, p. 126.
39. David Vincent, *The Rise of Mass Literacy: Reading and Writing in Modern Europe* (Cambridge: Polity Press, 2000), p. 144.
40. St Clair, *Reading Nation*, pp. 122–139.
41. St Clair, *Reading Nation*, p. 138.
42. Bate, *John Clare*, p. 104.
43. Clare, *By Himself*, p. 107.
44. St Clair, *Reading Nation*, p. 138.
45. St Clair, *Reading Nation*, pp. 132–133 (p. 133).
46. Blair's *Sermons* was a gift from Radstock, Clare, *By Himself*, p. 120.
47. St Clair, *Reading Nation*, pp. 268–292.
48. Thomson, *Autobiography of an Artisan*, pp. 64–65, pp. 79–80.
49. Vincent, *Bread*, p. 115.
50. Joseph Mayett, *The Autobiography of Joseph Mayett of Quainton (1783–1839)*, ed. by Ann Kusmaul, Buckinghamshire Record Society, No. 23 (Aylesbury: Buckinghamshire Record Society, 1986), p. 70.
51. Mayett, *Autobiography*, pp. 70–72 (p. 72).
52. Rose, *Intellectual Life*, p. 118.
53. Cooper, *The Life*, p. 59.
54. This survey is well known amongst historians of working-class literacy. See, Barry Reay, *The Last Rising of the Agricultural Labourers: Rural Life and Protest in Nineteenth-Century Britain* (Oxford: Clarendon Press, 1990). It is discussed along with other surveys in David Vincent, *Literacy and Popular Culture: England 1750–1914* (Cambridge: Cambridge University Press, 1989), pp. 73–94.

55. Frederick Liardet, 'State of the Peasantry in the County of Kent', in *Central Society of Education, Second Publication* (London: Taylor & Walton, 1838), pp. 87–139 (p. 89).
56. Reay, 'Context and Meaning', 89–129 (117).
57. Liardet, 'State of the Peasantry', p. 96. Further references are given in the text.
58. Reay, 'Context and Meaning', 116.
59. Liardet, 'State of the Peasantry', p. 91, pp. 92–93.
60. Quoted in Reay, 'Context and Meaning', 127.
61. Reay, 'Context and Meaning', 127.
62. Reay, 'Context and Meaning', 129.
63. [Wilkie Collins], 'The Unknown Public', *Household Words*, 18 (21 August 1858), 217–222, reprinted in Wilkie Collins, *My Miscellanies* (London: Chatto & Windus, 1874), pp. 249–264 (p. 251). Further references are given in the text.
64. Patrick Brantlinger, *The Reading Lesson: The Threat of Mass Literacy in Nineteenth-Century British Fiction* (Bloomington and Indianapolis: Indiana University Press, 1998), pp. 17–18.
65. Altick, *The English Common Reader*, p. 394.
66. Brantlinger, *The Reading Lesson*, p. 17.
67. [Margaret Oliphant], 'The Byways of Literature', *Blackwood's Magazine*, 84 (1858), 200–216 (202–203).
68. Henry Mayhew, *London Labour and the London Poor*, 4 vols (London: Griffin, Bohn, 1862).
69. Lorna Huett, 'Among the Unknown Public: *Household Words*, *All the Year Round* and the Mass-Market Weekly Periodical in the Mid-Nineteenth Century', *Victorian Periodicals Review*, 38, 1 (2005), 61–82; Deborah Wynne, *The Sensation Novel and the Victorian Family Magazine* (Houndsmill: Palgrave, 2001), p. 15.
70. Patricia Anderson, *The Printed Image and the Transformation of Popular Culture 1790–1860* (Oxford: Clarendon Press, 1991), p. 11.
71. Charles Knight, *The Old Printer and the Modern Press* (London: John Murray, 1854), p. 264.
72. Rose, *Intellectual Life*, p. 386.
73. *The London Journal*, 15 November 1851, p. 160.
74. Lynne Warren, '"Women in Conference": Reading the Correspondence Columns in *Woman* 1890–1910', in *Nineteenth-Century Media and the Construction of Identities*, ed. by Laurel Brake, Bill Bell and David Finkelstein (Basingstoke: Palgrave, 2000), pp. 122–134 (p. 127).
75. Gerrard, 'New Methods ', (56–57).
76. [Oliphant], 'Byways', 210–212.
77. Gerrard, 'New Methods', 60.
78. Gerrard, 'New Methods', p. 64; Rose, *Intellectual Life*, p. 386.
79. Warren, 'Women in Conference', p. 131; *London Journal*, p. 160.
80. Andrew King, *The London Journal, 1845–1883: Periodicals, Production and Gender* (Aldershot: Ashgate, 2004).
81. [Oliphant], 'Byways', p. 211.
82. For an overview of recent work, see Hilary Fraser, Stephanie Green and Judith Johnston, *Gender and the Victorian Periodical* (Cambridge: Cambridge University Press, 2003), pp. 68–76.

83. *The London Journal*, 15 November 1851, p. 160.

84. Warren, 'Women in Conference', pp. 129–134.

85. Leah Price, 'Reader's Block: Response', in *Victorian Studies*, 46, 2 (Winter 2004), 231–242 (233).

86. Garrett Stewart, 'The Mind's Sigh: Pictured Reading in Nineteenth-Century Painting', in *Victorian Studies*, 46, 2 (Winter 2004), 217–230 (226). Price and Stewart are mainly concerned with the unseen, untraceable, mental processes of reading (especially the reading of fiction).

87. Fraser, Green and Johnston, *Gender and the Victorian Periodical*, p. 49.

88. The book being considered was George Webbe Dasent's, *Annals of an Eventful Life* (London: Hurst & Blacket, 1870), *The Times*, 17 January 1870, p. 6, col. c.

89. Richard D. Altick, *The Presence of the Past: Topics of the Day in the Victorian Novel* (Columbus: Ohio State University Press, 1991), p. 460.

90. Isabella Todd, 'On the Education of the Girls of the Middle Class', *Leisure Hour* 19 (1870), pp. 202–203.

91. For the early history of bookstalls on the LNWR, see Stephen Colclough 'Station to Station: the LNWR and the Emergence of the Railway Bookstall', in *Printing Places: Locations of Book Production and Distribution Since 1500*, ed. by John Hinks and Catherine Armstrong (London: British Library, 2005), pp. 169–184.

92. 'Railway Literature', *Dublin University Magazine*, 34 (September 1849), 280–281 (280).

93. *The Literature of the Rail Re-Published by Permission from The Times of Saturday 9th August 1851* (London: John Murray, 1851), p. 5.

94. On the association of cheap literature with obscenity, see Lynda Nead, *Victorian Babylon: People, Streets and Images in Nineteenth-Century London* (New Haven: Yale University Press, 2000), pp. 149–161.

95. [Henry Mansel], 'Sensation Novels', *Quarterly Review*, 113 (1863), 481–514 (485).

96. 'Our Female Sensation Novelists', *Christian Remembrancer*, 46 (1863), 210–212.

97. Charles Dickens, *Oliver Twist*, ed. by Philip Horne (London: Penguin Books, 2002), p. 75.

98. Stephen Colclough, '"Purifying the Sources of Amusement and Information"?: The Railway Bookstalls of W. H. Smith & Son, 1855–60', *Publishing History*, 56 (2004), 27–51.

99. For contemporary photographs, see Jeoffry Spence, *Victorian and Edwardian Railway Travel from Old Photographs* (London: B. T. Batsford, 1985), p. 99.

100. Henry Sampson, *A History of Advertising from the Earliest Times* (London: Chatto & Windus, 1875).

101. 'Indenture Midland Railway Company and W. H. Smith, 28 July 1851', National Archives, Kew, Rail 793/10.

102. Charles Dickens, 'Bill-Sticking', in *Selected Journalism 1850–1870* (London: Penguin Books, 1997), pp. 283–293 (p. 284, p. 283).

103. For an example of a building in Leeds in the late 1860s, see *Victorian and Edwardian Yorkshire from Old Photographs*, ed. by A. B. Craven (London: B. T. Batsford, 1977), p. 106.

104. Dickens, 'Bill-Sticking', p. 284.

105. *The Language of the Walls and a Voice from the Shop Windows* (Manchester: Abel Heywood, 1855), p. 2, p. 57, p. 14.

106. 'Dickens, 'Bill-Sticking', p. 291.
107. On the attitude of Joyce towards advertising and commodity culture, see Thomas Richards, *The Commodity Culture of Victorian England: Advertising and Spectacle, 1851–1914* (London: Verso, 1991), pp. 205–222.
108. Charles Dickens, *Bleak House*, ed. by Nicola Bradbury (London: Penguin Books, 1996), p. 257.
109. Charles Manby Smith, *The Little World of London* (London: Arthur Hall, 1857), p. 9.
110. Clare, *By Himself*, p. 57.
111. Rose, *Intellectual Life*, p. 392.

Conclusion: Texts Consumed

1. Janice Radway, *Reading the Romance*, (London: Verso, 1987), p. 7.
2. H. J. Jackson, *Romantic Readers: The Evidence of Marginalia* (New Haven: Yale University Press, 2005), p. 303.
3. James Raven, Helen Small and Naomi Tadmor, 'Introduction', in *The Practice and Representation of Reading in England*(Cambridge: Cambridge University Press, 1986), pp. 1–21 (p. 15).
4. Gwyneth Tyson Roberts, *The Language of the Blue Books: the Perfect Instrument of Empire* (Cardiff: University of Wales, Press, 1998), 115–128.

Select Bibliography

Please note, this bibliography does not contain details of all the texts owned, borrowed or read by the readers studied in this book.

Primary sources

A. Manuscripts

Caesar, Charles. 'Commonplace Book of Charles Caesar, 1705', British Library, Add. MSS 43410.

Dawson, John. 'A Catalogue of My Books', Hackney Archives, London D/F/DAW-/2.

——. 'A Catalogue of the Books of Mr John Dawson of Hoxton Deceased, Left by Will to the Vicars of S. Leonard in Shoreditch, 1765', Hackney Archives, London D/F/DAW-/1.

——. 'John Dawson's Book; January 8, 1730', Hackney Archives, London, D/F/DAW-/2.

——. 'John Dawson's Diary, II', Hackney Archives, London D/F/DAW-/3/2.

——. 'The Life of John Dawson; Officer of Excise', West Yorkshire Archive Service, Kirklees, Huddersfield, MS: KC688.

Francis, Charlotte. 'Journal of What Passed in an Excursion to Brighton', British Library, Egerton MSS 3706A.

Freke, Elizabeth. 'Commonplace Book of Elizabeth Freke', British Library, Add. MSS 45718.

'Hackney Reading Society: Minutes, Records of Books Distributed, Accounts and Rules, April 1815–September 1828', Hackney Archives Centre, London, D/S/2/1.

'Hackney Reading Society: Minutes', 1828–1846, Hackney Archives, D/S/2/2.

Hunter, Joseph. 'The Journal of Joseph Hunter', British Library, Add. MSS 24,879.

'Indenture Midland Railway Company and W.H. Smith, 28 July 1851', National Archives, Kew, Rail 793/10.

Knight, Emma. 'Commonplace Book of Emma Knight', British Library, c.152.d.1.

Lister, Anne. 'Extracts From Books Read, 1814–1838', Calderdale Archives, Halifax Central Library, SH: 7/ML/Ex/1–11.

'Minutes of the Eclectic Book Society, 1812–20', Guildhall Library, London, MS 988A, f.124.

Savile, Gertrude. 'The Commonplace Book of Gertrude Savile', Nottinghamshire Archives, Nottingham, DD.SR 212/12.

——. 'Gertrude Savile's Journal, 1721–31', Nottinghamshire Archives, Nottingham, DD.SR 212/10–11.

'Walworth Book Society, 1835–1840', Southwark Local Studies Library, MS11220.

B. Annotated books

Atlas Geographus: Or a Compleat System of Geography Ancient and Modern, 2 vols (London: John Nutt, 1711), Hackney Archives, London. Annotated by John Dawson.

[Arbuthnot, John]. *Law is a Bottom-less Pit* (London: John Morphew, 1712), British Library [hereafter BL], 12314.aa.16. Anonymous annotations.

Boyer, Abel. *The History of the Reign of Queen Anne, Digested into Annals*, 11 vols (London: A Roper & F. Coggan, 1703–1713), Hackney Archives, London. Annotated by John Dawson.

[Collins, Arthur] *The Peerage of England, Or a Genalogical and Historical Account of All the Flourishing Families of this Kingdom … From Saxon Times to this Present Year, 1711*, 2 vols (London: Sanger and Collins, 1711), Hackney Archives. Annotated by John Dawson.

Echard, Laurence. *The Gazetter's; or, Newsman's Interpreter* (London: John Nicholson, 1704), Hackney Archives. Annotated by John Dawson.

Flavell, John. *Sacramental Meditations* (London: N. Crouch, 1700), BL, 875.a.10.

Laurence, Edward. *The Duty and Office of a Land-Steward* (Dublin: Samuel Fuller, 1731), BL, 1508/1236. Anonymous Annotations.

Holwell, John. *A Sure Guide to the Practical Surveyor, in Two Parts* (London: Christopher Hussey, 1678), Hackney Archives. Annotated by John Dawson.

The Merchant and Tradesman's Daily Companion (London: Midwinter, 1729), Hackney Archives. Annotated by John Dawson.

A New Commonplace Book: Being an Improvement on that Recommended by Mr Locke (London: Walker, 1799), BL, 8405.cc.21. Anonymous annotations.

The Peerage of England: or, an Historical Account of the Present Nobility, 4th edition, 2 vols (London: W. Taylor, 1717), Hackney Archives. Annotated by John Dawson.

[Peirce, J]. *An Essay in Favour of the Ancient Practice of Giving the Eucharist to Children* (London: J. Noon and J. Gray, 1728), BL, 117.g.56. Anonymous annotations.

Puffendorf, Samuel Von. *An Introduction to the History of the Principal Kingdoms and States of Europe* (London: J. Knapton, D. Midwinter [and 3 others], 1728), Hackney Archives. Annotated by John Dawson.

Salmon, Thomas. *The Chronological Historian* (London: W. Mears, 1733), Hackney Archives. Annotated by John Dawson.

Salmon, Thomas. *A Review of the History of England*, 2 vols (London: C. Rivington, 1724), BL, 598.e.16. Anonymous annotations.

Samber, Robert. *On the Passion of Our Blessed Saviour* (London: S. Battersbury, 1708), BL, 1608/5623. Anonymous annotations.

C. Books and periodicals

Arber, Edward. ed. *The Term Catalogues 1668–1709 A.D.; With a Number for Easter Term, 1711 A.D.*, 3 vols (London: Edward Arber, 1903–1906).

Aubin, Penelope. *The Noble Slaves* (London: E. Bell [and nine others], 1722).

——. *The Strange Adventures of the Count de Vinevil and his Family*, (London: E Bell [and nine others], 1721).

Austen, Jane. *Mansfield Park*, 3 vols (London: T. Egerton, 1814).

——. *Northanger Abbey*, ed. by Marilyn Butler (London: Penguin, 1995).

——. *Pride and Prejudice*, ed. by R. Irvine (Ormskirk: Broadview, 2002).

Bamford, Samuel. *Early Days* (London: Simpkin, Marshall, 1849).

Beadle, John. *The Journal or Diary of a Thankful Christian* (London: Thomas Parkhurst, 1656).

Behn, Aphra. *The Unfortunate Bride* (London: S. Briscoe, 1698).

——. *All the Histories and Novels of the Late Ingenious Mrs Behn* (London: A. Bettesworth and F. Clay, 1722).

Berkeley, George. *A Treatise Concerning the Principles of Human Knowledge* (Dublin: Jeremy Pepyat, 1710).

Bezer, John James. 'The Autobiography of One of the Chartist Rebels of 1848', in *Testaments of Radicalism: Memoirs of Working Class Politicians 1790–1885*, ed. by David Vincent (London: Europa, 1977), pp. 153–187.

[Bignon, Jean Paul]. *The Adventures of Abdallah Son of Hanif*, 3 vols (London: R. Newton, 1729).

Biographical Anecdotes of the Founders of the French Republic (London: R. Philips, 1797).

Bisset, Robert. *Modern Literature; A Novel*, 3 vols (London: T. N. Longman & O. Rees, 1804).

A Brief Character of the Protector Oliver Cromwell with an Account of the Slavery He Left the Nation under at his Death Comprehended in a Seasonable Speech, Made by a Worthy Member of Parliament, in the House of Commons … March 1659 (London: R. Taylor, 1692).

Burney, Fanny. Diary and Letters of Madame D'Arblay: Edited by Her Niece [Charlotte Barrett], 7 vols. (London: Henry Colburn, 1842–1846).

Byron, George Gordon. *The Complete Poetical Works*, ed. by Jerome McGann, 7 vols. (Oxford: Oxford University Press, 1980–1993).

Campbell, Thomas. *The Pleasures of Hope* (London: Longmans, 1819).

A Catalogue of the Library Belonging to the Book Society Held at the House of Esther Caterer in Surry Street, Sheffield (Sheffield: Pierson, 1798).

Clare, John. *John Clare By Himself*, ed. by Eric Robinson and David Powell (Ashington and Manchester: Carcanet, 1996).

——. *Sketches in The Life of John Clare*, ed. by Edmund Blunden (London: Cobden-Sanderson, 1931).

——. *John Clare's Autobiographical Writings*, ed. by Eric Robinson (Oxford: Oxford University Press, 1986).

——. *Poems Descriptive of Rural Life and Scenery*, 4th edition (London: Taylor and Hessey, 1821).

Cobbett, William. *The Life and Adventures of Peter Porcupine* (Philadelphia: William Cobbett, 1796).

Coe, William.'The Diary of William Coe, 1693–1729', in *Two East-Anglian Diaries 1641–1729*, ed. by Matthew Storey (Woodbridge: Boydell Press, 1994), pp. 203–260.

[Collins, Wilkie], 'The Unknown Public', *Household Words*, 18 (21 August 1858), 217–222.

Collins, Wilkie. *My Miscellanies* (London: Chatto & Windus, 1874).

Comber, Thomas. *A Discourse Concerning the Daily Frequenting of Common Prayer* (London: Charles Brome, 1687).

[Coombe, William]. *Fragments; in the Manner of Sterne*, (London: Debrett, Murray & Highley, 1797). Cooper, Thomas. *The Life of Thomas Cooper: Written By Himself* (London: Hodder and Stoughton, 1872).

'Correspondents on All Subjects of Literature and Science', in *Monthly Magazine* 51, (June 1821), 397–398.

Cradock, Samuel. *Knowledge and Practice, Or, A Plain Discourse on the Chief Things Necessary to be Known, Believ'd and Practised in Order to Gain Salvation. Useful for Private Families*, 3rd edition (London: Grantham, Mortlock and Miller, 1673).

Dallas, Robert Charles. *Adrastus, A Tragedy: Amabel and the Cornish Lovers and Other Poems* (London: James Cawthorn, 1823).

de Gomez, Madame [trans. Eliza Haywood]. *La Belle Assemblee, or, The Adventures of Six Days* (London: D. Browne Junr and S. Chapman, 1724).

de Segrais, Jean Regnauld. *Three Novels* (London: D. Browne Junr, 1725).

De Quincey, Thomas. 'Style', in *De Quincey as Critic*, ed. by John E. Jordan (London: Routledge, 1973), p. 78.

Dickens, Charles. 'Bill-Sticking', in *Selected Journalism 1850–1870* (London: Penguin Books, 1997), pp. 283–293.

——. *Bleak House*, ed. by Nicola Bradbury (London: Penguin Books, 1996).

——. *Oliver Twist*, ed. by Philip Horne (London: Penguin Books, 2002).

English Advice to the Freeholders of England (London: n.p., 1714).

Erasmus, Desiderius. *On Copia of Words and Ideas*, trans. by Donald B. King (Milwaukee: Marquette University Press, 1963).

An Essay Upon Study, More Particularly the Study of Philosophy (London: Richard Wilkin, 1713).

'Extracts from the Port Folio of a Man of Letters: Poetical or Prose Imitations and Similarities', *Monthly Magazine*, 5 (May 1798), 365–367.

Fenton, Elijah. *Mariamne: A Tragedy* (London: J. Tonson, 1723).

Ferrier, John. 'Comments on Sterne', *Memoirs of the Literary and Philosophical Society of Manchester*, iv (1793), 45–86.

[Flatman, Thomas]. *Heraclitus Ridens; or, A Discourse between Jest and Earnest, Where Many a True Word is Spoken in Opposition to All Libellers Against the Government*, 8 (Aug. 1682).

Freke, Elizabeth. *The Remembrances of Elizabeth Freke 1671–1714*, ed. by Raymond Anselment, Camden Fifth Series, Volume 18 (Cambridge: Cambridge University Press, 2001).

Gay, John. *The Beggar's Opera* (London: John Watts, 1728).

The Gentleman's Magazine 1731–51: The Lists of Books, Collected with Annual Indexes and the Index to the First Twenty Years, English Bibliographical Sources Series 1, No. 6 (London: Gregg Press, 1966).

Green, Muriel M. 'A Spirited Yorkshire-Woman: the Letters of Anne Lister of Shibden Hall, Halifax', Library Association Thesis, 1939.

Gregory, John. *A Father's Legacy to His Daughters* (Edinburgh. W. Creech, 1774).

A Guide to All the Watering and Sea-Bathing Places (London: Richard Philips, 1803).

Hall, Francis. *Travels in France* (London: Longman, Hurst, Rees, Orme and Brown, 1819).

Hall's New Margate and Ramsgate Guide (Margate: Joseph Hall, [1790]).

Haywood, Eliza. *The British Recluse* (London: D. Browne Junr, W. Chetwood, J. Woodman and S. Chapman, 1722).

——. *The Arragonian Queen* (London: J. Roberts, 1724).

——. *The Perplex'd Dutchess* (London: J. Roberts, 1727).

——. *The City Widow: Or, Love in a Butt. A Novel* (London: J. Roberts, 1729).

[Haywood, Eliza. trans.]. *Memoirs of the Baron de Brosse*, 2 vols. (London: D. Browne Junr and S. Chapman, 1725–1726).

Hemans, Felicia. *Records of Woman* (Edinburgh: Blackwood, 1828).

Herbert, George. *The Temple: Sacred Poems and Private Ejaculations* (London: Jeffrey Wale, 1703).

Hogg, James. *The Mountain Bard* (Edinburgh: A. Constable, 1807).

——. 'Memoir of the Author's Life', in *Altrive Tales: Featuring a 'Memoir of the Author's Life'*, ed. by Gillian Hughes (Edinburgh: Edinburgh University Press, 2005).

[Hunter, Sylvester]. *A Brief Memoir of the Late Joseph Hunter, F. S. A.* (London: John Edward Taylor, 1861).

Knight, Charles. *The Old Printer and the Modern Press* (London: John Murray, 1854).

The Language of the Walls and a Voice from the Shop Windows (Manchester: Abel Heywood, 1855).

Le Noble, E. *Zulima, Or, Pure Love* (London: J. Hooke and J. Roberts, 1719).

Liardet, Frederick. 'State of the Peasantry in the County of Kent', in *Central Society of Education, Second Publication* (London: Taylor and Walton, 1838), pp. 87–139.

Lister, Anne. *I Know My Own Heart: The Diaries of Anne Lister (1791–1840)*, ed. by Helena Whitbread (London: Virago Press, 1988).

——. *No Priest But Love: Excerpts from the Diaries of Anne Lister, 1824–1826*, ed. by Helena Whitbread (Otley: Smith Settle, 1992).

Lister, Martin. *A Journey to Paris in the Year 1698* (London: Jacob Tonson, 1699).

The Literary Souvenir (London: Longman, Rees, Orme, Browne and Green, 1828).

The Literature of the Rail Re-Published by Permission from The Times of Saturday 9th August 1851, (London: John Murray, 1851).

Locke, John. 'A New Method of a Commonplace Book', in *The Posthumous Works of Mr John Locke* (London: John Churchill, 1706), pp. 311–336.

London Catalogue of Books Published in Great Britain (London: Sampson Low, 1851).

The London Journal, 15 November 1851.

Lovett, William. *Life and Struggles of William Lovett* (London: Trubner, 1876).

Macky, John. *A Journey Through England* (London: J. Roberts and T. Caldecott, 1714).

Manby Smith, Charles. *The Little World of London* (London: Arthur Hall, 1857).

[Mansel, Henry]. 'Sensation Novels', *Quarterly Review*, 113 (1863), 481–514.

Mayett, Joseph. *The Autobiography of Joseph Mayett of Quainton (1783–1839)*, ed. by Ann Kusmaul, Buckinghamshire Record Society, 23 (Aylesbury: Buckinghamshire Record Society, 1986).

Mayhew, Henry. *London Labour and the London Poor*, 4 vols (London: Griffin, Bohn, 1862).

The Monthly Catalogue, 1723–30, English Bibliographical Sources Series 1, No. 2 (London: Gregg Press, 1964).

[More, Hannah]. *Hints Towards Forming the Character of a Young Princess* (London: Thomas Cadell, 1805).

The New Margate and Ramsgate Guide (London: H. Turpin and T. Wilkins, n.d).

Nunnery Tales Written by a Young Man (London: the Booksellers of London and Westminster, 1727).

[Oliphant, Margaret]. 'The Byways of Literature', *Blackwood's Magazine*, 84 (1858), 200–216.

'Our Female Sensation Novelists', *Christian Remembrancer*, 46 (1863), 210–212.

Penn, Marjorie. 'The Account Books of Gertrude Savile, 1736–58', *Thoroton Society Record Series*, 24 (1967), 99–152.

Pennington, Sarah. *An Unfortunate Mother's Advice To Her Absent Daughters* (London: S. Chandler and S. Bristow, 1761).

——. *A Mother's Advice To Her Absent Daughters* (London: Taylor and Hessey, 1811).

Percy, Thomas. *Reliques of Ancient English Poetry* (London: Dodsley, 1765).

Perrault, Francois. *The Divill of Mascon* (Oxford: R. Davis, 1659).

Philips, John. *Sportive Wit: The Muses Merriment – A New Spring of Witty Drollery, Joviall Fancies and a la Mode Lampoones* (London: Nath. Brook, 1656).

Pinkerton, John. ed. *Walpoliana*, 2 vols (London: R. Phillips, 1799).

Poems on the Affairs of State (London: n.p., 1703).

Poems on Various Subjects (London: Robinson, 1787).

Prior, Matthew. *The Literary Works of Matthew Prior*, ed. by H. B. Wright and M. K. Spears, 2 Vols (Oxford: Clarendon Press, 1959).

The Prude: A Novel in Three Parts, 3 vols (London: J. Roberts, 1724–1726).

Quarles, Francis. *Divine Fancies Digested into Epigrams, Meditations and Observations* (London: J. Williams and C. Skegness, 1687).

——. *The Shepherd's Oracles: Delivered in Certain Eclogues* (London: John Marriot & Richard Marriot, [1645]).

Radcliffe, Ann. *The Mysteries of Udolpho*, 4 vols (London: G. G. & J. Robinson, 1794).

——. *A Journey Made in the Summer of 1794, through Holland and the Western Frontier of Germany* (London: Robinson, 1795).

——. *The Italian: Or, the Confessional of the Black Penitents* (London: T. Cadell Jun and W. Davies, 1797).

'Railway Literature', *Dublin University Magazine*, 34 (September 1849), 280–281.

The Remarks on a Late Libel Privately Dispers'd by the Tories Entitled English Advice to the Freeholders of England, (London: J. Roberts, 1715).

Robinson, Anthony. *A View of the Causes and Consequences of English Wars* (London: Johnson, 1798).

[Robinson, John]. *A Directory of Sheffield Including the Manufacturers of the Local Villages* (Sheffield: James Montgomery, 1797).

Roscoe, Thomas. (ed.). *The Remembrance* (London: Jennings and Chaplin, 1831).

Ryder, Dudley. *The Diary of Dudley Ryder, 1715–1716*, ed. by William Matthews (London: Methuen, 1939).

Le Sage, Alain Rene. *The History and Adventures of Gil Blas* (London: Jacob Tonson, 1716).

Sampson, Henry. *A History of Advertising from the Earliest Times* (London: Chatto & Windus, 1875).

Savile, Gertrude. *Secret Comment: The Diaries of Gertrude Savile 1721–1757*, ed. by Alan Saville (Nottingham: The Thoroton Society, 1997).

de Scudery, Madeleine. *Clelia: An Excellent Romance* (London: Herringman [and eight others], 1678).

[Shirley, James]. *Double Falshood: Or, the Distrest Lovers ... Written Originally by W. Shakespeare* (London: J. Watts, 1728).

The Spectator, 1 (1711).

The Spectator, 37 (1711).

The Spirit of the Public Journals for 1797: Being an Impartial Selection of the Most Exquisite Essays and J'eux D'esprits (London: R. Philips [and four others], 1798).

Steele, Richard. *The Conscious Lovers: A Comedy. As it is Acted at the Theatre Royal in Drury-Lane* (London: Jacob Tonson, 1723).

Story, G. W. *A True and Impartial History of ... Ireland During the Last Two Years* (London: Chiswell, 1691).

Sturmy, John. *Sesostris: Or, Royalty in Disguise* (London: J. Crokatt, 1728).

Taylor, Mrs. *Practical Hints to Young Females* (London: Taylor and Hessey, 1815).

The True State of England. Containing the Particular Duty, Business and Salary of Every Officer, Civil and Military (London: King, Stagg, Francklin and Browne, 1729).

Thomson, Christopher. *The Autobiography of an Artisan* (London: John Chapman, 1847).

Todd, Isabella. 'On the Education of the Girls of the Middle Class', *Leisure Hour* 19 (1870), 202–203.

Villiers, Pierre. *Female Falsehood, or, The Life and Adventures of a Late French … Digested by Monsieur St. Evremont* (London: John Walthoe, 1722).

Voltaire. *Candide and Other Stories*, trans. by Roger Pearson (Oxford: Oxford University Press, 1990).

Wallas, Samuel. *The Good Angel of Stamford* (London: S.N., 1659).

Ward, Edward. *All Men Mad: or, England a Great Bedlam* (London: n.p., 1704), British Library, 164.1.67.

Ward, T. A. *Short Account of the Sheffield Library* (Sheffield: Bacon, 1825).

White, Robert. *Autobiographical Notes* (Newcastle: Newcastle University Library, 1966).

Williams, H. M. *A Tour in Switzerland; or a View of the Present State of the Government and Manners of Those Cantons, With Comparative Sketches of the Present State of France*, 2 vols (London: G. G. & J. Robinson, 1798).

Yearsley, Ann. *Poems on Several Occasions* (London: Thomas Caddel, 1785).

Zimmerman, Johann Georg. *Solitude Considered With Respect to Its Influence Upon the Mind and Heart … Translated From the French of J.B. Mercier* (London: C. Dilly, 1797).

Secondary sources

Alcorn Baron, Sabrina, Elizabeth Walsh and Susan Scola, eds *The Reader Revealed* (Washington: Folger Library, 2001).

Alsop, Derek and Chris Walsh, *The Practice of Reading: Interpreting the Novel* (Houndmills: Macmillan Press, 1999).

Alston, Robin. *Books with Manuscript: A Short Title Catalogue of Books with Manuscript Notes in the British Library* (London: British Library, 1994).

Alston, R. C. ed. *Order and Connexion: Studies in Bibliography and Book History* (Woodbridge: Boydell and Brewer, 1997).

Altick, Richard D. *The English Common Reader: A Social History of the Mass Reading Public, 1800–1900* (Chicago: University of Chicago Press, 1957).

——. *The Presence of the Past: Topics of the Day in the Victorian Novel* (Columbus: Ohio State University Press, 1991).

Anderson, Patricia. *The Printed Image and the Transformation of Popular Culture 1790–1860* (Oxford: Clarendon Press, 1991).

Anselment, Raymond A. 'Elizabeth Freke's Remembrances: Reconstructing a Self', *Tulsa Studies in Women's Literature*, 16 (1997), 57–75.

Backscheider, Paula and John Richetti, eds *Popular Fiction by Women 1660–1730: An Anthology*, (Oxford: Clarendon Press, 1996).

Baggerman, Arianne. 'The Cultural Universe of a Dutch Child: Otto Van Eck and His Literature', *Eighteenth Century Studies*, 31, 1 (1997), 129–134.

Ballaster, Ros. *Seductive Forms: Women's Amatory Fiction from 1684 to 1740* (Oxford: Clarendon Press, 1992).

Barchas, Janine. *Graphic Design: Print Culture and the Eighteenth-Century Novel* (Cambridge: Cambridge University Press, 2003).

Barnard, John. 'Introduction', in *The Cambridge History of the Book in Britain, Volume Four, 1557–1695*, ed. by John Barnard, D. F. McKenzie and Maureen Bell (Cambridge: Cambridge University Press, 2001), pp. 1–28.

——. and D. F. Mckenzie and Maureen Bell, eds *The Cambridge History of the Book in Britain: Volume IV, 1557–1695* (Cambridge: Cambridge University Press, 2002).

Barthes, Roland. 'The Death of the Author', in *The Norton Anthology of Theory and Criticism*, ed. by William E. Cain et al. (New York: W. W. Norton, 2001), pp. 1466–1470.

——. 'From Work to Text', in *The Norton Anthology of Theory and Criticism*, ed. by William E. Cain et al. (New York: W. W. Norton, 2001), pp. 1470–1475.

——. *Image, Music, Text*, trans. by Stephen Heath (London: Fontana, 1977).

Bate, Jonathan. *John Clare: A Biography* (London: Picador, 2003).

Beal, Peter. *In Praise of Scribes: Manuscripts and Their Makers in Seventeenth-Century England* (Oxford: Clarendon Press, 1998).

——. *Index of English Literary Manuscripts Volume II: 1625–1700* (London: Mansell, 1993).

——. 'Notions in Garrison: The Seventeenth-Century Commonplace Book', in *New Ways of Looking at Old Texts*, ed. by W. Speed Hill (New York: RETS, 1993), pp. 131–147.

Beetham, Margaret. 'In Search of the Historical Reader', *Siegener Periodicum zur Internationalen Empirischen Literaturwissenschaft [SPIEL]*, 19 (2000), pp. 89–104.

Bell, Bill, Philip Bennett and Jonquil Bevan, eds *Across Boundaries: the Book in Culture and Commerce*, (New Castle: Oak Knoll, 2000).

Bell, Bill. 'Bound for Australia: Shipboard Reading in the Nineteenth Century', in *Journeys Through the Market: Travel, Travellers and the Book Trade*, ed. by R. Myers and M. Harris (New Castle: Oak Knoll Press, 1999), pp. 119–140.

——. 'The Scottish Emigrant Reader in the Nineteenth Century', in *Across Boundaries: the Book in Culture and Commerce*, ed. by Bill Bell, Philip Bennett and Jonquil Bevan, (New Castle: Oak Knoll, 2000), pp. 116–129.

Benedict, Barbara. *Making the Modern Reader: Cultural Mediation in Early Modern Literary Anthologies* (Princeton: Princeton University Press, 1996).

Bennett, Andrew. 'Introduction', in *Readers and Reading*, ed. by Andrew Bennett (London: Longman, 1995).

——. ed. *Readers and Reading* (London: Longman, 1995).

Bloomfield, R. C. *A Directory of Rare Book and Special Collections in the United Kingdom and the Republic of Ireland*, 2nd edition (London: Library Association, 1997).

Brake, Laurel and Bill Bell and David Finkelstein. *Nineteenth-Century Media and the Construction of Identities* (Basingstoke: Palgrave, 2000).

Brantlinger, Patrick. *The Reading Lesson: The Threat of Mass Literacy in Nineteenth-Century British Fiction* (Bloomington and Indianapolis: Indiana University Press, 1998).

Brayman Hackel, Heidi. *Reading Material in Early Modern England: Print, Gender, and Literacy* (Cambridge: Cambridge University Press, 2005).

Brewer, John. *The Pleasures of the Imagination: English Culture in the Eighteenth Century* (London: HarperCollins, 1997).

——. 'Reconstructing the Reader: Prescriptions, Texts and Strategies in Anna Larpent's Reading', in *The Practice and Representation of Reading in England*, ed. by James Raven et al. (Cambridge: Cambridge University Press, 1996), pp. 226–245.

Brown, Cedric. 'The Black Poet of Ashover: Leonard Wheatcroft', *English Manuscript Studies*, 11 (2002), 181–202.

Brown, Tony. 'John Dawson: His Life and Library', Library Association Thesis, 1973.

Burnett, John and David Vincent and David Mayall, eds *The Autobiography of the Working Class: An Annotated Critical Bibliography*, 3 vols (Brighton: Harvester, 1984–1989).

Cain, William E. et al., eds *The Norton Anthology of Theory and Criticism* (New York: W. W. Norton, 2001).

Carey, William Wilfred. *The History of The Careys of Guernsey* (London: J. M. Dent, 1938).

Castle, Terry. *The Apparitional Lesbian: Female Homosexuality and Modern Culture* (New York: Columbia University Press, 1993).

Clark, Anna. 'Anne Lister's Construction of Lesbian Identity', *Journal of the History of Sexuality*, 7, 1 (1996), 23–50.

de Certeau, Michel. *The Practice of Everyday Life*, trans. by Steven Randall (Berkeley: University of California Press, 1984).

——. 'Reading as Poaching' in *Readers and Reading* (London: Longman, 1995), ed. by Andrew Bennett, pp. 150–163.

Chartier, Roger. *The Cultural Uses of Print in Early Modern France* (Princeton: Princeton University Press, 1987).

——. *The Order of Books: Readers, Authors and Libraries in Europe between the Fourteenth and the Eighteenth Centuries*, trans. by Lydia Cochrane (Cambridge: Polity Press, 1994).

——. *Publishing Drama in Early Modern Europe: The Panizzi Lectures 1998* (London: British Library, 1999).

——. 'Texts, Printing, Readings', in *The New Cultural History*, ed. by Lynn Hunt (Berkeley: University of California Press, 1989), pp. 154–175.

Colclough, Stephen. '"A Catalogue of my Books": The Library of John Dawson (1692–1765), "Exciseman and Staymaker", c.1739', *Publishing History*, 47 (2000), 45–66.

Colclough, Stephen. '"Designated in Print as Mr John Clare": The Annuals and the Field of Reading, 1827–1835', *John Clare Society Journal*, 25 (2005), 52–68.

——. '"Purifying the Sources of Amusement and Information"?: The Railway Bookstalls of W. H. Smith & Son, 1855–60', *Publishing History*, 56 (2004), 27–51.

——. *Reading Experience 1700–1840: An Annotated Bibliography of Sources for the History of Reading in the British Isles* (Reading: History of the Book On-Demand Series, 2000).

——. 'Recovering the Reader: Commonplace Books and Diaries as Sources of Reading Experience', *Publishing History*, XLIV (1998), 5–37.

——. 'Station to Station: the LNWR and the Emergence of the Railway Bookstall', in *Printing Places: Locations of Book Production and Distribution Since 1500*, ed. by John Hinks and Catherine Armstrong (London: British Library, 2005), pp. 169–184.

Cox, Jeffrey N. *Poetry and Politics in the Cockney School: Keats, Shelley, Hunt and Their Circle* (Cambridge: Cambridge University Press, 1998).

Craven, A. B. (ed). *Victorian and Edwardian Yorkshire from Old Photographs* (London: B. T. Batsford, 1977).

Cronin, Richard. *The Politics of Romantic Poetry: In Search of the Pure Commonwealth* (Basingstoke: Macmillan Press, 2000).

Dallenbach, Lucien. *The Mirror in the Text*, trans. by Jeremy Whitley and Emma Hughes (Cambridge: Cambridge University Press, 1989).

Darnton, Robert. 'Extraordinary Commonplaces', *New York Review of Books*, 21 December 2000, pp. 82–87.

——. 'First Steps Toward a History of Reading' (1986), in *The Kiss of Lamourette: Reflections in Cultural History* (London: Faber & Faber, 1990), pp. 155–187.

——. *The Great Cat Massacre* (London: Allen Lane, 1984).

Davidoff, Leonore and Catherine Hall. *Family Fortunes: Men and Women of the English Middle Class 1780–1850*, 2nd edition (London: Routledge, 1992).

Davison, Peter. ed. *The Book Encompassed: Studies in Twentieth-Century Bibliography* (Cambridge: Cambridge University Press, 1992).

Deacon, George. *John Clare and the Folk Tradition* (London: Sinclair Browne, 1983).

DeMaria, Robert. *Samuel Johnson and the Life of Reading* (London and Baltimore: Johns Hopkins University Press, 1997).

Donoghue, Emma. *Passions between Women: British Lesbian Culture* (London: Scarlet Press, 1993).

Eagleton, Terry. *Literary Theory* (London: Blackwell, 1983).

Eliot, Simon. *Some Patterns and Trends in British Publishing, 1800–1919*, Occasional Papers of the Bibliographical Society 8 (London: Bibliographical Society, 1994).

——. 'The Reading Experience Database; or, What are we to do About the History of Reading', *The Reading Experience Database*, <*http://www.open.ac.uk/Arts/RED/redback.htm*>

Engelsing, Rolf. *Der Burger als Leser: Lesergeschichte in Deutschland 1500–1800* (Stuttgart: Metzler, 1974).

——. 'Die Perioden der Lesergeschicte in der Neuzeit', *Archiv fur Geschichte des Buchwesens*, 10 (1969), pp. 946–1002.

Erickson, Lee. *The Economy of Literary Form: English Literature and the Industrialization of Publishing, 1800–1850* (London: Johns Hopkins University Press).

Feather, John. 'British Publishing in the Eighteenth Century: A Preliminary Subject Analysis', *The Library*, 6, 8, 1 (1986), 32–46.

Fergus, Jan. 'Eighteenth-Century Readers in Provincial England: The Customers of Samuel Clay's Circulating Library and Bookshop in Warwick, 1770–72', in *Papers of the Bibliographical Society of America*, 78: 2 (1984), 155–213.

Finkelstein, David and Alistair McCleery, eds *The Book History Reader* (London: Routledge, 2002).

Fish, Stanley. 'Interpreting the *Variorum*', in *The Norton Anthology of Theory and Criticism* (New York: W. W. Norton, 2001), pp. 2071–2089.

Flavell, M. Kay. 'The Enlightened Reader and the New Industrial Towns: A Study of the Liverpool Library, 1758–1790', *British Journal of Eighteenth Century Studies*, 8 (1985), 17–35.

Flint, Kate. *The Woman Reader, 1837–1914* (Oxford: Clarendon Press, 1993).

Fraser, Hilary, Stephanie Green and Judith Johnston. *Gender and the Victorian Periodical* (Cambridge: Cambridge University Press, 2003).

Freund, Elizabeth. *The Return of the Reader: Reader Response Criticism* (London: Methuen, 1987).

Gerrard, Teresa. 'New Methods in the History of Reading: "Answers to Correspondents" in the *Family Herald*, 1860–1900', *Publishing History*, 43 (1998), 52–69.

Ginzburg, Carlo. *The Cheese and the Worms: The Cosmos of a Sixteenth-Century Miller*(Baltimore: Johns Hopkins University Press, 1992).

Grafton, Anthony. 'Is the History of Reading a Marginal Enterprise?: Guillaume Bude and His Books', *Papers of the Bibliographical Society of America*, 91 (1997), 139–157.

——. 'Discitur ut Agatur: How Gabriel Harvey Read His Livy', in *Annotation and Its Texts*, ed. by Stephen A. Barney (Oxford: Oxford University Press, 1991), pp. 108–129.

Habermas, Jurgen. *The Structural Transformation of the Public Sphere*, trans. by Thomas Burger and Frederick Lawrence (Cambridge Mass.: MIT Press, 1989).

Hall, David. 'The uses of literacy in New England, 1600–1850', in *Cultures of Print: Essays in the History of the Book*, ed. by David D. Hall (Amherst: University of Massachusetts Press, 1996), pp. 36–76.

Harris, Frances. 'The Englishwoman's Private Library in the 17th and 18th Centuries', in *Libraries in Literature*, ed. by Peter Vodosek and Graham Jefcoate (Wiesbaden: Harrasowitz Verlag, 1999), pp. 189–203.

Hartley, Jenny. *Reading Groups* (Oxford: Oxford University Press, 2001).

Havens, Earle. *Commonplace Books: A History of Manuscripts and Printed Books from Antiquity to the Twentieth Century* (Yale: The Beinecke Rare Book and Manuscript Library, Yale University, and University Press of New England, 2001).

Hoggart, Richard. *The Uses of Literacy* (London: Chatto & Windus, 1957).

——. *A Sort of Clowning* (London: Oxford University Press, 1991).

Huett, Lorna. 'Among the Unknown Public: *Household Words, All the Year Round* and the Mass-Market Weekly Periodical in the Mid-Nineteenth Century', *Victorian Periodicals Review*, 38:1 (2005), 61–82.

Hunter, G. K. 'The Marking of *Sententiae* in Elizabethan Printed Plays, Poems and Romances', *The Library*, 5th Series, 6, 3–4 (1951), 171–88.

Hunter, J. Paul. *Before Novels: The Cultural Contexts of Eighteenth-Century English Fictions* (New York: Norton, 1990).

Hunter, Michael, Giles Mandelbrote, Richard Ovenden and Michael Smith, eds *A Radical's Books: The Library Catalogue of Samuel Jeake of Rye, 1623–1690* (Woodbridge: D. S. Brewer, 1999).

Iser, Wolfgang. *The Act of Reading: A Theory of Aesthetic Response* (Baltimore: Johns Hopkins University Press, 1978).

Jackson, H. J. *Marginalia: Readers Writing in Books* (London: Yale University Press, 2001).

——. *Romantic Readers: The Evidence of Marginalia* (New Haven: Yale University Press, 2005).

Jacob, Margaret, C. 'Sociability and the International Republican Conversation' in *Romantic Sociability: Social Networks and Literary Culture in Britain*, ed. by Gillian Russell and Clara Tuite (Cambridge: Cambridge University Press, 2002), pp. 24–42.

Janowitz, Anne. 'Amiable and Radical Sociability: Anna Barbauld's "Free Familiar Conversation"', in *Romantic Sociability*, ed. by Gillian Russell and Clara Tuite (Cambridge: Cambridge University Press, 2002), pp. 62–81.

Jardine, Lisa and Anthony Grafton. '"Studied for Action": How Gabriel Harvey Read his Livy', *Past and Present*, 129 (1990), 30–78.

Jauss, H. R. *Toward an Aesthetic of Reception*, trans. by Timothy Bahti (Minneapolis: University of Minnesota Press, 1982).

——. 'Literary History as a Challenge to Literary Theory' in *The Norton Anthology of Theory and Criticism*, ed. by William E. Cain et al. (New York: W. W. Norton, 2001), pp. 1550–1564.

Johns, Adrian. *The Nature of the Book: Print and Knowledge in the Making* (Chicago: University of Chicago Press, 1998).

Johnson, Kenneth R. *The Hidden Wordsworth* (London: Pimlico, 2000).

Jordan, John O. and Robert Patten. *Literature in the Marketplace* (Cambridge: Cambridge University Press, 1995).

Joynes, Sara E. 'The Sheffield Library, 1771–1907', *Library History*, 2, (1971), 91–116.

Kaufman, Paul. *Libraries and Their Users* (London: Library Association, 1969).

King, Andrew. *The London Journal, 1845–83: Periodicals, Production and Gender* (Aldershot: Ashgate, 2004).

Klancher, Jon P. *The Making of English Reading Audiences, 1790–1832* (Madison: University of Wisconsin Press, 1987).

Korsten, Frans. *A Catalogue of the Library of Thomas Baker* (Cambridge: Cambridge University Press, 1990).

Kugler, Anne. *Errant Plagiary: The Life and Writing of Lady Sarah Cowper 1644–1720* (Stanford: Stanford University Press, 2002).

Leader, Zachary. *Revision and Romantic Authorship* (Oxford: Clarendon Press, 1996).

Leavis, Q. D. *Fiction and the Reading Public* (London: Chatto & Windus, 1932).

Leedham-Green, E. S. ed. *Books in Cambridge Inventories*, 2 vols (Cambridge: Cambridge University Press, 1986).

Leitch, Vincent B. 'Reader Response Criticism', in *Readers and Reading*, ed. by Bennett (London: Longman, 1995), pp. 32–65.

Lethbridge, Stefanie. 'Anthological Reading Habits in the Eighteenth Century: The Case of Thomson's *Seasons*', in *Anthologies of British Poetry: Critical Perspectives from Literary and Cultural Studies*, ed. by Barbara Korte, Ralf Schneider and Stefanie Lethbridge (Amsterdam: Rodopi, 2000), pp. 89–104.

Library History Database: www.r-alston.co.uk

Liddington, Jill. 'Beating the Inheritance Bounds: Anne Lister (1791–1840) and her Dynastic Identity', *Gender and History*, 7 (1995), 260–274.

——. *Female Fortune: Land, Gender and Authority – The Anne Lister Diaries and Other Writings 1833–36* (London: Rivers Oram, 1998).

——. 'Gender, Authority and Mining in an Industrial Landscape: Anne Lister 1791–1840', *History Workshop Journal*, 42 (1996), 68–86.

Lindsay, David W. *The Beggar's Opera and Other Eighteenth-Century Plays* (London: J. M. Dent, 1993).

Lodge, Edmund. *Life of Sir Julius Caesar* (London: Hatchard, 1827).

Long, Elizabeth. *Book Clubs: Women and the Uses of Reading in Everyday Life* (Chicago: University of Chicago Press, 2003).

Love, Harold. *English Clandestine Satire 1660–1702* (Oxford: Oxford University Press, 2004).

——. 'How Personal is a Personal Miscellany? Sarah Cowper, Martin Clifford and the "Buckingham Commonplace Book"', in *Order and Connexion: Studies in Bibliography and Book History*, ed. by R. C. Alston (Woodbridge: Boydell and Brewer, 1997), pp. 111–126.

——. 'Oral and Scribal Texts in Early Modern England', in *The Cambridge History of the Book in Britain: Volume IV, 1557–1695* ed. by John Barnard, D. F. Mckenzie and Maureen Bell (Cambridge: Cambridge University Press, 2002), pp. 97–121.

——. 'Restoration and Early Eighteenth-Century Drama', in *The Cambridge History of English Literature, 1660–1780*, ed. by John Richetti (Cambridge: Cambridge University Press, 2005), pp. 109–131.

——. *Scribal Publication in Seventeenth-Century England* (Oxford: Clarendon Press, 1993).

Machor, James L. 'Historical Hermeneutics and Antebellum Fiction: Gender, Response Theory, and Interpretive Contexts', in *Readers in History: Nineteenth-Century American Literature and the Contexts of Response*, ed. by James L. Machor (Baltimore: Johns Hopkins University Press, 1993), pp. 54–84.

——. ed. *Readers in History: Nineteenth-Century American Literature and the Contexts of Response* (Baltimore: John Hopkins University Press, 1993).

Mandelbrote, Giles. 'From the Warehouse to the Counting-House: Booksellers and Bookshops in late 17th-Century London', in *A Genius for Letters: Booksellers and Bookselling from the 16th to the 20th Century*, ed. by R. Myers and M. Harris (Winchester and Delaware: St Paul's Bibliographies and Oak Knoll Press, 1995).

Manley, Keith. 'Booksellers, Peruke-Makers and Rabbit Merchants: The Growth of Circulating Libraries in the Eighteenth Century', in *Libraries and the Book Trade*, ed. by Robyn Myers, Michael Harris and Giles Mandelbrote (Delaware: Oak Knoll Press, 2000), pp. 29–50.

——. 'Lounging Places and Frivolous Literature: Subscription and Circulating Libraries in the West Country', in *Printing Places: Locations of Book Production and Distribution Since 1500*, ed. by John Hinks and Catherine Armstrong (London: The British Library, 2005), pp. 107–120.

Marotti, Arthur F. *Manuscript, Print and the English Renaissance Lyric* (London: Cornell University Press, 1995).

McGann, Jerome. 'The Text, the Poem and the Problem of Historical Method', in *Modern Literary Theory: A Reader*, ed. by Philip Rice and Patricia Waugh, 2nd edition, (London: Edward Arnold, 1989), pp. 289–306.

——. *The Textual Condition* (Princeton: Princeton University Press, 1991).

McHenry, Elizabeth. *Forgotten Readers: Recovering the Lost History of African American Literary Societies* (Durham: Duke University Press, 2002).

McKenzie, D. F. *Bibliography and the Sociology of Texts*, 2nd edition (Cambridge: Cambridge University Press, 1999).

——. *Making Meaning: 'Printers of the Mind' and Other Essays*, ed. by P. D. McDonald and M. F. Suarez (Amherst: University of Massachusetts Press, 2002).

——. 'Typography and Meaning: The Case of William Congreve', in D. F. Mckenzie, *Making Meaning: 'Printers of the Mind' and Other Essays*, ed. by P. D. McDonald and M. F. Suarez (Amherst: University of Massachusetts Press, 2002), pp. 198–237.

McKitterick, David. 'Book Catalogues: Their Varieties and Uses', in *The Book Encompassed: Studies in Twentieth-Century Bibliography* ed. by Peter Davison (Cambridge: Cambridge University Press, 1992), pp. 161–175.

——. *A History of Cambridge University Press: Printing and the Book Trade in Cambridge, 1534–1698* (Cambridge: Cambridge University Press, 1992).

——. 'Women and Their Books in Seventeenth-Century England: The Case of Elizabeth Puckering', *The Library*, n.s. 1, 4 (2000), 359–380.

Moore, Lisa. '"Something More Tender Still Than Friendship": Romantic Friendship in Early Nineteenth Century England', *Feminist Studies* 18, 3 (Fall 1992), 510–513.

Moss, Ann. *Printed Commonplace Books and the Structuring of Renaissance Thought* (Oxford: Clarendon Press, 1996).

Myers, Robin and Michael Harris, eds *Journeys Through the Market: Travel, Travellers and the Book Trade* (New Castle: Oak Knoll Press, 1999).

Myers, Robin and Michael Harris and Giles Mandelbrote, eds *Under the Hammer: Book Auctions Since the Seventeenth Century* (New Castle: Oak Knoll, 2001).

——. eds *Owners, Annotators and the Signs of Reading* (London: British Library, 2005).

Nead, Lynda. *Victorian Babylon: People, Streets and Images in Nineteenth-Century London* (New Haven: Yale University Press, 2000).

Pearson, Jacqueline. *The Prostituted Muse: Images of Women and Women Dramatists 1642–1737* (London: Harvester, 1998).

——. *Women's Reading in Britain 1750–1835: A Dangerous Recreation* (Cambridge: Cambridge University Press, 1999).

Pincus, Steve. ' "Coffee Politicians Does Create": Coffee Houses and Restoration Political Culture', *The Journal of Modern History*, 67 (December 1995), 807–834.

Price, Leah. 'Reader's Block: Response', in *Victorian Studies*, 46,2 (Winter 2004), 231–242.

——. 'Reading Matter', *PMLA*, 121.1 (January 2006), pp. 9–16.

Radway, Janice. *Reading the Romance: Women, Patriarchy, and Popular Literature* (London: Verso, 1987).

Raven, James. 'From Promotion to Prescription: arrangements for reading and eighteenth-century libraries', in *The Practice and Representation of Reading in England*, ed. by James Raven et al. (Cambridge: Cambridge University Press, 1996), pp. 175–201.

——. and Helen Small and Naomi Tadmor, 'Introduction: The Practice and Representation of Reading in England', in *The Practice and Representation of Reading in England*, ed. by James Raven et al. (Cambridge: Cambridge University Press, 1996), p. 1121.

——. *Judging New Wealth: Popular Responses to Commerce in England, 1750–1800* (Oxford: Clarendon Press, 1992).

——. 'New Reading Histories, Print Culture and the Identification of Change: The Case of Eighteenth-Century England', *Social History*, 23, 3 (1998), 268–87.

——. Helen Small and Naomi Tadmor, eds *The Practice and Representation of Reading in England* (Cambridge: Cambridge University Press, 1996).

——. 'Publishing and Bookselling 1660–1780', in *The Cambridge History of English Literature, 1660–1780*, ed. by John Richetti (Cambridge: Cambridge University Press, 2005), pp. 11–36.

The Reading Experience Database (RED): www.open.ac.uk/Arts/RED/

Reay, Barry. 'The Context and Meaning of Popular Literacy: Some Evidence from Nineteenth-Century Rural England', *Past and Present*, 131 (1991), 89–129.

——. *The Last Rising of the Agricultural Labourers: Rural Life and Protest in Nineteenth-Century Britain* (Oxford: Clarendon Press, 1990).

Rice, Philip and Patricia Waugh, eds *Modern Literary Theory: A Reader*, 2nd edition, (London: Edward Arnold, 1989).

Richards, Thomas. *The Commodity Culture of Victorian England: Advertising and Spectacle, 1851–1914* (London: Verso, 1991).

Richardson, Alan. *Literature, Education and Romanticism: Reading as Social Practice, 1780–1832* (Cambridge: Cambridge University Press, 1994).

Richetti, John. ed. *The Cambridge History of English Literature, 1660–1780* (Cambridge: Cambridge University Press, 2005).

Roberts, Gwyneth Tyson. *The Language of the Blue Books: the Perfect Instrument of Empire* (Cardiff: University of Wales, Press, 1998).

Rose, Jonathan. 'How Historians Study Reader Response: Or, What Did Jo Think of *Bleak House?*', in *Literature in the Marketplace*, ed. by John O. Jordan and Robert Patten (Cambridge: Cambridge University Press, 1995), pp. 195–212.

——. *The Intellectual Life of the British Working Classes* (New Haven: Yale University Press, 2001).

——. 'Rereading the English Common Reader: A Preface to a History of Audiences', in *The Book History Reader* (London: Routledge, 2002), ed. by David Finkelstein and Alistair McCleery, pp. 324–339.

Russell, Gillian and Clara Tuite, eds *Romantic Sociability: Social Networks and Literary Culture in Britain* (Cambridge: Cambridge University Press, 2002).

Scott-Warren, Jason. 'News, Sociability, and Bookbuying in Early Modern England: The Letters of Sir Thomas Cornwallis', *The Library*, n.s. 1, 4 (2000), 381–402.

Sharpe, Kevin. *Reading Revolutions: The Politics of Reading In Early Modern England* (London: Yale University Press, 2000).

——. and Steven Zwicker, eds *Reading, Society and Politics in Early Modern England* (Cambridge: Cambridge University Press, 2003).

——. 'Uncommonplaces? Sir William Drake's Reading Notes', in *The Reader Revealed*, ed. by Sabrina Alcorn Baron et al. (Washington: Folger Library, 2001), pp. 58–65.

Sherman, Stuart. 'Diary and Autobiography', in *The Cambridge History of English Literature 1660–1780*, ed. by John Richetti (Cambridge: Cambridge University Press, 2005), pp. 649–672.

——. *Telling Time: Clocks, Diaries, and English Diurnal Form, 1660–1795* (Chicago: Chicago University Press, 1996).

Sherman, William. *John Dee and the Politics of Reading and Writing in the English Renaissance* (Amherst: University of Massachusetts Press, 1995).

——. 'Toward a History of the Manicule', in *Owners, Annotators and the Signs of Reading*, ed. by Robin Myers et al. (London: British Library, 2005), pp. 19–48.

Skelton-Foord, Christopher. 'Surveying the Circulating Library Scene: Popular British Fiction, 1770–1830', in *Bibliotheken in der Literarischen Darstellung: Libraries in Literature*, ed. by Peter Vodosek and Graham Jefcoate (Wiesbaden: Harrassowitz Verlag, 1999), pp. 89–113.

Smyth, Adam. *'Profit and Delight': Printed Miscellanies in England, 1640–1682* (Detroit: Wayne State University Press, 2004).

——. '"Read in One Age and Understood i' th' Next": Recycling Satire in the Mid-Seventeenth Century', *Huntington Library Quarterly*, 69, 1 (2006), 118–126.

Speck, W. A. *Literature and Society in Eighteenth-Century England: Ideology, Politics and Culture, 1680–1820* (London: Longman, 1998).

Speed Hill, W. ed. *New Ways of Looking at Old Texts* (New York: Renaissance English Texts Society, 1993).

Spence, Jeoffry. *Victorian and Edwardian Railway Travel from Old Photographs* (London: B. T. Batsford, 1985).

Spufford, Margaret. 'First Steps in Literacy: the Reading and Writing Experience of the Humblest Seventeenth-Century Spiritual Autobiographers', *Social History*, IV (1979), 407–435.

St Clair, William. *The Reading Nation in the Romantic Period* (Cambridge: Cambridge University Press, 2004).

Stewart, Garrett. *Dear Reader: The Conscripted Audience in Nineteenth-Century British Fiction* (Baltimore: Johns Hopkins, 1996).

Stewart, Garrett. 'The Mind's Sigh: Pictured Reading in Nineteenth-Century Painting', in *Victorian Studies*, 46, 2 (Winter 2004), 217–230.

Tuite, Clara. 'The Byronic Woman: Anne Lister's Style, Sociability and Sexuality', in *Romantic Sociability*, ed. by Gillian Russell and Clara Tuite (Cambridge: Cambridge University Press, 2002), pp. 186–210.

Vincent, David. *Bread, Knowledge and Freedom: A Study of Nineteenth-Century Working Class Autobiography* (London: Methuen, 1982).

Vincent, David. *Literacy and Popular Culture: England 1750–1914* (Cambridge: Cambridge University Press, 1989).

Vincent, David. *The Rise of Mass Literacy: Reading and Writing in Modern Europe* (Cambridge: Polity Press, 2000).

Vodosek, Peter and Graham Jefcoate, eds *Libraries in Literature* (Wiesbaden: Harrasowitz Verlag, 1999).

Warner, William B. 'Novels on the Market', in *The Cambridge History of English Literature 1660–1780*, ed. by John Richetti (Cambridge: Cambridge University Press, 2005), pp. 87–105.

Warner, William Beatty. 'Staging Readers Reading', *Eighteenth-Century Fiction*, 12, 2–3 (January–April 2000), 391–416.

Warren, Lynne. '"Women in Conference": Reading the Correspondence Columns in *Woman* 1890–1910', in *Nineteenth-Century Media and the Construction of Identities*, ed. by Laurel Brake, Bill Bell and David Finkelstein (Basingstoke: Palgrave, 2000), pp. 122–133.

Weatherill, Lorna. *Consumer Behaviour and Material Culture in Britain, 1660–1760*, 2nd edition (New York: Routledge, 1996).

Webb, R. K. *The British Working Class Reader 1790–1848* (London: Allen & Unwin, 1955).

Williams, Raymond. *Culture and Society, 1780–1950* (London: Chatto & Windus, 1958).

Woolf, D. R. *Reading History in Early Modern England* (Cambridge: Cambridge University Press, 2000).

Woolf, Daniel. 'News, History and the Construction of The Present in Early Modern England', in *The Politics of Information in Early Modern Europe*, ed. by Sabrina Baron and Brendan Dooley (New York: Routledge, 2001), pp. 80–118.

Wynne, Deborah. *The Sensation Novel and the Victorian Family Magazine* (Houndsmill: Palgrave, 2001).

Zwicker, Steven N. 'The Constitution of Opinion and the Pacification of Reading', *Reading, Society and Politics in Early Modern England*, ed. by Kevin Sharpe and Steven Zwicker (Cambridge: Cambridge University Press, 2003), pp. 295–316.

——. 'The Reader Revealed', in *The Reader Revealed*, ed. by Sabrina Alcorn Baron et al. (Washington: Folger Shakespeare Library, 2001), pp. 11–17.

Index